THE SOUTH SEA BUBBLE

THE
SOUTH SEA
BUBBLE

BY JOHN CARSWELL

*

LONDON
THE CRESSET PRESS
MCMLX

Published in Great Britain by
The Cresset Press, 11 Fitzroy Square, London W.1.

First published 1960

Printed in Great Britain by
The Camelot Press Ltd., London and Southampton

Preface

SOME PEOPLE HAVE attributed the events from which this book takes its title to sun-spots. But more usually the South Sea Bubble is treated as a grotesque incident, a kind of fantastic outcrop on the smiling landscape of the Age of Reason.

In fact, the South Sea Year was the culmination of the intensely active period in our history which I have called in this book the Commercial Revolution. It was followed by the pause which we often call 'the eighteenth century', though in fact it lasted barely fifty years: the pause between the end of one revolution and the beginning of the Industrial Revolution that opens our own time. I have therefore felt obliged to give the earlier part of this book to a description of that Commercial Revolution and the way in which the events of the South Sea Year rise naturally out of it.

This seems a fairly obvious way of approaching the subject, but there are several reasons, I think, why such an attempt to consider the South Sea Bubble in its context has not been made before. For one thing, it left an uncomfortable scar in a tender place. During the eighteenth century people did not care to think about it at all except as an unaccountable piece of collective folly; and perhaps, obscurely, it is still the subject of a kind of historical repression. The personalities of those who took a leading part in it—Craggs, Aislabie, Sunderland, Blunt—do not figure even as villains in our historical memory. Then it stands on the borderline between political, social, and economic history. When parliamentarians go on the stock exchange there is no specialist to follow them there. Scholars are not attracted by business men, as one can see from the fact that only half a dozen of the men who served as South Sea directors down to 1720 are noticed in *The Dictionary of National Biography*. This has forced me to include as an appendix such biographical particulars of the South Sea directors as I have been able to recover.

v

But the historian cannot complain that materials are lacking. Their very abundance has probably deterred intending students, for the South Sea Bubble is the glory hole of English history. There can hardly be a manuscript collection bearing on the period at all that has not some relevance to the events that affected nearly every pocket in the country. The pamphlet literature is vast and excruciating. The bulky financial documents are even worse.

I make no apology, therefore, for having attempted no bibliography. References, which I have tried to keep to a minimum, give my sources for quotations (except in obvious cases) and for less familiar facts. Certain large collections of material are, however, so important, that I should briefly mention them here.

The official records of the South Sea Company are preserved in the British Museum as Add. MSS. 25,494 to 25,581. For the period up to and including the Bubble they are singularly uninformative, and some of the crucial volumes are not there. Far more important for the Company's formal proceedings are the extracts included, with other important South Sea material, in the Goldsmith Collection (Goldsmith MS. 89), and in the Records of the House of Lords.

The disclosures after the Bubble had burst are contained in the printed Journals of the two Houses of Parliament. Those of the House of Lords are supplemented by original documents requisitioned by the House for their inquiry, which form the most important surviving collection of South Sea papers and are now in the Record Office of the House of Lords. I therefore owe much to the kindness of Mr. M. F. Bond, the Clerk of the Records, and his staff. The same is true of the staff of the London University Library, where I was able to examine, not only the manuscripts I have already referred to, but the beautifully kept Goldsmith collection of early economic literature. The papers of Sir Robert Walpole, which are at present in the Cambridge University Library, also contain important material, and I acknowledge the generosity of their owner, the Marquess of Cholmondely, in making them available, as well as the kindnesses I have received from Dr. J. H. Plumb.

Four secondary works, as being the only ones dealing at any length with the Bubble, should also be mentioned. W. R. Scott's great work *Joint Stock Companies to 1720* (now extremely hard to obtain) will not soon be superseded, though it was published nearly fifty years ago. It contains a very full account of the South Sea Company and is indispensable for the whole period of the Commercial Revolution. Nevertheless, it is old and in some respects incorrect; and Scott, writing from an exclusively economic point of view, neglects the political and social. Lewis Melville's *South Sea Bubble* (1921) has the distinction of being the only full-length book hitherto written on the subject, and is therefore not useless; but it goes to the opposite extreme from Scott, being, like most of Melville's work, anecdotal, inaccurate, and superficial. The present Marquess of Reading published a lively, but short, account of the Bubble in 1932. Mr. Eric Wagstaff, whose unpublished thesis of 1934 entitled *Political Aspects of the South Sea Bubble* is deposited in the London University Library, is the only author who has tried to unravel the mixture of politics and business which is one of the Bubble's chief interests. I am much indebted to his research. There are a few shorter studies, among which that of Wolfgang Michael, *Der Südseeschwindel vom Jahre 1720 (Vierteljahrschrift für Sozial— und Wirtschaftsgeschichte VI—1908)*, is the best.

No passage in history, perhaps, could illustrate more clearly the unity of economic with general political and social history than the South Sea Bubble and the Commercial Revolution; and the attempt to combine the two, even if it can only touch the fringe of what could be said, must, I am sure, enlarge our understanding of ourselves as a commercial nation. In the Augustan Age at any rate commercial greatness was the core round which the other manifestations of this country's genius flourished.

The London Library was indispensable.   J. C.

BERINS HILL.
11 September 1959.

Note on Dates and Figures

DURING THE PERIOD covered by this book England was using a calendar 11 days behind that used on the Continent, which must have complicated business dealings considerably. To preserve chronology I have redated Continental events—except where otherwise indicated—to conform with the contemporary English calendar. But I have throughout used the familiar years beginning on 1 January, and not the contemporary English year beginning on 25 March.

Inevitably there are a good many figures. Eighteenth-century business men loved to calculate even the largest sums down to farthings, but where millions are concerned this endearing but bogus precision has, I think, a bemusing effect. Unless, therefore, it is necessary to quote an exact figure to make a specific point, I have rounded to the nearest thousand.

Contents

List of Illustrations

xi

CHAPTER I

The Commercial Revolution

IN 1689 THE Reverend Robert Kirk, who had travelled from his Perthshire cure of Aberfoyle in search of a publisher for his new Gaelic Bible, set down his impressions of London in his notebook. 'The city', he wrote, 'is a great vast wilderness. Few in it know a fourth part of its streets, far less can they get intelligence of a hundredth part of the special affairs and remarkable passages in it, unless by the public printed papers, which come not to every man's notice. The most attend their business.'[1]

During the thirty years up to the Revolution of 1688 London had become the biggest town in Europe. Amsterdam had perhaps a quarter of a million people, Paris 400,000. Half a million people—one Englishman in eleven—lived in London, over twice as many as in Cromwell's day; and this had been achieved although far more Londoners died than were born. The Temple, which not so long before had been the western limit of the main arc of buildings rising from London's principal thoroughfare, the Thames, was now the central point of an arc curving from Millbank to Stepney. The old palaces of the nobility, running back to the Strand from their main entrances on the waterside, were already being broken up by such speculative builders as Nicholas Barbon, son of Cromwell's Praise-God Barebone, to make way for smaller houses. Northwards, too, Barbon's building was covering the fields beyond Holborn, and in St. Giles's, Thomas Neale, Master of the Mint and promoter of lotteries, was putting his money into the bricks and mortar of the star-shaped housing estate known as Seven Dials. Further west, following the line of the river, the quality were fanning out into Kensington and

Chelsea villas. Eastwards 'it may be said without vanity, that no river in the world can show a braver sight of ships than are commonly to be seen (like a floating forest) from *Blackwall* to *London Bridge*'.[2]

London was a double town. One end was a royal and parliamentary capital, governed, so far as it had a government, by an obscure condominium of palace officials and nominees of the Dean and Chapter of Westminster. The other end was virtually a mercantile republic. Its great men were as proud and as independent—especially since the solemn confirmation of their privileges which had been one of the first acts of the Revolution Government—as the merchant princes of Venice, Hamburg, or Amsterdam. They had long been used to knight-hoods. Many were allied by blood or marriage, with good country families: the goldsmith Actons of Leadenhall St. and their neighbours, the linen-draper Gibbons, with whom they intermarried, were related to the Actons of Shropshire, hearty Tories with a baronetcy for their services to Church and King. The City returned four Members to Parliament, and whereas in the rest of England sheriffs and lieutenants nominated by the Crown intervened between the local magistrates and the central government, there was no such restraining hand on the Corporation of London. The City's right to elect its own sheriffs had been vindicated in a great tussle with the monarchy only a few years before, and the powers of lieutenancy were discharged into a commission of citizens. And for the times the government the City gave its citizens was an efficient one.

London had an army on which the King could not call, composed of the Orange, Blue, Red, Yellow, and Green Regiments and the Honourable Artillery Company, all officered by leading citizens. This force was not yet a joke. Kirk had heard that at three hours' warning the City could command '120,000 men, with a continuous recruit of men and supply of ammunition and victuals'. This was an exaggeration, but the thought of London effectively in arms was not.

There was every reason for the Lord Mayor to be counted as important a personage in the kingdom as most dukes. On

2

state occasions the aldermen's gowns of scarlet, green or violet, depending on the occasion, simultaneously displayed the City's grandeur and the fruitfulness of the trade in woollen cloth, which was still the foundation of old-style business prosperity. Manufactured wool was the largest export, and the most respectable line of business, on which the prosperity of no less than five of the twelve major livery companies had been built. Dyer, the poet patronized by Heathcote, the great merchant banker, chose wool for his best-known work:

> The care of sheep, the labours of the loom,
> The arts of trade, I sing. Ye rural nymphs!
> Ye swains and princely merchants, aid the verse![3]

Many, perhaps most Londoners, had strongly-growing country roots, and the successful Londoner's dearest ambition was to retire into rural gentility—though not necessarily to his native soil. One could be a country gentleman at Wanstead, Leyton, or Carshalton. But whatever the Londoner's dreams, his business outlook and the orientation of his City's interest lay south and east, across the narrow seas.

From the seaward side London was one unit in the ever more closely integrated commercial system disposed along both sides of the waters which connected Britain, the Netherlands, and France. It was easier and quicker for the Londoner to get to Amsterdam than to Exeter or Carlisle: two days of comparative comfort against the best part of a disagreeable week. But it was not so much personal travel that bound the commercial community of 'the middle seas' together, though that was important. It was ease of communication. What happened in Hamburg or Amsterdam registered more speedily in London than events in foreign Scotland or colonial Dublin. All the year round the North Sea was speckled with little ships, and most of them carried news or business mail, as well as cargo.

Very often both sender and recipient would be an Englishman, especially where the Baltic was concerned, and sometimes they would be relatives, like the Joyes of Stockholm, Danzig,

3

Gothenburg, and London.[4] There were British business men at Riga and Archangel, and the Deputy Governor of the British Baltic Company was permanently stationed at Hamburg, where the municipality feasted him and his colleagues annually on sturgeon.[5]

So far as the system had a financial capital it was Amsterdam. Its highly developed if old-fashioned banks had grown up in freedom from even the breath of state interference; and they were deeply interested in the commerce of London. As time passed, and London's prosperity advanced, the biggest men in the City found it necessary to have money and credit in Amsterdam, and the exchange rate there was considered the index to the strength of sterling.

To the south, staring across the Channel, lay the directed economy of France, whose King had once said that 'no right was better established or more inseparably attached to my crown than that of universal subordination and direction within my territories'.[6]

The English business man knew that this was no mere boast. It had substance in the subsidized looms of Abbeville and Carcassonne, in the subsidized fleet operating from the planned port of Havre, in the elaborate and minutely enforced regulation of commerce which was the legacy of Colbert. The Dutch were competitors, but the French were an organized business enemy; and formidable not only because organized. England had an advantage over Holland in possessing a productive hinterland and the framework of a nation-state; France was the biggest, most homogeneous, most populous nation-state in Europe.

A directed economy, Englishmen noted, went hand in hand with religious persecution. By 1690 there were many Londoners who knew the meaning of this at first hand. The revocation of the Edict of Nantes in 1685 was merely the climax of a mounting campaign of discrimination and terror which had driven Huguenots to seek homes in England for more than a century. John Houblon, who dominated the Bank of England from its foundation until his death in 1712, and Thomas

4

Papillon, who led the great onslaught on the old East India Company in the 1690s were London Huguenots of the second and third generations. The ancestor of Sir Edward Desbouverie the great Turkey merchant and his sons, William, Edward, and Christopher (the first two of whom became baronets and the third a knight), had been naturalized under James I. Among more recent arrivals were Theodore Janssen, who had come over eight years before the Revolution at the age of twenty-two with the small fortune he was to build into one of the largest London had seen. About the same time Joseph Bateman had arrived from Flanders and settled down as a small banker. His family was a spreading tree. James, his eldest son, was to be Lord Mayor, a baronet, and Sub-Governor of the South Sea Company; and his grandson would marry a Spencer, and be raised to the peerage as master of one of the great houses of the West Country.* Even today, when Shobdon Court is in ruins, the family's suburban estate, engulfed in Soho, is commemorated in Bateman Street.

When the refugees, for whom this word was first coined, began to pour across in the 1680s, the bridgehead was well established. They brought valuable skills with them—valuable especially because in 1689, for the first time in English history, trading with the national enemy was formally prohibited. Their settlement stiffened the native hostility to France; but it created bonds of a kind between France and England which were not to be forgotten. The Huguenot had been used to a bigger world, a broader horizon, than most Englishmen; and, perhaps even more important, he often had relatives who had stayed at home in Aquitaine or Flanders, conforming, very often, for the sake of the family property. There were, for example, John Lambert, the Huguenot fellow-pupil of Defoe at the Camberwell Academy, who was to carve out a great business career for himself, marry a French wife, and act as London agent for a great Paris banking house; and John Ligonier, the future Field-Marshal and Commander-in-Chief

---

* George I is reported to have said he could make Bateman a peer, but not a gentleman.

of the British Army, whose family remained in France.

The Huguenot immigration is the most celebrated instance of mobility in seventeenth-century Europe, but it was by no means the only foreign stream that fed revolutionary London to make it the cosmopolis which Defoe first earned fame by satirizing in *The True-born Englishman*:

> *Your Hermans, Papillons, and Lavalliers,*
> *Pass now for true-born English knights and squires,*
> *And make good senate members and Lord Mayors.*[7]

There was the large Dutch business community, and an important German one. In the 1680s Thomas Jacobsen, London agent of the Hanse, had his nephew Jacob naturalized so as to inherit the family fortunes and in time became one of London's biggest dealers in metal.

Jews were uncommon in the London of the 1690s, but appeared in increasing numbers with the turn of the century. Most of them were Spanish- or Portuguese-speaking, and it is not unusual to find a London stockbroker's account kept in those languages. Just as alien to the Londoner as the Sephardic Jews, and like them suspected of clannishness, were the already common Scotch, who provide two of the most remarkable and characteristic careers of the age. In 1691 William Paterson, the intellectual parent of the Bank of England and author of the grandiose and disastrous plan for an emporium serving the two hemispheres from the Isthmus of Darien, was engaged on a scheme for supplying water to London from the heights of Hampstead, where the ponds he built as reservoirs can still be seen. Soon afterwards his younger fellow-countryman, John Law, then aged twenty, settled in the new suburb of St. Giles's.

Law possessed in an extraordinary degree the characteristic gifts of his age.

It was an age in which the theorist was typically also a man of action. Locke and Newton, Addison and Swift, all had considerable public careers, with which their intellectual gifts harmonized. John Law was the equal of at any rate three of these in originality and profundity of intellect, and his powers of thought and deed were almost equally balanced. This sagacious, daring man was tall, imposing, dark, and long-nosed. He combined the highest ambition and unshakeable self-confidence with a peculiar sincerity and longing to clear from the minds of others those barriers to the exploitation of the world's wealth from which he had freed his own. Different though their spheres were, one might select Marlborough among Law's own contemporaries as offering the same combination of ambition, boldness, and charm; yet the soldier had a taint of falseness and self-love which was not in the financier.

Law's origins were certainly no humbler than Churchill's. His father, after acquiring a substantial fortune as a goldsmith and banker to the best names in Scotland, had become a landed man, Laird of Lauriston. Through his mother, John Law was related to the family which the Revolution made the most powerful in Scotland, the House of Argyll. The kinship might be remote, but Campbells remembered cousins.

In London with his patrimony, Law combined education with pleasure in a way talented men often do. One of his masters was certainly his landlord, Thomas Neale, whose part in the history of English finance has been curiously neglected, though he was Newton's predecessor as Master of the Mint and Montagu's confidential adviser at the Treasury, as well as official purveyor of dice and playing-cards to both James II and William III. Neale was the promoter of the first English State lottery, launched while Law was in London and called, in perfect accord with the spirit of an age which for the first time was thinking in seven figures, 'The Million Adventure'. He probably suggested our earliest Government-emitted paper money, the Exchequer bill,* which (except for the fact that

---

* 'The Million Adventure' of 1694 was based on Venetian experience. Like a later promotion of the same kind, its attraction was that one could not lose, only win—'a profitable venture to the fortunate', as Neale put it, 'and can be unfortunate to none'. The subscriptions represented a fund lent to the Government for sixteen years at moderate interest, with a bonus rate of interest for the prize tickets. It proved an expensive way of borrowing.

7

it bore interest, like most contemporary paper) was what we would call a Treasury note, though by the time it was introduced in 1697 Bank of England paper had already established itself, and the government machine was in any case inadequate to get the bills into circulation without the help of the City.

Law had gambled and flirted, and in 1695 had the misfortune to kill a fashionable young man named Wilson in a duel, for which he was condemned to death. In the ordinary way such a killing would not have been a serious matter, but the young man had powerful friends, and Law was a foreigner. The question whether he should be hanged or not developed into a tussle of some political importance, with Law's influential Scotch relations intervening vigorously on the other side. 'What!' said William III when one of them tried to enlist his sympathy by saying that Law had been very frank at his trial. 'Scotchmen suffer for their ingenuousness? Was ever such a thing known?' No pardon was forthcoming, but in the end the authorities were induced to connive at an escape.[8] It is one of the ironies of history that during the generation of the British Commercial Revolution England was closed, under penalty of death, to one of the greatest economic and financial minds this country has produced.

*   *   *

There was nothing cosy or quaint about revolutionary London, but its inhabitants had only to look about them to see that this was, indeed, the 'opulent city' of the contemporary handbook.[9] The dome of the new cathedral was rising, and service would be sung there before the century was out. Most of the streets were new also, and the principal ones were wide enough for the newly introduced hackney carriages, whose steadily increasing number was a source of profit to the government-appointed licensing commissioners as well as the owners. Better water supplies were being organized, and the new Convex Lights Company was providing better street lighting than London was to have a century later. There was a new sociability, whose symptom was the coffee-house, a new thirst for information, whose symptom was the newspaper.*

As Kirk had noticed, most Londoners were intent on business. As never before, London was possessed by an urge to make money. It was passion for business, not increase in leisure, that made coffee-men and journalists thrive. The foreign news, the business announcement, and the prices of stocks sold papers, and the coffee-house conference was not only the precursor of the business lunch: the coffee-house often provided, in its private rooms, the only office accommodation many business men possessed.

Plague, fire, war, plot, and, worst of all, the deliberate default of the Stuart government on its borrowings in 1672, had not prevented the making of great fortunes and a great advance of national prosperity in the thirty years after the Restoration. In that time national wealth had increased by a quarter, and savings had doubled.[10] In 1662 London had shipped exports worth about £2 million; by the last years of the century the annual average was 75 per cent. higher, at £3½ million.[11] In 1638 the average size of coal cargoes arriving in London had been 139 tons; by 1701 it was 248 tons.[12] Between 1660 and 1685 a holding of East India stock multiplied (if one takes account of bonus issues) ninefold in value, and even at that price the dividend gave the purchaser 10 per cent. on his money. Improved production had contributed to these remarkable figures, but the prime source, as everyone knew, was commerce.

Until the Revolution the old reservoirs still seemed big enough to contain the new floods of wealth. Such old 'regulated' companies, for instance, as the Muscovy and Levant Companies, had been worn into mere rings of privileged merchants specializing in certain sectors of foreign trade; the new joint stock companies, of which there were only three of any

---

* By 1690 there were several hundred coffee-houses in London and Westminster, including the celebrated business forums of Jonathan's and of Garraway's (which eventually became the Stock Exchange). Apart from government sheets, there were at least five tri-weekly London newspapers by 1695. The first daily (*Daily Courant*) appeared in 1702, and the first evening (*Evening Post*) in 1706. By 1709 London had eighteen newspapers.

importance, traded, it is true, as corporations on borrowed capital represented by their stock and bonds. But even as late as 1693 there were only 499 holders of East India stock, and eighty-four men held three-quarters of it. One East India shareholder in three had in that year held his stock for the past sixteen years or more.[13] The market in share values came into existence remarkably quickly.

Moreover, incorporation, even as a joint stock, was still considered a privilege, not merely a matter of business organization, and it was not thought in the least unfitting that a joint stock company should describe itself as honourable. Such privilege had to be justified on the ground that some particular line of business was best exploited by incorporation, and the idea of two corporations competing in the same field, though it was to happen soon enough, seemed anomalous to both lawyers and business men. And just as incorporation was a privilege, so was membership of a corporation. The East India Company could and did seek to control the ownership of its stock.

In the years immediately following the Revolution pent-up wealth and initiative burst their banks. By 1695 there were more than 100 joint stocks in existence, a number hardly exceeded in the bumper promotion year of 1720 itself.[14] They had a nominal capital of £4m.—one-ninth of the whole estimated personal property of the country—and the market in shares was brisk, if ill-organized. It was calculated that the turnover of such East India stock as came on to the market in 1691 and 1692 was equal in face value to the whole of the Company's paid-up capital.[15]

Apart from major economic trends and the business euphoria which followed the installation of the revolutionary régime there were two immediate spurs to all this activity. A good share or bond, people were beginning to see, was an excellent substitute for land, and in some ways a more convenient way of securing a future for oneself or one's family. This new form of property, with which the law had not yet got to grips, was readily saleable, it needed no husbandry, and above all, unlike land, which since the Revolution had been taxed at 4s. in the pound, its yield was not taxed. In the second place, for those who possessed landed estates already, the share provided a means of avoiding charges on the rent-roll for married daughters, and a form of property which a married woman could properly retain as a personal estate. Already in 1685 20 per cent. of the holders of India and Africa bonds (what we should call preference stock) were women; and between 1675 and 1691 the number of women holding the ordinary shares of the East India Company doubled.[16]

It is dangerously easy, by using modern economic terms, to be misled about the realities and the atmosphere of the eighteenth-century business world. The reactions we have come to expect were not only unascertained; they very often failed to occur simply because things were so incoherent. As always, phenomena preceded grammar; the players were eagerly at the game before the rules had been agreed. Economic theory there was in plenty; and an even greater plenty of economic and financial experiment; but union of the two into a systematic pattern of economic behaviour was lacking. Like a pack suddenly released from their kennel, the hounds of business snuffled after false scents and bayed up blind alleys as eagerly as they followed true game.

According to the first business directory of London, which was published in 1677, the City and Westminster contained 1,786 merchants, and by the Revolution there must have been close on 5,000 London traders above the rank of ordinary shopmen.[17] They ranged from giants like Josiah Child, with his £50,000 holding in the East India Company, or Robert Clayton, the estate agent, down to modest men trading on capital of £1,000 or so.* The big man would have a country

---

* Relative values have changed so much that it is almost impossible to give an adequate idea of what seventeenth- and early eighteenth-century money was worth in our own £.s.d. Clothes, newspapers, books, imported luxuries such as tea, coffee, pepper, cochineal (used for faces as well as confectionary) cost a great deal, often more in cash terms than they do today. Home-grown food, on the other hand, and all kinds of personal services were extremely cheap. Foreigners commented on the high consumption of meat by the poor. The Bristol Workhouse found it could provide a good diet, including meat and beer, for 16d. per head per week in 1714, so that the

place—Essex usually, or Surrey—as well as a City establishment which would have handsome living quarters over the counting-house. Most merchants could be assigned to some particular trade—by the City guild in which he had served his apprentice-ship, or by the 'walk' he frequented out of the twenty-three into which the Royal Exchange was divided if he dealt in overseas markets. But in practice there were very few business men of consequence whose interests were entirely concentrated in one speciality. A sixteenth share of a trading voyage, a few bags of such scarce, compact, and non-perishable commodities as pepper or cochineal,* a little discounting of out-of-town bills or advancing of money to customers were common items to find passing through the books of a draper or a timber merchant. The import of drugs against the export of cloth was a highly recommended branch of the Levant trade.[18]

We know something about the merchant, but almost nothing about his clerks beyond the monumental and beauti-fully engrossed accounts and business correspondence that flowed from their pens; yet even at that time what we should call the white-collar population of London must have been large, and it was steadily growing. The great business flotations of the 1690s required hundreds of copyists and tellers. The organization of these large clerical operations, and the time they took, were among the most important limiting factors on the business ingenuity of the age.†

Yet there is no evidence of difficulty in finding literate, trained men for the meagre wages offered. Hatton's *Merchant's*

---

typical labourer's wage of 1s. a day (less in remoter areas) was far from contemptible (cf., in particular R. N. Salaman, *History and Social Influence of the Potato*, 1949, p. 464). As a very rough guide, especially where salaries are concerned, multiplication by ten will give some sort of relativity with present-day standards throughout our period.

* Cochineal, in particular, occupied a peculiar place in the financial system. Worth approximately £1 a lb., at which price it was fairly stable, it was treated almost as if it was bullion. Most City men held some, and as late as 1740 it is the only com-modity for which a price is quoted in Lloyd's List.

† A little later advertisements for absconding clerks begin to give us a few portraits: 'Thomas Williams, aged 22 years, a tall thin black man, sickly complexioned, a mole on his cheek, a cut in his forehead, stoops in the shoulders, with a cinnamon-coloured coat, another coat over it, wriggles as he walks.' *London Gazette* 13.1.1719.

Magazine assured its readers that office life was quite compatible with gentility, and there were even commercial colleges, such as Pickering's in Paternoster Row, which offered both a full-time course and evening classes.[19] It was not accidental that this was the great period of the English writing-master. For one piece of clerical work alone, in 1720, the South Sea Company needed, and quickly found, seventy additional clerks. Many clerks were apprentices; but the secret of the unfailing supply undoubtedly lay in the fact that the business world of that time drew no clear distinction between the office employee and the agent. One could buy a man's services, but not his subordination: the conception of loyalty to a firm, as distinct from obligation to an individual, which is so engrained in our business system, was quite alien. Thus to be a clerk was not merely to have set one's foot on the lowest rung of the commercial ladder; it was a recognized invitation to create the germ of a business for oneself.

This especially was true of any post which involved the handling of money. Here law and habit alike tended to put even the most humble office-worker in the position of an independent agent, and to consider any money he held as his so long as he held it, even though he might be accountable for it to someone else. It was this atomization of business life that made it at the same time cumbersome and fertile. It led to endless internal accounting between individuals in what we should regard as the same firm, but ensured that money rarely lay idle on anyone's hands. What we should call embezzlement and fraudulent conversion flourished in consequence—but these crimes were unknown to the English law until the end of the eighteenth century; such habits were indispensable if banking was to progress beyond the stage it had reached in Amsterdam, whose banks, for all their prestige, were little more than safe deposits issuing a convenient paper currency.

Instead of subordination and law there was credit, a habit of mind, and a cement of the business world established long before economic theories began to be built upon it. It is this which explains the profound response of the commercial world to theories of credit when they came to be propounded, and the almost passionate worship of the idea of public credit by those who imperfectly understood its intellectual implications.

They clung to the conception of credit the more eagerly because the law gave little protection to the weak or foolish. Civil recovery was expensive and disappointing, and there was little satisfaction to be got from the criminal law—savage though it was in other respects—unless 'false tokens' or plain forgery could be proved. The victim of a bogus prospectus or a fraudulent agent had only himself to blame for lack of 'common prudence'. False pretences was not an offence until 1757. In 1703 a man was charged with getting money from a debtor by pretending to be the creditor's agent. 'Shall we', Lord Chief Justice Holt exclaimed to the Grand Jury, 'indict one man for making a fool of another?'[20]

★   ★   ★

Sometimes borne up on the tide of commerce, sometimes stranded when it ebbed, were the cockleshells of the projectors, each with his cargo of ingenuity. No age has been richer in such men, or more fertile in solutions to all human problems. There were financial projects for banks of all kinds, for insurance, for pawnbroking; innumerable salvage schemes with patent diving apparatus, one of which, Sir William Phipps's expedition to the West Indies, yielded the huge dividend of 4,700 per cent. There were ideas with a great future, like Savery's steam pump, Tyzack's burglar alarm, Yarranton's tin-plate process, which established the South Wales industry, and Puckle's machine-gun, with its six revolving chambers and his patent plastic wood; East's pianola, Neale's pin-table, Austin's 'musket-proof chariot', Sutton's waterproofs; and there were ideas with no future, like making salt water fresh. It was patronized by Boyle and recommended to James II in a long poem by Edmund Arwaker, called *Fons Perennis* which suggested that by adopting it James would succeed where Canute had failed:

Boyle *our good Angel, stirs the sov'reign Pool*
That makes the Hydrophic-Leprous Seaman whole.[21]

Between 1660 and the end of the century 236 patents were
taken out—thirty-two more than in the succeeding forty
years—and of these more than a quarter were granted in the
three years 1691-3. We shall see most of these—even the one
which led to one of the most startling manifestations of
Parliamentary omnipotence in the 'Act to Make Salt Water
Fresh'—riding once more on the crest of the wave in which
most of them were at last to founder, in 1720.

In a successful project the patent was only the first story.
The second was a joint stock company, and most of the joint
stocks that leapt into existence in the wake of the Revolution
were for the exploitation of patents. Some of the most promising were for the monopoly of naturalized processes in war
conditions, such as making the fancy French fabrics known as
lustrings and alamodes, or white paper, which was in growing
demand.* Like a patent, a joint stock, once created, had a long
life, though patent and joint stock might be separated and go
their different ways as money makers. Water and textile
companies, as we shall see, were transmuted under new
management to insurance offices and real estate investment
trusts. As time passed a market grew up in moribund charters
of incorporation. Above all abundance of companies created
the necessary conditions for a market in stocks. Hand in hand
with the inventor and promoter went the stock-jobber.

Nobody had a good word to say for the stock-jobber as he
emerged during the 'nineties into public notoriety. Yet he was
ineradicable. In 1697 the parliamentary Committee which
condemned his 'pernicious' practices saw no way of getting rid
of him, though an Act was passed for registering brokers and
limiting their number. Defoe, ever in tune with public opinion,
aimed a broadside at them, 'The Villainy of Stock-Jobbers

---

* The first patent for manufacturing white paper was granted in 1685, and the joint
stock was authorized in the following year. Substantial production did not begin
until 1690, and by 1697 nearly half the white paper used was made in England.
Theodore Janssen early appreciated the possibilities of this trade, and was prosecuted
by the patentees for breach of their monopoly in 1687.

Detected', and they were formally (though not in practice) excluded from the dignified merchants' walks of the Royal Exchange, whereupon they emigrated to Exchange Alley, a few hundred yards away. The centre of business moved with them.

The miniature labyrinth of lanes called Exchange Alley is still there, in the acute angle formed by Lombard Street and Cornhill. Two main lanes make a crude cross, with a third attached to its western tip. The whole maze, with its six entries (two in Lombard Street, two in Cornhill, and two in Birchin Lane) and two great trading coffee-houses, Garraway's and Jonathan's, covered an area rather smaller than a football pitch.

There, it was universally believed, the jobber lurked to fleece the unwary with bogus promotions, false rumours, and, above all, technical patter. And yet 'Change Alley fascinated people with the charm of a new toy. Houghton's 'Price of the Stocks', started in the 1690s, found ready buyers, and the jobber could reasonably insist that his gains were precarious and his bargains far from easy to enforce. Markets were not so easily rigged as journalists made out. When the new toy went wrong, as it often did, a scapegoat was needed, and it would not be a serious exaggeration to say that after the revolution the stock-broker gradually replaced the jesuit as everyman's idea of a conspirator.*

*   *   *

The money on which the Londoner was so intent now took many forms: gold, silver, paper, and wood. Economists already perceived this; but to the ordinary man money still meant a specific weight of silver, coined only as evidence of its fineness, the monetary unit being the crown, weighing one ounce of sterling silver. The rest of the currency, even including gold, was regarded as a promise to pay silver, and as such

* See, for example Hogarth's celebrated cartoon on the South Sea Bubble, which shows the monument commemorating the Great Fire with the anti-papist inscription erased and an anti-stockbroker inscription substituted:

was discounted or given a premium according to the bullion market (in the case of gold) or the credit of the issuer (in the case of paper and the wooden tallies representing government borrowing).

The national habit of discounting extended to transactions in silver itself, for nobody but a simpleton would accept 1s. at its face value if it weighed less than one-fifth of an ounce, which was the case with most shillings down to 1696, owing to the profitability of exporting silver bullion to France and the incessant drain on silver from the Indian trade. As a result it was said that money was scarce. But since good money was hoarded or melted, and bad, light money and unregulated paper was plentiful, people were usually paying more than the nominal price for what they bought. This meant that there was a sort of inflation, although not of the kind we are used to today.

William Lowndes, the Secretary of the Treasury, was disposed to recognize this inflation by abolishing the crown and substituting a 'heavy crown', which he called a 'sceptre', of 6s. 3d., divided into five testoons of 1s. 3d. each, and so get the gold guinea down from its market price of about 24s. to four ounces of silver. His celebrated controversy with Locke ended with the rejection of this plan, and instead a decision on the part of the government to accept old silver at face value regardless of weight up to May 1696, and then to count it at bullion value only. This surgical operation, which involved complete recoinage, and great loss to anyone who could not get his silver to the Mint by the time appointed, could never have succeeded but for the great underlying strength of the economy. The result was to make sterling the hardest currency in Europe. In 1696, before the recoinage began, sterling at Amsterdam varied between 31 and 27 Dutch florins to the silver pound. From 1698 to 1703 it never fell below 34, and sometimes touched 37. The way was clear for the silent transition from a silver standard to a gold one, which was implicit in Newton's recommendation in 1717 that the government, instead of fixing a maximum value for the guinea in terms of silver, should settle the number of shillings to a guinea, the number adopted being twenty-one.[22]

Neither recoinage nor expanding trade could have been financed without paper money, which was issued during the war in increasing quantity from the Exchequer, the Bank of England, and the innumerable goldsmiths and running cashes of Lombard Street. The £6 million at which Lowndes estimated the face value of the silver in circulation in 1695, was absurdly inadequate for even personal transactions. It could not possibly support an economy that already talked in millions. The paper circulation, even at that time, was estimated at £15 million, and all of it, according to received economic theory, was credit. When men spoke, as they increasingly did, of the 'public credit', they were speaking primarily of the new, chaotic, paper and wooden currency.

Paper might be common, but it was far from being unquestioned, as the fate of one promissory note will show. In 1691 a man named Joseph Williams, who had invented a diving machine, drew a promissory note payable to his manager, Daniel Foe, who was as yet unknown and unprefixed. The amount was £12. 10s., but no doubt when Foe cashed it at the shop of Thomas Williams, goldsmith, of 76 Lombard Street, he got rather less than that for it. When the goldsmith presented the note to his namesake the diver, payment was refused on the technical ground that endorsed paper only passed between merchants, a status to which the diver and his manager made no pretensions. The goldsmith took the matter to court—by which time Foe, now Defoe, was keeping house quietly at Bristol after failing in a business for manufacturing tiles, and writing an Essay on Projects—and got his money; but although *Williams* v. *Williams* underpinned paper currency for some years, it was not until Chief Justice Holt tried to reverse it by holding promissory notes to be 'a new sort of speciality unknown to the Common Law, and invented in Lombard Street to give laws to Westminster Hall', that Parliament had to step in and set matters right by statute.[23]

Business documents of all kinds were the peculiar province

of the scrivener, a calling which rose to its peak of influence in the second half of the seventeenth century, and had fallen from grace by the second decade of the eighteenth. The scrivener's paper expertise made him the natural agent, who knew where demand lay, and where supply. 'Let me see,' the scrivener is made to say in Powell's *Art of Thriving*, 'there comes in the night Sir Samvan Skynker's money, five hundred, and tomorrow much more. I can supply you one hundred to a thousand out of that as your occasions require: how do you say?' Money was not the only commodity for which the scrivener acted as an agent. He dealt (or might specialize) in land, leases, businesses, reversions—anything, in fact, which would yield a commission and fees for documents. He was not a banker, for he did not himself lend or borrow, but only introduced lender to borrower; but he was simultaneously the solicitor, the estate agent, and the business agency of that enterprising age. His habits and ingenuity dictated business practice, and set business fashions. He produced the 'fine print' which it is peril to leave unread.

Among the entrants to this promising profession in the year of the Revolution was John Blunt, who at the comparatively late age of twenty-five was made free of the Merchant Taylors' Company after apprenticeship to Daniel Richards, scrivener, of Holborn, on 5 March 1689.[24] Like his father, who was a prosperous shoemaker in Rochester, Blunt was a Baptist. Burly and overbearing, glib, ingenious, and determined to get on, he was well fitted to make his way in the business jungle, and from the first he was successful. Only four months after setting up as a scrivener he was able to marry a lady of respectable Warwickshire family named Elizabeth Court, and in 1691 he became a liveryman. In the techniques of his profession he was unequalled: and his coarse character contained just that trace of titanism which was to carry him for a moment or two to the summit of politics and finance.

Some six months before Blunt qualified as a scrivener, at the end of James II's last summer as King, a person describing himself as 'John Craggs of Newland, in the County of Dublin,

Gent.', swore a curious document before a Master in Chancery. Its purpose was to provide a pedigree for a confidential servant of the Duke of Norfolk, named James Craggs, whose uncle John Craggs claimed to be. The account he gave of the ancient Durham family of warriors and landlords to which he claimed to belong was rather scanty, since he admitted that all its muniments had been lost in the Civil War and the only evidence he produced of its gentility was an armorial signet ring; and whatever his more remote ancestors may have been, James Craggs's parents were acknowledged to have been a landless farmer from the obscure hamlet of Wyersly, near Wolsingham, and the daughter of a Prebendary of Durham. It was, however, enough for James Craggs, two years afterwards, and now private secretary to the Earl of Marlborough, to establish his right to bear 'upon a Fess, between three mullets, as many cross crosslets'. It was a decisive step upwards for one of the most ambitious men of his time.[25]

The pedigree never completely smothered the taint that hung about Craggs's origins. He had been born in 1675, and some said that when he first came to London in 1680 he had kept a barber's shop, and that his first employment with the Duke of Norfolk had been as a footman. It was also said that his son, who was two years old at the time of the Revolution, and for whom the father was as ambitious as he was for himself, was not the offspring of Mrs. Craggs, the handsome daughter of a Watford corn-chandler, but of Mary, Duchess of Norfolk, sister of Henry Mordaunt, subsequently Marlborough's favourite lieutenant as Earl of Peterborough. Certainly Craggs knew the secrets of more than one great family, and his son was in time to be the darling of the best people; but the more probable explanation of Craggs's success lies in the fact that, as Somerset Herald said in his memoir of him, 'he was remarkable for his talent in reading men, and by a peculiar way gaining on the minds of those he dealt with'.

At about the time of the Revolution—it is not certain exactly when—Craggs transferred his loyalty from the Catholic Duke of Norfolk to the rising star of the Churchills.

PLATE I

JOHN BLUNT

PLATE II

POSTMASTER–GENERAL JAMES CRAGGS,
aged 58

Thereafter he made his way quickly in the borderland of business and politics for which his talents suited him so well. By 1695 he was combining the duties of confidential secretary to Marlborough with a valuable contract for military clothing which involved him in a brush with the House of Commons and a brief period of imprisonment for refusing to produce his accounts. For the next twenty years he was never far from Marlborough's (and Sarah's) elbow. In Marlborough's entourage he was ably supported by Mrs. Craggs's two brothers, Colonels Jacob and Michael Richards, both brilliant military engineers and technicians of the new class of self-made men.

Blunt and Craggs were making their way to fortune in an England that was advancing in power and civilization at a rate never equalled before. It was an age of giants, great achievement, unparalleled confidence. Among the statesmen of the next twenty years there were at least nine who would have towered above any ordinary political world. Newton and Locke were transforming science and philosophy; Swift and Defoe language; Addison and Steele, journalism and manners. English law moved on from the age of Jeffreys to that of Somers and Holt and began to play its traditional part above the battle. In Cornwall steam power was set to work. The whole of the British Isles was finally brought under a single political system—Ireland by force, Scotland by diplomacy. For the first time in modern history the English armies that Craggs helped to clothe and the Blunts to shoe campaigned over the Continent and won a series of land victories against the greatest European power in battles on a scale not to be seen again for nearly a century. No wonder that for the rest of the eighteenth century Englishmen looked back on its earliest years as 'Augustan'. Augustan England was the Britain of the commercial as well as the political revolution, charged with a new and, as it was to prove, intoxicating energy.

Without wealth and the means of transforming it into national power, none of this would have been possible. Our first concern must be a closer look at the agencies by which this transformation took place, their origins, and their operators.

CHAPTER II

The Sword Blade

A PROFOUND ALTERATION in the traditional relationship between business men and the government over money matters was one of the most impressive changes brought about by the Revolution. The Stuart kings, without enough prestige to take, like their contemporaries in France, or enough credit to borrow on a large scale, had never managed effectively to mobilize national wealth for public purposes. They gained little in power from the buoyancy of the economy over which they presided. When they did succeed in borrowing, their subsequent behaviour confirmed the contemporary maxim that business men should not put their trust in princes —a maxim which, it was generally believed, made it impossible for banks to flourish except in republics. The City never forgave the Stuarts for their seizure of the bullion deposits in the Mint on the outbreak of the Civil War and the default of 1672 which ruined the great banker, Sir Robert Vyner, along with half Lombard Street.

In twenty years of rising prosperity under the last two Stuarts the total income of the government from all sources, including loans, increased from just over a million a year in 1668 to £2·3 million in the last financial year of James II. Nearly all of it came from taxes. In 1692-3 the government's income was £5·6 million, and nearly a fifth of this was borrowed.[1]

This was not because the moneyed classes as a whole preferred the political ideas of 1689 to those of 1685 or 1660. The business man's views on the great questions of Church and State were as often traditionalist as they were Whig. The difference arose from the security he was offered. Down to

1688 the King borrowed on his personal responsibility alone, and there was no way of binding him, let alone his successors, to honour his debts, as Charles II's creditors found. He owed a million in the City when he died, and neither his brother nor his cousin paid either principal or interest.* We can only begin speaking of a National Debt in 1693, when the borrowings of the government were first guaranteed by Parliament.

This revolutionary association of Parliament with the borrowings of the State goes far towards explaining the passionate interest in public finance which is the leading characteristic of political life during the next thirty years. And now that financial expertise, as never before, was the key to the highest offices of all, a new type of parliamentary politician began to emerge. Montagu, Godolphin, Harley, and Walpole all made their names and, once they had made them, spent most of their official time, dealing with financial questions. At the level of civil servants, the career and importance of William Lowndes, who served at the Treasury from 1680 to 1724, most of the time as Secretary, have no parallel in earlier English history, and few later. At lower levels the business and official worlds interpenetrated to multiply the class of men who combined commerce and government service with great profit to themselves—whether, like Edward Gibbon, a Commissionership of Customs had followed on success in banking, or, like Francis Hawes, a stockbroking business had grown out of a clerkship at the Treasurer of the Navy's office.

It was fashionable to distinguish in the new political world between a Tory, or traditionalist, 'landed interest' and a 'moneyed' one which supported Revolution principles. This antithesis had its importance as a political slogan; and it is undoubtedly the case that the new class of business men were finding it worth their while to find and occupy seats in Parliament. By 1702 there were at least sixty of them in the Commons. But many other Members who were either landed

* This was the so-called 'Banker's Debt'. After lengthy negotiations, Queen Anne's Government agreed in 1704 to resume payment of interest on the capital written down by 50 per cent. Further unpaid debts of Charles II's time were being hopefully brought to the notice of Parliament as late as 1710.

proprietors or lawyers—two of the most heavily represented callings in the House—also had sizeable business interests, like John Hungerford, the fire-eating legal adviser to the East India Company. The antithesis does not correspond to the facts. Walpole, for instance, the embodiment of the moneyed interest, was a comparatively poor squire; Foley, the professed champion of the squires, came of a rich family of iron-founders. The great politico-economic struggles that lay ahead—the duel between the two East India companies, the birth-pangs of the Bank of England, the catastrophe of the South Sea—were fought out between rival business groups, each with its 'lobby' or core of parliamentarians and publicists. Each side in these struggles tried to use the contestants for high political office, and in turn was used by them. In at least one election a lobby openly sponsored its own political candidates; and by recipro-city the control of the major enterprises in the City—for there too there were elections—became a matter of the highest interest to politicians.[2]

The attitude of the independent gentleman, who still set the tone of the back benches in the House of Commons, alternated between admiration for the marvels the new finance seemed to achieve, and a kind of half-baked hostility to what he did not usually understand. In particular he was oppressed by his status as guarantor of the National Debt, and irritated by the thought that he and those like him paid most of the taxation which went to service it. These mixed feelings, if skilfully worked upon, could often be rallied to support, not the old ways, but ways espoused by business syndicates opposed to those which for the time being enjoyed the favour of the government.

The machinery for collection and expenditure of public money was unsystematic, and, as the war developed, became labyrinthine. Very little of it was under the direct control of responsible ministers. Indeed, apart from the government's maid-of-all-work, the Customs, on whom it depended for frontier policing, coastguard, quarantine, lighthouses, naval recruitment, and the enforcement of the Navigation Acts, as well as the collection of revenue, the various items of collection and expenditure were assigned to *ad hoc* agents or boards, each of which enjoyed a measure of independence. Even in the Exchequer itself each teller accounted separately for, and was entitled to trade in, his own cash. The more independent spending agencies—Paymaster of the Forces, Treasurer of the Navy, Commissioners of Victualling, and so forth, were virtually bankers, and their credit depended as much on the nature of the particular service and the personality of the agent, as on government credit in general. It was always easier, for instance, to raise money for the Navy than it was for the Army, because ships, cordage, and tar, with their prospect of easy conversion to civilian use, were a better security than military stores. Moreover, the Army had to pay its soldiers more or less regularly, and often abroad, while the Navy took the view that seamen did not need pay until they came safely home. Even then it usually took the form, not of cash, but of the Treasurer of the Navy's promises to pay, known as seamen's tickets.

The obligations of government agencies, such as seamen's tickets, Army debentures, and tallies,* formed a tangled thicket of public indebtedness which was always distinguished from the well-tended plantation of the National or 'funded' Debt— so called because it was statutorily secured on the yield of a

---

* Tallies were hazel faggots, rather shorter than broomsticks, split down the centre according to a medieval procedure which remained unchanged from the fourteenth century to the nineteenth. Before being split, the faggot was notched in a code expressing the amount paid into the Exchequer, so that the notches appeared both on the 'foil' given to the depositor and the 'counterfoil' retained in the Exechequer. The Treasury was very pleased with this as 'absolutely the best way that ever was invented; for it is morally impossible so to falsify or counterfeit a tally, but that upon rejoining it with the counterfoil, it will be obvious to every eye'. Although the form of the tally remained unchanged, its use (owing to its security) was much developed during the seventeenth century. Originally no more than a receipt to accounting officers, it turned first into a receipt for money advanced and ultimately into a notification that something (often interest) was due from the Exchequer. In such cases the tally's redemption was assigned to the product of some tax due perhaps years ahead, the tally being, as the phrase ran, 'struck on the Customs' for a given year. The tally would then be accepted by the tax-collecting agency for cash (as and when available) and end up again at the Exechequer as a voucher in the agency's account. Until redemption, tallies naturally circulated at a discount depending on the state of credit and the remoteness of the revenue on which they were struck; and, equally naturally anyone accepting tallies from the Exchequer expected some consideration in addition to the face value of the tallies he received.

particular tax; and it formed an important part of the financier's stock-in-trade. It was said in 1694 that bundles of tallies were to be found in every goldsmith's in Lombard Street. John Blunt's relation, Charles, who carried on the family bootmaking business at Bristol, held large sums in Army debentures issued against his contract for ammunition boots. In Deptford taverns the rising stationer, Thomas Guy (whose father had been a lighterman), discounted the tickets of needy seamen for cash as a sideline to his profitable trade in pirated bibles.[3]

By far the biggest investor in government securities of all kinds was the City syndicate associated with the name of Gilbert Heathcote. He had started life as a wine merchant, and was in his prime when the Revolution threw the business world open to a man of his outstanding shrewdness and tenacity. In all his dealings, whether he was assaulting a monopoly or creating one, merciless concentration was his rule. To the *Spectator* he was 'Sir Andrew Freeport', the embodiment of what was best in English business; to his enemies 'the meanest man in England'. His favourite aversions were simpletons and clergymen, for whose tithes he had a rooted hostility. When a hostile government curtailed his Lord Mayor's show on land, he rode on horseback to the Mansion House to be sworn and ordered the procession to follow him by water. In 1693 he fought and won the test case of the interloping sloop *Redbridge*, which broke Sir Josiah Child's grip on the East India trade. In 1694 he played a leading part in the foundation of the Bank of England.

It is usually said of this celebrated operation that it consisted of making a loan to the government in return for a charter to act as a national bank. This, however, conceals the ingenious answer which Heathcote and his associates found to the problem of carrying on a banking business when the whole authorized capital of £1·2 million was technically on loan to the government. Although Heathcote, the three Houblon brothers, Theodore Janssen, Sir William Gore, and Michael Godfrey, brother of the Sir Edmund whose murder had lit the bonfires of 1679, were very rich men, the loan which they made as bankers did not consist of cash, but of Bank of England notes. The cash put up by the shareholders was retained for banking. Indeed, only 60 per cent. of the authorized capital was called up in the first instance, and even of this amount one-seventh did not consist of actual cash, but of promises to pay. What had been done was to supplement the currency in a more acceptable way than by a fresh shower of distrusted Exchequer wood. Tallies corresponding to the new debt were struck indeed, but they were retained permanently by the Bank as what they grandly called their 'Fund of Credit', and never appeared in the market at all.

The reward of the Bank was very great. In return for creating £1·2 million new currency for the use of the government, it received a guaranteed 8 per cent. (£100,000 a year) on it, plus management charges; or over 13 per cent. on the £720,000 they actually raised. In addition, since the note issue was fixed at the same figure as the capital, and the capital was always the amount lent to the government, they in effect secured the right to create new money at the same rate as the government borrowed money from them.

From 27 July 1694, when the books were opened with the words 'Laus Deo in London', the Bank was surrounded with an aura of prestige and mystery which has never entirely evaporated—a sense that it was not as other businesses, yet as businesslike as any. It was like some great ship, with its watch of directors always on duty during business hours, and its studied display of operational efficiency. The un-English title of 'director',* the Italianate contraction 'Compa' on its notes, were deliberate touches of the exotic and modern, showing those who handled the new currency or dealt with the Bank that, though this was something new in England, it had borrowed its tradition from the glorious banks of Genoa and Amsterdam. And although the Bank had grown from, and

---

* In 1673 the business sense of 'director' was still regarded as a foreign usage: 'He is still one of the chief of the Court of Committees, which a foreigner would call directors' (O.E.D.).

continued as the preserve of, a particular business syndicate who as a group and as individuals had many other interests, it bred and drew a particular type of man, capable of sustaining its gravity. No institution is less easy to see through to the men behind it.

In the early years of the Bank's existence the undergrowth of unsecured government debt naturally went on sprouting round the little plantation of funded debt tended by the Bank. By 1697 tallies were at a discount of 40 per cent. and even the Bank's notes commanded rather less than their face value. In this situation the Bank undertook to relieve the market of £800,000 tallies at par and £200,000 in bank-notes, against a new issue of £1 million new stock authorized by Act of Parliament. In the horticultural metaphor from which 'stock' itself comes, this new stock was said to be 'engrafted', like a new shoot on an old tree, and the government undertook not only to pay the Bank interest on the tallies subscribed, but to redeem them over a period of years, the 'engrafted' stock being cancelled *pari passu* with the redemption.*

This operation was a complete success from every point of view. By freezing a large block of its tallies, the government improved its own credit; and the holders of tallies were eager to subscribe a security on which interest was not easy to extract in cash, in exchange for shares with a regular dividend and voting rights. The advantages to the syndicate operating the Bank were even greater. They were themselves large holders of tallies, and it is said that they used their inside knowledge to add to them when tallies were still at a heavy discount, afterwards exchanging them at par for stock. The coup was alleged to have enriched Heathcote alone by £50,000.

The Bank's share of the bargain was victory over the various rival banking schemes which had sprung from the fertile minds of Barbon the builder and Chamberlayne the projector.

---

*An important detail was the government's undertaking to redeem one-fifth of the tallies subscribed at once, thus permitting an expansion of the Bank's capital by £200,000 without any equivalent holding of Debt.

These schemes had made considerable headway, encouraged by such opposition politicians as Harley and Foley, and founded for purposes of publicity on the credit of land, in contra-distinction to the moneyed interest the Bank was supposed by its enemies to symbolize. But by the Act providing for the Engraftment the existence of the Bank was prolonged from 1706 (the original date on which it could be wound up) to 1710, and its privileged position was not only confirmed but extended in the most solemn terms:

> During the continuance of the Corporation of the Governor and Company of the Bank of England, no other Bank, or any corporation, society, fellowship, company, or constitution in the nature of a bank shall be erected, established, permitted, suffered, countenanced, or allowed by Act of Parliament with-in this Kingdom.[4]

During the sixteen years while first Montagu, then Godol-phin, presided at the Treasury the Bank became indispensable to the government. It underwrote the recoinage and the financial aspects of the Union between England and Scotland; and although it did not actually underwrite the eight issues of annuities by which the government raised almost £10 million between 1700 and 1710, the annuities themselves were payable and transferable at the Bank, which thereby became the pay-master of the new rentier class.

Its credit and influence spread over the whole community of the narrow seas, and not least through the demands of Britain's Continental war. Pay and provisions for the forces overseas, and subsidies for their allies were arranged through the Bank's correspondents in Amsterdam, Antwerp, Lisbon, Oporto, Hamburg, and Berne. So too, foreign business men came to hold large quantities of British government securities, and the British government required advice on foreign tastes and opinions in financial matters, as well as agencies abroad for maintaining service to foreign Debt-holders. All this the Bank supplied. The great corporation was the wonder and envy of the business world. It and its future were undoubtedly among the most important questions in the politics of the first two decades of the new century.

*   *   *

By the monopoly clause in the Engraftment Act of 1697 the Bank destroyed all its obvious rivals; but not a seed which had already been planted, and would in time be the most dangerous competitor of all. It was to all appearances one of the many scattered in the fertile soil of the 1690's, but it happened to be a magic bean.

One of the most prominent promoters of the eager age was Sir Stephen Evance. He was an American, and the sign of the Black Boy which hung above his goldsmith's shop in Lombard Street probably referred to his transatlantic parentage (his father had been born in New England) and his own familiarity with the coast of North America. Although professionally a goldsmith, his interests were more diverse than usual even for those times. They included salvage (with one of the patent diving machines of the period); a lead-mine; a privateer; mineral prospecting in Canada; fisheries off the coast of Ireland, in which he was concerned with Sir James Houblon, of the Bank, and Samuel Ongley, the rich linen-draper who was to preside over the South Sea Company in its early years. The wealth to be obtained from fishing was almost as much an article of faith among promoters as searching for sunken treasure.

Evance's most interesting venture, however, was in the field of manufacture. The old-fashioned English rapier with its heavy flat blade had now been losing favour for some years, both as a military arm and a gentlemanly adjunct, to the handier grooved, or 'hollow', blade. These were made in France, and with the war embargo were hard to get. In 1691, therefore, Evance promoted a scheme for importing a group of Huguenot technicians to make them in England, and on 13 October he and certain others received a charter of incorporation as the Governor and Company for Making Hollow Sword Blades in the North of England, with perpetual succession, the right to hold land, a common seal, a personality to sue and be sued, and the power to issue stock.* Forges were established near Shotley Bridge in Durham; and as usual the charter was matched by a loan from the promoters to the government. The sum (which covered two other patents taken out by Evance about the same time) was £50,000, advanced by Evance in association with Sir Francis Child in August 1692.[5]

For a time the new company prospered straightforwardly enough. They auctioned their product in London and from time to time confiscated smuggled blades by virtue of their charter. For a time, also, Evance prospered. He became an Excise Commissioner, and succeeded his associate and fellow-goldsmith, Sir Francis Child, as jeweller to William III. But soon after that King's death 'he failed in the world and shott himself in the temple . . . being no longer able to keep shop'. At about the same time the foreign blacksmiths in their Durham forges disappear from history. His affairs were left in such a tangle that they had not been cleared up in 1718, nearly twenty years later.[6]

By the turn of the century, the Sword Blade Company had passed into other hands, who meant to employ it for a very different purpose. Its offices were in Birchin Lane, a step from Exchange Alley, in premises occupied by the Company's new secretary, the scrivener John Blunt. The intermediary had in all probability been Evance's old colleague, Francis Child, whose son Stephen, also a banker, was to have a long and close association with Blunt.†

For those who fancy genealogical associations there may be something attractive in the thought that the great rival of the Whiggish Bank of England had these affinities with

* Evance was the first Governor. The Court of Assistants named in the Charter included three French Protestants—Peter, John, and William Reneau—and a certain Francis Tyssen, indicating an early association between that name and the armaments industry.

† For details of the family and business associations of Blunt and Child, see Appendix under Blunt, Child, and Tudman. Stephen Child's business was at 76 Lombard St., in succession to the firm of Williams, with whom Defoe had cashed his dubious promissory note (see p.18

a syndicate which had financed the Stuarts, for Sir Francis had been in partnership with Alderman Backwell, whose bank at the Marygold had been one of the props of Charles II.

But ideology played little part in the outlook of Blunt or the syndicate for whom he was acting as secretary. Apart from Blunt himself, there were three of them, Elias Turner, Governor of the Company, Jacob Sawbridge, the Deputy Governor, and George Caswall.[7]

Turner, though the senior, is also the most elusive of this trio. He was a goldsmith whose family had long traded under the ambiguous sign of the Fleece in Lombard Street. Being a reticent man, with a dignified manner, he managed to avoid most of the odium which fell on his more forthcoming partners. Nevertheless, he was said to have the impudence of one and the craft of the other. He provided the experience, and probably most of the capital, for the new enterprise.[8]

The birthplace of Sawbridge was Canterbury, where he began in 1706 to build up a landed estate, but his father had been in business in London, and the family sprang, like Mrs. Blunt's, from Warwickshire, although, being non-armigerous yeomen, they were rather lower in the social scale. Among his relations was the bookseller Sawbridge, whose shop was a favourite haunt of Swift's. The Deputy Governor's character was not a strong one, but what he lacked in will-power he made up in intelligence and activity.[9]

The only member of the group bred outside London was George Caswall. His family were leading people in Leominster, whence he had come to seek his fortune, and Members of the name had sat in Parliament for the place as long ago as Queen Elizabeth's time. James Caswall, George's father, was Bailiff (or Mayor) no less than five times between 1698 and 1710, besides being Receiver of the Land Tax for neighbouring Monmouthshire. For his municipal office he had to qualify by attending the established form of worship 'with the usual formalities'—for the Caswalls, like the Blunts, were Baptists, and the nickname 'Lemsterdam' had been conferred on the place, not only on account of the number of its streams, but of its sects. It was an important place, economically and politically: busier than now, and in the heart of the best wool country in England, 'a town of brisk trade in manufactures . . . in hat-making, leather, and many others . . . in a valley luxuriant beyond measure'.

On the whole, as one would expect from its multiplicity of chapels, the atmosphere there was Whiggish, and for some years after the Revolution its affairs were dominated by the eccentric and extreme Whig Thomas Coningsby from his country seat at Hope under Dinmore, a few miles away. Feudal in outlook, Coningsby was a republican in principle. He was the last English gentleman to keep a jester, and preserved in a glass case the handkerchief with which he had stanched the slight wound King William had received at the Boyne. In his stormy career he quarrelled with nearly everybody, especially the two rising opposition Whig families of the southern marches, the Harleys and the Foleys. He also quarrelled with that 'united and loving body' the Corporation of Leominster, who in 1692 elected Robert Harley's lawyer brother Edward as their Recorder to defend their privileges.* In 1698, in the teeth of the Coningsby interest, Edward Harley became one of the members for the town, initiating a struggle between the two families which was to go on for fifteen years, with much expenditure of money and manipulating of sects.[10]

Clearly such a man as George Caswall was highly qualified to move in the corridors of politics as well as finance. The tussle between Coningsby and the Harleys, moreover, was not the only link between Caswall's corner of Herefordshire and the greater scenes at the capital. In 1705 one of Heathcote's oldest associates, the second-generation Fleming, Sir James Bateman, bought the handsome country seat of Shobdon Court, a few miles from the town. He was Deputy Governor

---

* Harley retained this office until his death in 1732, when it passed to his son, and then to his grandson, so that a Harley was responsible for the privileges of Leominster down to the beginning of the nineteenth century.

of the Bank when he bought it, and in the same year became Governor.

Since 1700 George Caswall had been in partnership with a goldsmith named Brassey at 71 Lombard Street, just opposite the principal mouth of Exchange Alley, and from the first he had specialized in market business. His methods were bold and bustling, and his days were crammed with engagements, for which he was invariably punctual. Wherever he was—and he loved to do business for the best people—he carried a whiff of Exchange Alley with him, and addressed his audience like a shareholders' meeting. 'A man of brass', it was said, 'sufficient for much more business than he can be trusted with; famed for more fire than flegm; fitter to drive than to lead.'

Defoe summed up the trio whom he called the 'three capital sharpers of Britain': 'Sawbridge is as cunning as Caswall is bold, and the reserve of the one with the openness of the other makes a complete Exchange Alley man. Turner . . . acts in concert . . . and makes together a complete triumvirate of thieving.' But the driving force behind them was Blunt, with his scrivener's skill. He was now in the prime of life, with powerful jowl and heavily-lidded eyes, an industrious, domineering man whom it was equally difficult to like and to resist. The enterprise on which the new owners of the Sword Blade charter were embarked in the early years of the eighteenth century was to annex for themselves as large a part as they could of the politico-financial empire that had been carved out by the Bank of England.[11]

Just when the process of beating swords into ploughshares began cannot be stated with certainty. The Company were still auctioning their old product as late as 1703, but this was probably a clearance sale, for by that time the reconstruction as a finance corporation must have been well advanced. In 1702 Blunt was sufficiently well known at the Treasury to offer them his 'sentiments' on the way to keep public accounts in a letter that does not seem to have been answered, and the first moves in the new game may well have been the spate of pamphlets in 1700 urging a reform in the disposal of the estates confiscated from Jacobites during the conquest of Ireland.[12]

After the conquest these estates had been parcelled out among the officers and hangers-on of the expeditionary force such as Caswall's neighbour Coningsby, who was among the larger beneficiaries of the distribution. The idea that they should have been sold for the benefit of the public rather than given away for the King's, which was put forward in vigorous language in the pamphlets, naturally attracted country Members of Parliament, and the result was a statute cancelling many of the grants made in the heat of victory and turning them over to Commissioners, with instructions to sell them at public auction.

At these auctions the Sword Blade Company, empowered by their charter to hold land, were large buyers, and altogether by the autumn of 1702 they had acquired estates with a rent-roll of £20,000 a year for about £200,000 or ten years' purchase—a bargain price. To pay for these, the Company used another charter privilege—the power to issue stock. The stock created, however, was not issued for cash but, on the pattern of the Bank's 'Engraftment' operation a few years before, against depreciated, unsecured, Government obligations. The class of floating debt chosen was Army Debentures, the paper issued by the Paymaster of the Forces, which then stood at 85 on the market, and for which the holders were offered Sword Blade stock, backed by landed security, at 100. The government thus received the price of its land in its own obligations, which it could cancel.[13]

There can be little doubt that the Sword Blade syndicate imitated Heathcote by laying out large sums in debentures as private individuals before the offer was made, and so were able to unload them profitably on to an appreciative market or the Company itself as the price rose. If even one-half of the debentures required to make the price of the land was found in this way by the promoters themselves their personal profits would have been over £25,000 in the summer of 1703, when the subscription was taken.

The government, by cancelling £200,000 worth of Debt and an interest charge of £15,000 a year in return for assets they could not profitably use themselves, was also a gainer. What was more, they extracted a loan in cash from the promoters. The terms—£20,000 at 5 per cent. with a royal stock of Cornish tin as security—were settled at the Treasury by Blunt and the Company's legal adviser Lake on 1 June 1704. The amount is remarkably near the syndicate's probable private profit, which was no doubt the basis of the Treasury's estimate.[14]

Naturally, this operation did not escape the vigilance of the Bank, who were still more concerned when they found the Sword Blade Company launching out, not only as a land corporation, but as a land bank. On the strength of their 'fund of credit' in land and tin, they were granting mortgages to other purchasers of Irish land, accepting deposits, discounting bills, and even issuing notes. In the spring of 1704 the Bank served notice on the Treasury that in their view the monopoly clause of the Act of 1697 was being infringed. The embarrassed Treasury referred the question for a legal opinion, which was initially on the Bank's side, but no action against the Sword Blade followed. Apart from the Treasury's reluctance to spoil a profitable deal, there was a curious legal obstacle, which no doubt Blunt and Lake pointed out (there is no evidence that they did so, but they were not prone to miss points of the kind). The Act of 1697, for all its sonority, only protected the Bank against rival corporations set up 'by Act of Parliament'; and although (as the law required technically in the case of all joint stocks) directions for preparing a Bill to authorize the Sword Blade charter had been given in September 1691, no such Bill had ever been passed.[15]

So matters dragged on until May 1707, when the Bank, with a favourable turn in the political situation, extracted a promise from the Treasury that proceedings would be taken against the Sword Blade and the Bank's privileges further fortified by legislation. For the Bank this was one in a much larger series of moves, on which their whole future depended. In the past

PLATE III

JAMES CRAGGS THE YOUNGER,
aged 22

PLATE IV

GILBERT HEATHCOTE,
aged 60

few years their services to the government had been immense. They had financed the Union with Scotland, and their directors had been prominent in raising for Marlborough's ally, Prince Eugene, the first loan to a foreign government ever floated on the London market. Their existing charter had only a further three years to run, and in return for its renewal for another twelve years they were offering to lend the government a million and a quarter at 5 per cent. Having made this offer, they were dismayed to find another syndicate were offering to lend the government a million and a half.

Whether or not the Sword Blade were concerned in this rival bid, they were certainly behind the volley of propaganda that was now directed against renewal of the Bank's charter as privileged financier to the government. The publicity, naturally, was ostensibly addressed to country gentlemen, every one of whom, according to *A Short View of the Apparent Dangers and Mischiefs from the Bank of England*, knew that one should lop the big trees to give the underwood a chance to develop. ' 'Twould be wonderful, if those gentlemen who refused to trust King William with a standing army when there was some appearance of conveniency in it, should consent to vest such power in the Lord knows who.' The Sword Blade Company, its apologists maintained in another pamphlet, were being threatened with the loss 'not only of the franchise inherent in them as a corporation, which they are in the actual use and exercise of', but of the right to subject the Bank to the blasts of healthy competition. Since they had set up as a bank, and discounted tallies at 4 per cent. when the Bank asked 5, interest rates had never been so low.[16]

Nevertheless the Bank won, though only after raising their loan offer to a million and a half, and lowering the interest on it from 5 to $4\frac{1}{2}$. Their charter was prolonged until 1732, and their privileges were reaffirmed in language specifically designed to put the Sword Blade out of business, making it illegal for—

any body politic or corporate whatsoever, erected or to be erected (other than the said Governor and Company of the

Bank of England) or for any other persons whatsoever united or to be united in covenants or partnerships exceeding the number of six persons, in that part of Great Britain called England, to borrow, owe, or take up any sum or sums of money on their bills or notes, payable at demand, or at any less time than six months from the borrowing thereof.[17]

Nor was this the full measure of the Sword Blade's discomfiture. Their Irish business was not prospering. The trouble here was title. Professedly loyal relatives of the original Jacobite owners of land owned by or mortgaged to the Company kept on making their appearance with title deeds which seemed to have been assigned to them before the forfeitures came into force; and when the Company tried to enforce their rights the Irish courts and Parliament were unsympathetic. The Company managed to get an Act from the British Parliament in spring, 1708, setting a time limit on the right to raise these disputes as to title; but in April of that year their stock was down to 51, and those who had refused the offer to exchange their Army Debentures (which still stood about 85) were congratulating themselves on their prudence.

It took the Sword Blade partners nearly four years to extricate themselves from their Irish venture, and in the process they came perilously near bankruptcy. They blamed the Bank, and never forgave it, nursing 'the measure of their revenge, not to cool, no not till the charter of the Bank shall expire'.[18]

Their only consolation was in contemplating the struggles of the government to raise money with the aid of the financial monopoly to which they had chained themselves. The year 1707 had seen a third mortgage (by way of tally-splitting) of the Customs revenue; 1708 saw a fourth, 1709 a fifth, and 1710 a sixth, which hypothecated revenue as far ahead as 1720 and raised only £150,000 ready money—in Switzerland.* For the main parliamentary loan of 1710 the Government was driven to abandon the usual plan of selling straightforward annuities,

---

* Blunt followed all these struggles with the greatest care, and was able to furnish Swift with an exact memorandum of them, which he inserted verbatim in *The History of the Last Four Years of the Queen.* Swift acknowledges the authorship of the passage in a marginal note on the original MS.

and revived the expedient, disused since the lamentable failure of the Malt Lottery Loan thirteen years before, of baiting the issue with prizes.

In the business world of 1710 the Sword Blade partners were not alone in waiting hungrily for the charmed circle set up by Godolphin's Treasury and the Bank to break. Many were excluded from it. There were, for instance, Samuel Ongley, now richer than ever, for whom Blunt acted; the adventurous Samuel Shepheard, Heathcote's former colleague, who had recovered from the damage done him by the Bank in the great East India battle of 1702; Edward Gibbon, a linen-draper like Ongley, and even richer and more gifted financially; Sir Richard Hoare, private banker to the best people, who combined strong High Church views with inveterate hostility to the Bank and all it stood for; the banking house of Tudman and Child; and Swift's old schoolfellow at Kilkenny, Francis Stratford, who had once been a Bank director, and was now a leading man in the Baltic trade. And behind these there were men even bigger who would not be unwilling to replace the Bank if a government unfriendly to it should replace Godolphin's.

CHAPTER III

The South Sea Company

IN THE SPRING of 1710 it began to be apparent that those in the wilderness would not have to wait much longer. The system built round Godolphin's financial skill and Marlborough's victories was beginning to crumble. In August Godolphin himself was dismissed from the Treasury, and Robert Harley, for the time being as Chancellor of the Exchequer, not Lord High Treasurer, took his place.

The Bank had never believed such a thing was possible, and had, in consequence, overplayed their hand. At the first sign of political trouble Heathcote, then serving as Governor, had taken the extraordinary step of insisting on a private interview with the Queen, during which he lectured—almost threatened —her about the terrible financial consequences that would follow any change of ministers. Harley saw to it that this attempt to put pressure on the sovereign should be widely known; and it was not the only way in which Heathcote contributed to the débâcle, for he assured Godolphin to the last that Harley's adventure could never succeed for lack of financial backing. Even when, as a result, Godolphin was taken unawares by his own dismissal, the ex-ministers still spoke confidently of Harley as struggling 'in a sculler alone against wind and tide, without any person to assist him'.[1]

There was an element of truth in this, and although during that summer Harley had to prepare for a general election and throw out the first secret casts in his great policy of peace with France, he gave no less attention to gathering financial advice and support. Advice, indeed, tended to come unasked, once he was installed. He heard from his old protégé, Chamberlayne, of the Land Bank days, and the unwearied Paterson, still with

American dreams. More to the purpose was the long, secret correspondence with the banker Drummond at The Hague, through whom he kept in touch with business opinion in Holland and received many hints about constructing a financial system without the Bank. Drummond did not think much of Harley's own banker, Shepheard—'an excellent merchant for shipping, and in foreign trade by far the first in England, but no banker'. 'Get such a man', he wrote, 'who has credit abroad, as Sir James Bateman, or Sir Theodore Janssen . . .'— significantly, ex-directors of the Bank. 'I have made several entertainments', he went on, 'to get the best people together to put them right, for your adversaries are industrious . . . they all say they will be convinced . . . providing when the Parliament comes to sit, the funds be provided before you quarrel. If they see the land tax, and malt tax, and a new lottery or annuities for one two and three lives granted before Christmas, they will all join and venture as fast as ever.'[2]

Elections, and not only parliamentary ones, were the other great preoccupation. Great efforts were put out at Leominster, where, with the help of the Baptists headed by the Caswalls, the Harleys for the first time succeeded in capturing both seats. Just as much trouble was taken with the election of East India directors, which was also on party lines. Among the new directors chosen were Arthur Moore, one of Harley's closest financial cronies, the rising Edward Gibbon, and John Blunt, who in the course of the autumn was to be seen more and more frequently at the Treasury, to the distress of Secretary Lowndes. It was all part and parcel of an advance into office of Harley's business backers—Hoare, as banker to the Civil List; Gibbon, as a Commissioner of Customs.

The new Parliament elected in October, was remarkable rather for its atmosphere than for any startling change in its composition. It was possessed with a strong, if muddled, feeling that the time for dramatic changes in policy at home and abroad had now arrived. This feeling had its focus in the large and noisy group of members who called themselves the October Club. They were perhaps 200 strong, and by no means

all of them were country gentlemen; but they were fond of the
High Churchmanship and xenophobia which were supposed to
be typical of squires. They were the key to the new Parliament,
because they had agreed to vote as a block on all major questions
—an unusual step to take at this stage of parliamentary history.

There was no particular reason why the October Club
should have been enthusiastic about Harley. High Churchmanship hardly fitted this ex-Dissenter, who was 'always careful
to have a clergyman of each kind to Sunday dinner', so as not
to offend his Baptist supporters in the West Country. Nor was
peace, by itself, a particularly attractive slogan for men who
prided themselves on their patriotism. Malplaquet might have
been bloody, but it had been won.[3]

The 'butcher's bill' of Malplaquet and the Sacheverell case,
in fact, hurt Harley's opponents more than they helped him. In
the Queen's closet Mrs. Masham's victory over the Duchess
of Marlborough had given Harley an indispensable tactical
advantage, but no materials for a ministry or a policy. And if,
in Swift and Defoe, he had two of the most gifted propagand-
ists in English history, his opponents, in Addison and Steele,
had the other two. Altogether, without high skill and a large
allowance of luck, it seemed unlikely that Harley would
succeed in consolidating his hold on power.

Harley was not only skilful and lucky, but extremely skilful
at turning what seemed to be bad luck into good. During his
first six months of office an attempt by a Frenchman to murder
him made him a national hero; the Whig junto's favourite
commander, Stanhope, was compelled to surrender in Spain;
and the Emperor Joseph, who seemed set for a long reign,
suddenly died, leaving his throne to be filled by his brother,
the Archduke Charles, whom it had been the chief British war
aim to promote to the throne of Spain in order to exclude the
Bourbons. Arguments about the balance of power in Europe
took a different turn, and there seemed little to choose from
that point of view between condoning the dynastic connexion
between France and Spain, and recreating Charles V's Empire
for Charles VI.

None of these events, however, had happened by the autumn of 1710, and in any case they were the waves that helped Harley forward, not the tide that carried him. The changes of 1710 were the political expression of the first fully-fledged crisis in the commercial and financial revolution through which the nation was still passing. Business and politics were now so closely intertwined that no political grouping could hope for success without business support. Godolphin knew that as well as Harley; but what Harley had gauged, as Godolphin and Heathcote had not, was the degree to which the Bank—so one of the Sword Blade pamphleteers had put it—had acted as a dam on the accumulating enterprise of the nation.

The war had encouraged, not checked, the advance of wealth and the multiplication of paper. It was no uncommon thing, now, for a man to have made a 'plum', as current slang described £100,000. Foreign visitors were astonished by the ready circulation of paper money, the efficiency of the banks and public offices, and the crowded advertisement columns of the exuberant Press. The enormous output of bricks—29 million in 1711—was reflected in a London whose inhabited arc now curved from Vauxhall to Stepney. London's population in twenty years up to 1710 had risen, despite increasing death-rates, by over 25 per cent., to over 675,000 people. If the torrent of ingenuity did not flow quite so freely as in the 'nineties, it certainly showed no signs of drying up. In 1713 the literary man Aaron Hill published his scheme for extracting edible oil from nuts; in 1714 a typewriter was patented. 1710 itself was marked by a burst of enthusiasm for insurance, in the course of which the Sun Insurance Office was launched by Charles Povey.* The compiler of the contemporary directory

* Povey started as a coal-merchant, and the range of his activity is more extraordinary than Defoe's. Apart from founding the Sun Fire Insurance Office, he developed at different times a pirate letter-carrying service (prosecuted by the Post Office); a free newspaper, dependent entirely on advertisements; a salvage corps; a water-bomb for putting out fires; a commercial agency; and a weaving factory at Belsize Park. He was also a currency reformer, a Commissioner for Sick and Wounded Soldiers, and the author of some 600 pamphlets on every conceivable topic, from Low Churchmanship to the immorality of Richardson's *Pamela*.

gave religion only a courtesy precedence: 'Next to the purity of our religion', he wrote, 'we are the most considerable Nation in the World for Vastness and Extensiveness of Trade.'[4]

The traditional rulers of the countryside, who made so much noise in the October Club, rejoiced in the commerce but resented the pushing business world that thrived on it. It was in every way disagreeable to find some rich City knight, whose father had been a tradesman or even a foreigner, settling down as a country neighbour, like Bateman in Herefordshire and Lambert Blackwell, the merchant grandson of the Parliamentarian general, who by 1710 was already an extremely big landowner in Norfolk, sending up prices and robbing the old families of respect with his untaxed fortune. People of the same kind had burrowed, during the Godolphin régime, into the heart of the national administration. Craggs, for instance, thanks to Marlborough, was Clerk of the Deliveries to the Ordnance and Member of Parliament for Grampound in Cornwall, where he was working hard to build up a local influence of his own by alliance with the ancient, but for the time being enfeebled, county family of Eliot of Port Eliot. With all this he still remained the great Duke's confidential emissary from his headquarters at The Hague; and had placed his promising son, a thorough gentleman, with charming manners which were exerted with great effect at the Court of the Elector of Hanover, in the same sort of confidential and profitable employment with Stanhope in Spain.

In particular, with all their comings and goings, the Craggs, Cardonells and Solomon de Medinas emphasized how closely war and business now united the two sides of the Midland Sea. It was no consolation to ordinary Englishmen in their new mood that England dominated both sides of it. They still felt the Continentals were older and more cunning in commerce and politics. They were lining their pockets as they supplied the British forces and bought British government securities. It seemed especially intolerable that Dutchmen and Portuguese Jews should have a lien on British taxation. It was no accident that the Sacheverell mob tried to burn down the Bank.

So it was that the English gentleman's social and political resentments came to crystallize on the question of national finance and public indebtedness. To him it was a simple matter. The nation was an estate and the National Debt an encumbrance to it, so that the owner's freedom of action was hampered until it was paid off. Where debtor and creditor can be represented as divided by national and social boundaries there is the opportunity for manufacturing a powerful political propellant. So far as Parliament was concerned, Harley founded his power on the proposition that for the past ten years the public purse had been scandalously mismanaged for the glory of the Duke of Marlborough and the benefit of foreigners and the Bank of England.

He was far better qualified for this role than as a rescuer of the Church of England. From 1690 to 1697 he had served a seven-year apprenticeship in finance as a Commissioner of Public Accounts. In 1695 he had been the hero of the Land Bank scheme. One of his brothers, Nathaniel, was a leading figure in the Levant trade, and the other, Edward, had since 1702 been one of the Auditors of the Imprest, a post which entitled him to examine every detail in the transactions of the war-time spending agencies. The other Auditor was Harley's brother-in-law, Paul Foley, so that when the time came the new Government was able very quickly to cast a beam into the murkiest corners of their predecessors' doings. Harley himself had taken some pains to appear during the election campaign as an expert and orthodox financier. Two essays were published under his name (they were actually by Defoe), one dealing with credit, the other with loans. A third, on the danger of national banks, was contemplated.

*   *   *

Homespun—or apparently homespun—finance for the squirearchy was one item in the programme leading to a peace which Harley was to make appear preferable to victory; but it was not a theme to impress such men as Bateman, Janssen, or

45

Shepheard. They harboured no crude morality about debtor and creditor, and politically were very far from being isolationists. But with the transformations of the past twenty years before them they cherished the ambition of almost limitless expansion in overseas commerce. For its sake they had so far supported the war with voice and purse. If Harley was to carry with him an influential segment of the business community, he had to convince them that the war had been carried on without regard to British commercial interests.

In this he was much helped by what had happened after Malplaquet. Whatever Englishmen might believe, the heaviest losses there had fallen on the Dutch, who had lost the flower of their infantry in a series of murderous charges. To keep the Dutch in the war at all, the Whig Townshend, in October 1709, had felt obliged to make them some remarkable concessions. One was that they should occupy the Spanish Netherlands when these were reconquered; the other that they should have an equal share with Britain in the trade with Spanish America.

The South Sea trade, as commercial enthusiasts were fond of calling it, was considered the choicest commercial prize the war had to offer. It answered every popular economic maxim. South America was more accessible than India, and less civilized. Instead of being a drain on silver, like India, it would take traditional English manufactures like cloth and ironmongery and pay in bullion or the not much less precious commodities of dyestuffs, logwood, and cochineal.

South America was the more tempting because the Bourbon King Philip, like his Habsburg predecessors, did not allow foreigners to carry on ordinary trade with his colonies. It had been the hope that the British candidate for the throne of Spain would relax this rule in favour of Britain alone—and he had in fact secretly agreed to do so. But the Whig slogan of 'No peace without Spain', which had in consequence stirred the British merchant for so long, had a hollow ring now that the fruits were to be shared with the Dutch.

The British trader was not wholly ignorant of South

America. There was one loophole for the foreigner, through which he was able to glimpse its possibilities. Partly, at any rate, because of the protection given by the Church to the native peoples, South America had an inexhaustible appetite for African slaves. Heathcote, whose globe-encircling interests included a profitable contract for remitting money to the West Indies for the British forces there, put the point with his usual pith: 'We exchange our goods for nothing but gold and silver and the goods we traffick with them are onely wearing apparel and negroes for their mines.' The right to import slaves was put out to tender by the Spanish authorities, and since the 1680s this concession, the celebrated Asiento, had been granted to foreign business syndicates, first of Italians, then of Portuguese.

Neither the Dutch nor the British had so far been formal concessionnaires, but they had come to have an important stake in the trade because their island possessions of Curaçao and Jamaica were convenient depots for the 'refreshment' of the negroes between their hideous voyage from Africa and the last stage of their journey across the Caribbean and the Isthmus to the mines of Lima at £17 to £22 each 'free on board'. Until the slave reached the islands he usually belonged to the British or Dutch slavers who had brought him from Africa, not to the Asientists. Nor did British and Dutch interests end in the island slave markets. The Asiento ships to the mainland were used to cover highly profitable contraband cargoes of textiles and other manufactured goods. On all counts, slaving was held to be the key to the whole South American trade.

Since the Portuguese had succeeded the Italians as Asientists, the British had had the lion's share of the slave trade. Something of its scale can be gathered from the figures for the ten years from 1698 to 1708, during which 44,000 negroes were imported into Jamaica—a number far in excess of the local demand—and the Jamaica trade, in the last year of the ten, was reckoned to be yielding bullion at the rate of £200,000 a year. These highly satisfactory results had been achieved in spite of the new French King of Spain's transfer of the Asiento from the Anglophile Portuguese to the French Guinea Company, and a British war embargo on trade between Jamaica and any Spanish possession.

Heathcote had made short work of this last difficulty. 'This might be done', he wrote to the authorities in 1703, 'by intimating to the Governor [of Jamaica] to wink or look through his fingers and when they bring silver and gold to ask no questions.' In 1704 the embargo was formally lifted so far as Jamaica was concerned, and in 1708 the Governor thought that 'if there can be a method found out to prevent the French trading to Lima and the South Seas, trade here will soon be in a flourishing condition'.[5]

*   *   *

All this was in Harley's mind when he met the new Parliament for the first time on 25 November 1710. But first he had to establish himself as the cleanser of the Augean stables of war finance, and the scourge of moneyed men. So he would destroy the reputation of his predecessors, canalize the energies of the October Club, and extract the supplies with which to carry on. Only when this had been effectively done could his own moneyed allies, along with the recruits the assurance of supplies would bring in, be safely brought on the scene. In the meantime, on the commercial front, business men must not be frightened, and the secret peace feelers with France must make it clear that an essential feature of the settlement would be a privileged position for British trade in South America.

The Speech from the Throne, therefore, was artistically colourless, with a single prominent highlight. As soon as she had referred to her determination to pursue 'this expensive war' to a successful conclusion, the Queen expressed her concern 'that the Navy, and other offices, are burdened with heavy debts, which so far affect the public service that I must earnestly desire you to find some way to answer these demands and to prevent the like for time to come'.

The Commons took the bait eagerly, and, having assured the Queen that they would 'endeavour to trace the source of this great evil, and to apply a remedy suitable to it', began sending for figures of all kinds. These came forward very promptly, for Harley had set officials to work compiling them in August, as soon as he moved into the Treasury. On 4 December Walpole's responsibility, the Navy debt, was revealed as over £6 millions; next day disclosed the Exchequer borrowings during the current year alone as £6·3 millions; on the 7th that Marlborough's army in the Low Countries was costing £1·5 million a year; on the 8th that Craggs estimated the debt on Ordnance services at a quarter of a million; and on the 11th that half a million was owed for transportation, mostly for Stanhope's Spanish campaign.

As soon as Christmas was past, Harley heaped more fuel on the blaze. He chose 3 January, the day after Stanhope's disaster at Brihuega had been solemnly announced in a royal message, to reveal that with the connivance of the Victualling Commissioners the public had been swindled out of large sums by the ring of brewers who contracted to supply the British sailor with beer. Next day he blandly presented estimates of the sums to be found for Britain's Continental allies—the Duke of Savoy, the Margrave of Hesse, the Elector Palatine, the Archbishop of Trier, the King of Portugal (666,666 pattacoons, 33 stivers), and the King of Prussia, whose requirements included an amount described with an irony that can hardly not have been deliberate as: 'More, to enable her Majesty to satisfy her share of the pretensions of the King of *Prussia* to a further allowance for the extra charge he has been at in recruiting the body of his troops in *Italy*—£11,141. 2s. 3d.' There was more to come, but the horrified House had heard enough to make them turn from the October Club's favourite projects of stopping moneyed men from sitting in Parliament and building fifty new churches, to appoint a committee to go into the whole question of public indebtedness.

On the whole it was a committee of experts: Harley himself, the two Auditors, the indispensable Lowndes. But it had to include one leading member of the October Club, and for this reason it was convenient to include William Aislabie, the

Member for Ripon. He had once been a keen Whig, and had no particular claims to gentility (his father had been an ecclesiastical official and his ancestors were Baltic merchants), but he had had early premonitions about the way the political wind would veer, and in the last year or two had become a rabid High Churchman. Throughout the preceding summer and autumn he had badgered Harley for a post in the new administration, and from Harley's lack of response one can guess that he did not think much of this sly, domineering, ambitious, but basically stupid Yorkshireman. His good will in his county had eventually been thought worth a seat on the Board of Admiralty, which Aislabie, who had a high opinion of himself, thought much less than he deserved.[6]

Once this committee had seriously set to work the cauldron could be left to simmer with only an occasional extra puff, such as the revelation that about half the guardsmen who signed for pay never appeared on parade, and a supplementary estimate for £20,000 to provide foreign troops with 'forage, wagon money, recruits, douceurs, and other extraordinaries'. With Parliament behind him, Harley could turn to the problem of finding money in the City and abroad without recourse to the Bank of England.

The immediate question of finding the autumn quarterly remittance for Marlborough's army had been solved by Harley's first line of financial supporters, including Gibbon, Caswall, and Hoare's bank, who between them had remitted £300,000 through Drummond at The Hague. This alone must have made the Bank of England, who so far had kept their hands firmly in their pockets, very uneasy; but they persisted in non-cooperation as dangerously as ever, and can reasonably be blamed for the comparative failure of the lottery they had undertaken to manage for Godolphin.* A German visitor was shown the great drum for the draw revolving under elaborate precautions in the Inigo Jones banqueting hall, which

* So complete was to be the Bank's management that the proceeds were not even to be paid into the Exchequer. The Bank was to hold them as a credit for spending departments to draw upon—a novel arrangement which was as unsound as it was unpopular.

governments have used for so many purposes. Another lottery was projected for 1711, and the Bank was to manage this too. Hermitage, the Dutch envoy, considered that it too would be undersubscribed.[7]

A change had, however, been suggested in the presentation of this lottery which 'Mr. Lowndes ... called unintelligible, and was with great difficulty brought to comply with it' when it was put forward by Auditor Harley. The lottery of 1710 had simply been a draw for annuities, with some—the prizes—larger than the rest. The new version was designed to make the mouth water by expressing the prize money as lump sums of up to £12,000. It is true that the effect was the same as if they had been prize annuities, because the lump sums were kept by the government as part of the loan and only the interest on them was actually paid; but it was understood that even the capital would eventually be paid in full.[8]

John Blunt had undoubtedly been Auditor Harley's technical adviser in this victory over the official Treasury; and when the Bank again showed signs of failing to fill their old enemy's project quickly enough, Blunt and his associates undertook to fill it themselves. Their books opened on 3 March 1711, and by the 7th they were more than filled. Orders were pouring in from Holland and Germany too late to be registered, and the Bank was desperately reversing its engines to retrieve its mistake.* It was the first successful English State lottery, and Blunt's first triumph in the field of public finance.

A day afterwards Harley was stabbed at the examination of the Frenchman Guiscard, and during his convalescence his brother Edward and Blunt shared virtually complete control at the Treasury. Blunt never lacked expedients or the courage to reinforce success. The first lottery was no sooner marketed than he was ready with a new one of even more dazzling pattern. From the amount it raised it was grandly known as 'The Two Million Adventure' or, more technically, as The

* Like most financial projects of the time, the 'subscription' of promises to take up tickets preceded the actual issue of the tickets and, in this particular case, the Act of Parliament establishing the lottery. The price of the tickets was paid by instalments, so that the whole sum took a year or more to get in.

Classis. Its inventor regarded it as his masterpiece, and as ushering in a new era of finance, not only in England, but in Western Europe. It may be said that it did.

For one thing, it was on a much bigger scale than the old lotteries. The tickets cost £100 each instead of £10; and the big prize was the unprecedented sum of £20,000, a fortune as large, in contemporary values, as even the biggest football pool today. What was more, every ticket, even the so-called 'blanks', carried a prize of some sort, ranging down to £10. The effect of this was to raise the rate of interest used for calculating the annuities, which was 6 per cent. as before, to a guaranteed minimum yield of $6\frac{1}{2}$ per cent. on the investment. But the most novel device of all was the division of the draw into five 'classes', containing different numbers of tickets for different scales of prizes. Thus the first 1,330 tickets out of the draw qualified for prizes ranging from £1,000 down to £10; while the last 6,600 qualified for prizes from £20,000 down to £30. This gave the speculator the attraction of entering for five lotteries at the same time, and not knowing which one Chance would assign him to.

Taking the prizes into account, the Government was offering under these arrangements to pay an average of something like 8 per cent., and it is not surprising that the subscription was made in nine days, or that other securities fell correspondingly. Much of the marketing was done through the Sword Blade syndicate and their associates. Gibbon alone disposed of a tenth of the tickets, for which he paid cash to the Exchequer and received discount of £4,500. Blunt himself sold tickets to the tune of £993,000. Charles Blunt was made Paymaster of the lottery, with an expense account of over £5,000. Samuel Ongley's son was chief clerk. The Bank was wholly excluded from the management.[9]

While they were planning these operations, Auditor Harley and Blunt were also at work, in the strictest secrecy, on a yet more spectacular project. Harley himself had prepared the ground for it the day before he was stabbed, when he announced to derisive opposition cheers that the total public Debt for which no funds had been assigned by Parliament came to the impressive total of £9 million. Six weeks later, on 26 April, he reappeared to an ovation and received the Speaker's formal congratulations on his recovery. Swift was sure he would be made a peer.

By this time the Members who were closest to the Government already knew the master plan, and the Bill had been prepared when, on 2 May, Harley unfolded his proposal to incorporate the holders of the whole unsecured £9 million as a company to carry on the South Sea trade. The House was enthusiastic. The bonfires blazed in the City. It was, as Lady Dupplin wrote to her aunt, 'a glorious thing'.[10]

*　　*　　*

Politically speaking the South Sea scheme was a marvellous synthesis of finance, commerce, and foreign policy. It pleased both the October Club and the City, which by itself was an achievement, but the magic of it was in giving a foretaste of the sweets of peace before the policy of peace itself was openly announced. By publishing the South Sea scheme Harley established an understanding between himself and the nation that peace there would have to be.

Defoe has been given the credit for this scheme, as for so much else; but this is undeserved. Defoe was almost exclusively occupied with Scottish affairs that winter. Paterson, the Darien projector, has a better claim to have brought it to Harley's mind. 'What my mind is now most intent upon', he had written to the Chancellor on 4 September 1710, 'is sufficiently to apprise myself of the state of the public revenues and debts, in order to the putting an effectual stop to this immense running loss and waste therein . . . one half of which sum applied towards the extraordinaries of Spain and the Indies will make a happy conclusion of the affairs abroad, as the saving of the other will much contribute to the quiet and satisfaction at home.'[11]

Paterson received no recognition, either then or later; but before the end of May, Harley was an Earl and Lord High

Treasurer; and was even referred to as Prime Minister. With the South Sea scheme carried, he felt able to send Prior to Paris to begin peace negotiations—in secret, admittedly, but in earnest.

The provisions of the Bill for setting up the South Sea Company, which passed rapidly through all its stages, were quite simple. The £9 million worth of unfunded Government securities were to be exchanged compulsorily for shares at par in a joint stock company to be set up under the Act to carry on 'the sole trade and traffick, from 1 August 1711, into unto and from the Kingdoms, Lands etc. of America, on the east side from the river Aranoca, to the southernmost part of the Terra del Fuego, on the west side thereof, from the said southernmost part through the South Seas to the northernmost part of America, and into unto and from all countries in the same limits, reputed to belong to the Crown of Spain, or which shall hereafter be discovered'. In addition to the monopoly of this trade the Company was guaranteed by statute an annual payment from the Exchequer of £568,279. 10s., or 6 per cent. on the Debt taken over, plus management charges. This annuity, like the Bank's, was secured on indirect taxes.[12]

Although the South Sea Company was very far from being a 'Tory rival' to the Bank, it never escaped the consequences of its origin in the very heart of party politics, and the rewards it conferred fell to the business men who had backed Harley from the beginning or were now prepared to throw in their lot with him. It thus marked the establishment, in a field till now reserved for the Bank, of the Bank's most determined rivals.

They now secured national mercantile status on a par with the Bank and the East India Company—a status which had come to be so powerful that some supposed the great companies might one day bulk even larger than Parliament itself in prestige and power. Those with inside knowledge also reaped the customary rewards from buying in the securities to be converted before the announcement was made. The scale of these gains was very large—how large will be seen shortly— since the market prices had recently been as low as 55 for some forms of Debt. There can be little doubt that they played an important part in rallying to Harley's business nucleus the really big men Drummond had recommended: James Bateman and Theodore Janssen.

This great stroke was not achieved without the magnifying effect of propaganda. Much of the seeming infatuation of the public during the next ten years can be explained by the rapid rise of a journalism that operated on a public who were still comparatively unsophisticated. The government press, from Swift in *The Examiner* downwards, made full use of their opportunities, pointing with one hand to the triumphant solution of the financial problem and with the other to the need for expansion 'for the support of our established way of living'. Enthusiastic lists of prospective exports to South America were published. Colchester bays, the public learned, were 'universally worn' there, and a strong demand existed for silk handkerchiefs, worsted hose, sealing wax, spices, clocks and watches, Cheshire cheese, pickles, and 'scales and weights for gold and silver'. The venture would 'buoy up' the slave trade, and divert the fabulous profits which had enriched the pirates of Madagascar.[13]

The Company, as its apologists freely admitted, would have to embark on this trade entirely on credit, since the Parliamentary annuity (unless the shareholders were prepared to make sacrifices) was only enough to pay the interest on the Debt taken over. The Company could, it was true, call on its shareholders for another £10 per £100 stock, but, out of respect for the position of the Bank of England, it was provided that the interest on any such call—and indeed on any sums borrowed by the Company—should be a charge on their Exchequer annuity, and so would diminish the dividend.

Blunt and his associates were aware that all this was beside the point. Just as they had employed the Sword Blade charter to run a bank, they now meant to use the South Sea Company's privileges as a façade behind which they could continue the business of financial manipulation which they really understood. The fundamental weakness of the scheme was not the shortage of active capital or the chimerical nature of the trade itself—though, as Defoe pointed out only a year later, 'Unless the Spaniards are to be divested of common sense, infatuate, and given up, abandoning their own commerce, throwing away the only valuable stake they have left in the world, and in short, bent on their own ruin, we cannot suggest that they will ever, on any consideration, or for any equivalent, part with so valuable, indeed so inestimable a jewel, as the exclusive power of trade to their own plantations.'[14]

Almost because it was so brilliant as a financial and political stroke, the scheme as a business proposition was from the first a sham. Apart from the earnest Auditor Harley, nobody closely concerned with its creation or management ever gave it the single-minded loyalty Child had given the East India Company and Heathcote gave the Bank. Its promoters valued it not for its own sake, but for the advantage it gave them in other capacities in the creation of credit, and the management of financial operations for the government. Lamb, in his famous passage on the South Sea House, said its 'soul had long since fled'. The truth was that it never had a soul.

The dispirited Whig opposition made only feeble gestures against what was trumpeted as 'the Earl of Oxford's master-piece'. Any fight that was left in them by early May was stamped out by the reception of the report of the Committee of Public Debts, which contained, among much else, some very unpleasant reflections on Heathcote personally, and a round condemnation of the money spent by the previous Government on 'necessitous and useless foreigners'—the Protestant refugees from Germany. Before adjourning, the Commons voted a grand remonstrance to the Crown condemning the former ministers as 'guilty of a notorious breach of trust'. The opposition, especially Walpole, did not forget the phrase, but their only demonstrations against the South Sea scheme were attempts to prevent the Crown nominating the first directors, and to make the conversion voluntary. Both were unsuccessful, as was a petition by the East India Company against the Bill. The Bank, though it appointed a committee to watch the situation, did not even petition. They had learned their lesson, and their monopoly was at any rate formally preserved by a specific ban in the Bill against the new Company issuing notes or accepting deposits.

The conversion was in five phases. Blunt's energy was such that two of them were complete by the time the charter passed the seals in September. Private banks, of which the Sword Blade was the chief, were employed to take them.

Altogether these two subscriptions came to just over two and three-quarter millions, or a quarter of the whole. Of this three quarters of a million came from government departments, thus inaugurating the curious practice of the government holding securities in a private enterprise and receiving its own money by way of interest on them. The rest was found by about 200 names, among whom were twelve professional goldsmiths, thirty-four merchants, forty-nine 'gentlemen' or better, and thirty-seven Dutchmen, Italians, or Jews.

The commissioners taking the subscriptions reported in detail to Harley himself, who converted £8,000 worth of securities personally, probably to qualify for the Governorship. It was a modest holding compared with that of Blunt and his associates, notably Caswall and Sawbridge, which came to over £65,000; and these again were outstripped by names which Harley could read with real satisfaction. Janssen not only converted £25,000 of his own, but headed an international syndicate, which included a Piedmontese banker, for nearly a quarter of a million. Bateman and Shepheard also subscribed large sums, as did the powerful Anglo-Dutch banker Decker (£49,271) and the well-connected ironmaster, Sir Ambrose Crawley (£36,791). If even part of these holdings of Debt had been recently acquired, the profits must have been very large indeed.[15]

The Charter creating the Company in form and appointing its first Court of Directors was sealed on 10 September 1711, only a few days before the preliminaries of peace were signed in Paris. Harley himself was Governor, Bateman was Sub-Governor, and Ongley, Blunt's most respectable business associate, was Deputy Governor. In addition there were thirty ordinary directors of whom no fewer than nine, including Benson, the new Chancellor of the Exchequer, and Secretary St. John, were political nominees.* Perhaps one should also include in this category Francis Stratford, for Swift took the credit for the nomination of his old school friend. Five places were reserved for the Sword Blade group,† and seven for the bell-wethers of Harley's growing financial flock.‡ The remaining eight were men of lesser account who were yet to make their way, or soon to fall by the wayside, though one piece of Herefordshire patronage may be noticed among them in Samuel Clarke, Receiver of Land Tax for that county. On the whole the 'South Sea cullies' of whom an opposition versifier wrote, were an impressive, if lopsided collection:

> *We are a wretched motley crew,*
> * More various than the weather,*
> *Made up of debtors old and new,*
> * Jumbled and rocked together;*
> *Tars, soldiers, merchants, transport, tallies,*
> *Chained in a row like slaves in galleys.*

> *We furnished beer, we guns and balls,*
> * We ships or money lent,*
> *With hemp enough to serve them all;*
> * O may it so be spent.*
> *And since his payments are so few,*
> *Give Caesar what is Caesar's due.*

Apart from their stock they had only one thing in common. Not a single one of them had any experience of the South American, or even the West Indian trade, unless one counts Blunt, who had a cousin in Buenos Aires to whom he once lent £100, but never got it back.[16]

* Benson, Auditor Harley, Secretary St. John, Arthur Moore, Admiral Sir James Wishart (who was to command the Mediterranean fleet with 'restraining orders'), Joseph Martin (a Commissioner for the French commercial treaty), William Gore, Sir Thomas Vernon (Aislabie's brother-in-law), and George Pitt of Strathfieldsaye. All these were Members of Parliament.

† John and Charles Blunt, Tudman, Sawbridge, Caswall.

‡ Beachcroft, Decker, Crawley, Dolliffe, Hoare, Janssen, Shepheard.

He had personally drawn up the charter of the Company for a fee of 58 guineas, using the Bank charter, with sincere flattery, as his model. There was the same triennial election of directors, and the same twice-yearly meeting of shareholders. The salaried officers—Cashier, Secretary and Accountant—had the same titles as at the Bank; but, looked at more carefully, it can be seen that the constitution was admirably framed for manipulation by a caucus. The Governor was honorific. The full board of thirty-three (against the Bank's twenty-four) was too unwieldy to do detailed business. The key provision was that a duly constituted committee of directors could do anything committed to them by the Court as fully as the Court itself.

Window-dressing of the charter for the benefit of the October Club was provided by the rule that no director of the Bank or East India Companies could hold a directorship, and the elaborate regulations for the government of the Company's future commercial empire. Every trading station, and every ship in their fleet of over 500 tons, was to have a clergyman of the Church of England qualified in Spanish or Portuguese and approved by the Archbishop of Canterbury and the Bishop of London. Few if any of these livings were ever filled. On the other hand, the Baptist John Blunt's gains, measured in simple cash for professional services alone, had solid substance. His fees from the government and the Company in connexion with the promotion came to £3,846. 5s. 6d. It was a sum which labourers, at rates of wages then current, could barely have earned by working from the date the South Sea Company was founded to our own time.[17]

CHAPTER IV

Harley's Ditch

THE COMPETITIVE PROGRESS of the Commercial
Revolution was not interrupted by the political upheavals
of the last years of the Queen, the Peace, and the
change of dynasty. The transition of the South Sea Company from Stuart to Hanoverian England was not without
incident, but the business men concerned had no intention of
following their political sponsors into the wilderness. They
survived to see what Auditor Harley, in his disgust, came to call
his brother's 'dirty ditch' swimming with money.[1]

The minute books for these first years show the directors in
enthusiastic, but not always effective action. A great deal of
their time was spent on fostering the Company's prestige.
They took out a coat of arms, though the motto provided by
the heralds—'*A Gadibus usque ad Auroram*' (from Cadiz to the
dawn)—seemed to ignore the fact that the Company's concession lay towards the setting, not the rising sun. The Company was, indeed, very careful to avoid any possibility of
offending the East India Company, and on that account
rejected the proposal of the ingenious Captain Welbe to finance
the exploitation of what he called '*Terra Australis Incognita*' to
the far west of South America, which he felt sure was there
and must contain valuable gold-mines.[2]

For the time being the domestic front was more important
than voyages. An impressive house in the City was rented and
prudently insured against fire; and the board-room was
handsomely furnished with two and a half dozen black Spanish
upholstered chairs in beechwood frames and gilt nails. The
meetings there were club-like affairs, with coffee served at the
Company's expense and half-crown fines for non-attendance.

But from the first these meetings of the full Court were mainly for formal business. Initiative lay with *ad hoc* bodies of directors or the seven standing committees, of which the most important was the 'Committee for the Affairs of the Company'. They handled liaison with the government of the day and all questions of raising fresh finance, and even their minutes were not disclosed to the other directors.[3]

One subject, however, was too important to be handled outside the full Court of Directors. This was patronage. Nothing excited the job-hungry eighteenth century more than a new consignment of this commodity. There were several candidates for every post the Company had to bestow, from the senior appointments down to the porters, watchmen, and chars, and balloting for them occupied many of the early meetings. Then there were many candidates for professional and business patronage: a legal adviser; foreign correspondents (Harley's friend, Drummond, was willing to act for the Company at The Hague); a printer. This last appointment went to Swift's friend, John Barber, who had printed *The Examiner* and whom Harley had made printer of the *London Gazette*. The arrangement had the advantage of catering indirectly for Barber's mistress, Mrs. Delia Manley, who had worn out her reputation in writing Tory propaganda and wearied the government with her applications for recognition. The Company also required a banker, which was, of course, the Sword Blade.[4]

The chief posts in the salaried hierarchy were those of Secretary, Accountant, and Cashier. The emphasis on the financial side, though understandable in these early years, when the conversion was still going on, is noteworthy in an institution forbidden by law to act as a bank. No provision was made for any official other than the Secretary to co-ordinate the Company's trading activities, and he was the least important of the three. He had only two subordinates in the office, and the duties required a compliant witness rather than a man with drive. The original Secretary, James Pym, was removed very quickly, ostensibly because his security was inadequate, but actually because he took too high a view of his responsibilities. Ury, his successor, was a nonentity.

The two other officials were much more significant people, and stayed with the Company until 1721. Both were brought to the Company's notice by Blunt, who provided their considerable securities.

The Accountant Grigsby was already getting on in years. He had made his way out of the obscurity of the 1690s as proprietor of a City coffee-house, and then graduated to be a licensed stockbroker under the Act of 1697 which regulated that calling for the first time. He was thus well qualified for the main function of his branch, which was the registration of changes in the ownership of stock, and the making of new issues. The exotic commodity in which he had once dealt, the sinister profession he had later adopted, and his gnome-like appearance combined to give him a vague reputation for dabbling in black magic and the nickname of 'The Necromancer'.[5]

Robert Knight, the Cashier, was an altogether sunnier figure. He was thirty-five when he got this coveted post. He had already made his way in the world, as can be gathered from his personal contribution to the Company's first conversion of floating debt, which was over £5,000. Moreover, though City-born, he was a gentleman. The Knights of Barrells, near Henley-in-Arden, were a respectably ancient family that had once intermarried with the Raleighs, and although Robert's branch of it had settled down to a commercial life in London in the second half of the previous century, his cousin William, an elderly bachelor, was still in possession of the family estates. Too much stress should not be put on it, but it is interesting that the Knights of Barrells were also remote connexions of the first Mrs. Blunt and neighbours of Sawbridge's Warwickshire forebears. There may also have been a relationship with John Knight, the prosperous former Bank director, Member of Parliament for St. Germans, and a close crony of James Craggs.[6]

Altogether, for £200 a year, later raised to £250, the

Company acquired in Knight one of the most eligible men in the City: well-connected, well-mannered, good-looking, and possessed of a remarkable gift for carrying complicated transactions in his head. If he had not the sagacity and scope of his contemporary, Law, Knight had some of the requisites of a great financier. Certainly, although he was Blunt's protégé and confidant, he was as ambitious as his master.

In the summer of 1712 the shareholders who had so far converted were called upon to elect successors to the directors nominated in the charter, whose term of office was limited to one year. Six of these thereupon disappeared from the Court, one being Swift's old friend Stratford. Drummond had never thought much of his business head, and Swift had done his nominee no good by letting him into the secret of the peace negotiations. He 'graspt at too many things and that was his ruin'—in other words, he over-extended himself buying for a rise on inside information. He landed in the Queen's Bench Prison for a time, and then had to go abroad—a first casualty which might have been a warning.[7]

Illness, which ended in death, removed the goldsmith and army clothing contractor, Benjamin Tudman, from the scene, and Blunt, now a widower, consoled himself for the loss of a colleague on the Court by marrying Mrs. Tudman and her substantial fortune, derived from two earlier husbands. The union added eleven of her children to the seven of his own for whom the vigorous Baptist had to provide.*

He could, however, contemplate with satisfaction the progress of the Sword Blade Bank. Now thoroughly entrenched with the government, they were able to defy their old rival

---

* It is fair, in assessing Blunt's career, to take account of the host of dependents who looked to him, and the care he took to provide for them. Of his own seven children, John, the eldest, was placed with the East India Company and went out to India; Henry worked in the Sword Blade Bank; Charles was apprenticed to a City friend; Rachel was married to Blunt's nephew Samuel, Sword-bearer to the City; William Thomas, and Elizabeth, who were still growing up, were at good schools. The second Mrs. Blunt, however, brought handsome endowments with her. Her father, Richard Craddocke, had held office under the East India Company in Bengal and was a director of the Royal African Company, 1684-6 and 1689-95. Her first husband, John Banner, was a salter in London, but may have been related to the prosperous Birmingham cutler John Banner, for whom see K. G. Davies, *The Royal African Company*, p. 178.

and its Act of Parliament by issuing notes, and had the additional pleasure of acquiring a large block of Bank shares, with corresponding voting rights. They also controlled, under various names, shares in the South Sea Company entitling them to thirty-two votes in the choice of directors.

Two of the other retirements in 1712 were a serious loss to the Court. Sir Robert Beachcroft and Sir Matthew Decker had lent much prestige to the original flotation—one as an ex-Lord Mayor of great wealth and respectability, and the other as a financier with international connexions who was one of the shrewdest business brains of his time. Beachcroft probably gave up on grounds of age, but Decker, one suspects, had already formed his own opinion about the new Company's prospects. At any rate, he chose to rejoin the Court of the East India Company, which disqualified him. None of the new directors was comparable with these two in calibre. They came from the middle stratum of City tradesmen whose war contracts had made them large holders of Debt now converted into stock, and if anything they mark a movement away from the intimate association with the régime that had been so noticeable in the original appointments. This trend was confirmed when a casual vacancy towards the end of the year was filled by the son of a Bank director and a neighbour of Heathcote's at Low Leyton, Fisher Tench. Harley, however, remained Governor, and all the original political nominees retained their directorships.

*   *   *

The Court might be tending towards neutrality in politics, but they were not uninterested in them, and they had long discussions at their unwieldy meetings, in their uncomfortable Spanish chairs, about how they should manage the Spanish trade when the Government's tortuous diplomacy should finally confer it on them. In the meantime, the payment from the Exchequer, which was the Company's sole income, dragged sadly, the dividend record was poor, and the stock hung miserably below par. It did not escape their notice that

Harley's Treasury raised as many new loans as Godolphin's had done. Altogether, between 1711 and 1714, Harley added £9 million to the funded Debt—all of it by lotteries. The amount was, by an odd coincidence, the same as the floating Debt it was his boast to have abolished.

Confidence between the Government and its creation had sunk very low by the time the Asiento Treaty was signed as part of the settlement of Utrecht on 26 March 1713. Harley and his brother thought the business men ungrateful for the great opportunity they were being given. The business men were in the mood of a menagerie where the mealtime is long overdue.

The privileges conferred on the Company by the peace, though not so glittering as they had seemed in prospect, were not insubstantial. In particular, the contract for supplying negroes was of the unprecedented duration of thirty years. During this period the Queen (who was the nominal contractor though it was understood she would sub-contract to the Company) would furnish the Spanish colonies with 4,800 negroes a year under conditions of great elaborateness and complexity. In furtherance of the contract, the Company was to be allowed establishments (but not, as had been hoped, extraterritoriality) at the seven ports of Buenos Aires, Caracas, Cartagena, Havana, Panama, Portobello, and Vera Cruz. Finally, they would be allowed to send on a direct trading voyage to one of these stations a ship of not more than 500 tons, one-quarter of the profits being reserved for the King of Spain. As a special bonus, two cedulas or licences for ships to sail at once were also granted, and the British Government undertook not only to find ships for this purpose from the demobilized fleet, but to provide naval protection.

Once more the Company were roused. By July they had made a contract with the Royal African Company to supply 'healthful, sound negroes of all sizes, in such condition as to be able to go over the ship's side' at Jamaica. Nine-tenths (at £10 each) were to be over sixteen, and the rest (at £8 each) over ten years of age. Two-thirds were to be males. The margin between buying and selling prices of 150-200 per cent. will be noted—it was to prove inadequate.[8]

For the second leg of the slaving voyage the Company commissioned its own ships, and by the end of the year three had sailed for the carriage of 1,230 negroes, subject to the usual commission for the captains—4 per cent. of the slaves delivered alive. These figures assumed that the captains did not add to their earnings by loading extra negroes for sale on private account, a practice disapproved of by the Company, since it led to overcrowding, and what was called in the trade 'dead freight'. In the following year seven more ships, among them the *Hope* and the *Liberty*, sailed with commissions for no less than 2,680 slaves. To finance them the Company raised £200,000 in bonds.

The enthusiasm was to be shortlived. The Company soon found that its faith in governments on both sides of the Atlantic was misplaced. The Court of Madrid naturally charged its royalty for the Asiento from the date on which it was granted in May 1713; but their officials in America, whose tradition was profoundly hostile to foreign enterprise, refused to admit the Company's first shipments on the ground that the formalities of promulgating the Asiento in America had not been completed. These cargoes had eventually to be disposed of at heavy loss in the West Indies.

The Company persisted in the slave trade, but it was never to prove profitable to them. Thirteen ships sailed in 1716, twenty in 1717, and at least twelve in 1718, carrying more than 13,000 negroes altogether. They naturally blamed Spanish obstructiveness for the poor return, and the ingenuity of the bureaucracy was certainly remarkable. The import duty of $33\frac{1}{2}$ pieces of eight per head was rigorously exacted, although for purposes of the contract the authorities insisted on classifying the negroes so that they came to fewer '*piezas de India*', or standard slaves, than their actual number. Their fee of 6 pieces of eight for burying a dead negro was also regarded as an unreasonable burden. Nevertheless, the Company must bear a great deal of the responsibility for not making money out of this criminal and complicated traffic, which involved heavy overheads for the inexperienced. It is horrible to think that human suffering should have been made even worse by commercial inefficiency bred from meretricious politics. Mortality on the South Sea Company's slavers was heavier than on those of the more experienced Royal African Company.

They were just as clumsy and fussily inefficient in handling the direct trade. One of their two special ships of 1714 was loaded entirely with woollens, which, in defiance of the warnings sent by the Company's agent in Madrid, were discharged at Cartagena, where no fair was to be held for two years and the market was overstocked with French textiles, instead of Vera Cruz, where there was an immediate demand. The woollens were still lying at Cartagena two years afterwards, 'subject to the moth and other vermin which abound there'.[9]

Still worse was the faithlessness of the government at home, which was now gripped in the crisis of the succession. During St. John's brief predominance the relationship between government and Company was plunged into an atmosphere of bickering and open scandal. First, to the great indignation of the shareholders, the government abruptly announced early in 1714 that in sub-contracting the Asiento the Queen would reserve 25 per cent. of the profits for her own Civil List. Then it came out that a further $7\frac{1}{2}$ per cent. had been conferred privately on St. John's mysterious financial adviser, Manuel Mannasseh Gilligan, so that the proprietors, after financing the whole enterprise, were to share only two-thirds of the profits of slaving and (allowing for the King of Spain's share) less than half the profits of the direct trade.

When all this was discussed at a General Court of proprietors on 24 February 1714 nearly a third of the 1,200 present were against accepting the Asiento at all on the terms offered, and the government eventually had to withdraw. But the atmosphere was now thoroughly poisoned, and the last straw was the discovery, at the height of the dynastic crisis which put an end to the ministerial careers of Harley and St. John, that Arthur Moore, whom they had made a director, had been trying to load 60 tons of goods on private account into one of the Company's precious direct trade ships. Moore was ejected from the Court of Directors almost at the same moment as Harley's staff as Lord High Treasurer was taken from him by the dying Queen, and that indefatigable Whig traveller, James Craggs the Younger, set out with the good news for Hanover on behalf of the Junto.

*   *   *

Harley had risen to power by careful husbanding of a City connexion, on which he had hoped to confer permanent form by chartering it as the South Sea Company. By alienating the Company, he deprived himself of a form of support he himself had always regarded as indispensable, and when he fell the Court of Directors, of which he was still technically the chief, hurried to congratulate King George.

It was very much in the interest of their shareholders that they should do so. By this time there were between 2,000 and 3,000 of them, a much greater number than had shares in either of the other two great companies.* There is little doubt that most of them, like Lady Cowper at the new King's coronation, felt strong emotion at the thought of 'our holy religion thus preserved, as well as our liberties and properties'. Such was the general satisfaction that in May 1715 the Company's stock reached par for the first time since it was issued.[10]

The new King and his heir had taken an early opportunity to acquire large holdings themselves, and the improvement in the Company's shares was much assisted by the friendly relations which from the first prevailed between the South Sea and the new royal family. In 1715, when the election of directors had again come round, the shareholders showed their loyalty by removing all prominent Tory politicians from the

---

* Among the shareholders at Christmas 1714 were several prominent Whig politicians—James Craggs, Charles Earl of Halifax, and Sir Joseph Jekyll; a considerable sprinkling of Dutch and Sephardic financiers; and many modest tradesmen, not only in London, but in the provinces. There were also a large number of women. Among the intelligentsia who held stock may be noticed Newton, Kneller, Swift, and Arbuthnot. (*List of the Corporation, 1714. British Museum press mark 1887.b.63.*)

Court of Directors and replacing most of them with neutral business men. Only ten of Harley's original nominees now survived. Symbolic of the new state of affairs was the election of the Prince of Wales as Governor instead of Harley. The Prince was very interested in adding to his income in any way he could, mainly to make him independent of his father, who, in accordance with the pattern reproduced again and again in the history of his House, detested and envied his heir. Doubtless the Company, in electing the Prince, had no intention of taking sides in the quarrels which in 1717 produced an open rift in the Royal Family, but it is interesting that the only two politicians who became directors in 1715 belonged to the group which was soon to back the Prince against the King and go into opposition: Horatio Townshend, Walpole's brother-in-law and brother of his closest political friend; and James Campbell, Duke of Argyll.

The Duke of Argyll's becoming a director was almost as remarkable, in its way, as the adoption of the Prince as Governor. It is true that Argyll and his brother, Islay, were deeply interested in financial transactions, not only in London, but in Paris in conjunction with their kinsman, Law. The Scotch nobility had acquired an unenviable reputation since the Union for dabbling in finance of all kinds, high and low, and Lord Cowper had doubted whether a single one of them could afford to live in London without a subsidy from the Queen. Argyll, according to Horace Walpole, was a miser as early as a hero, as well as a lover of books and a patron of inventions. Nevertheless, it was practically the first time that a man of such high rank had deigned to accept a working directorship in a joint stock company. That a duke—even a duke who had married beneath him for money, as Argyll had—should be willing to sit at the same board, and have the same voice, as Astell the timber merchant, Page the brewer, and Francis Hawes, who not so long ago had been a mere clerk in the Treasurer of the Navy's office, was a notable sign of the times. Blunt well knew the value of associating men of birth and fashion with his enterprises.

The Company might congratulate itself on having successfully shot the rapids of the change of dynasty, but the new
government expected some consideration from the former
backers of their opponents. In 1715 the new Court of Directors
was prevailed upon to write off the last two years' annuity due
to the Company, which had never been paid and came to
over £1 million, in return for a statute authorizing them to
increase their capital by that amount. The effect of this manœuvre was to substitute a bonus distribution of shares for a
dividend and bring the issued capital up to just over £10
million—half the entire joint stock capital in the country and
considerably more than the whole of that capital as recently
as 1703.

Of the politicians few had survived these difficult years so
successfully as James Craggs and his son. The father had
indeed lost his seat for Grampound and his jobs at the Ordnance
in the election of 1713; but the next year had seen his return to
both. In 1715 he was installed as Joint Postmaster-General, an
office which was both profitable and, in his hands, influential.
The government, like its predecessors, depended on tampering
with the mail for private information about politics and
finance; and from his office in the City, Craggs, who was by
now exceedingly rich, was in a position to supplement this
source of information by direct contact with the market. His
son, now also in Parliament for the Cornish borough of
Tregony, had risen in the train of his patron, Stanhope, and
ingratiated himself ceaselessly with the new King's German
harem. He became Cofferer to the Prince of Wales in 1715,
Secretary at War in 1717, and with Stanhope's arrival at the
summit of power in 1718, Secretary of State.

As consistent Whigs the Craggs could reasonably claim
their rewards in the change of political luck. Aislabie, the
former apostate to Toryism, had to display more agility.
Nevertheless, his sense of when a ship was sinking had not
deserted him. As early as April 1714 he had foreseen that
Harley and St. John could not last, and had resigned his
Commissionership of the Admiralty. In October he was

rewarded with the Treasurership of the Navy. For a man so deeply committed it was a remarkably neat pirouette, and he quickly showed that he knew what was expected of him. He was vociferous in pressing for the impeachment of his old leader, Harley; and personally undertook the proceedings against his old departmental chief, Lord Strafford—a task which particularly appealed to him, since he had always felt strongly that he should have been First Lord himself under the previous administration. So it came about that in April 1717, with the victory of Stanhope and Sunderland over the Walpole faction, Aislabie received his reward and became Chancellor of the Exchequer. One of his first acts on this appointment was to promote Francis Hawes, his cashier as Treasurer of the Navy and a South Sea director since 1715, to be, additionally, Receiver-General of Customs.[11]

* * *

James Stanhope, the man round whom these political adventurers were clustering, was himself a man of lofty, even glorious ideas. As a colleague he was neither simple nor loyal, but there is nevertheless something attractive and profound about his character. Like Marlborough before him, he understood the new status as a great power in Europe that war and wealth had conferred on Britain since the Revolution, and when he fell that vision was to vanish for many years. As a political strategist he was daring and original, with no qualms about departures from tradition if they seemed likely to pay dividends. *Quieta non movere* was certainly not his motto. Few ministers have dared to suggest such fundamental changes in the Constitution as Stanhope, or such radical reforms of cherished institutions.

Abroad he followed in the path opened up by Harley, and was the architect of the celebrated Anglo-French entente which forms such a curious interlude in the normal pattern of our diplomatic history between the Revolution and the Crimean War. This great project first took shape at an interview between Stanhope and the Abbé Dubois, former tutor to the French Regent Philip, at The Hague in March 1716. The English minister was in attendance on King George, who was travelling to Hanover. Dubois was incognito, in the character of a collector of curios and rare books. Conversations took place under colour of Stanhope inspecting Dubois' collection, and during them the idea of a mutual guarantee of the *status quo* in the two countries was mooted. The relative strengths of the two nations were also discussed, Stanhope describing how the English National Debt was capable of almost unlimited expansion, and Dubois replying that the French king must be the stronger because 'he really owns all the land in his kingdom'. So the rival theories on which the two countries were to launch their shots at the financial moon and bring a halt to the Commercial Revolution were compendiously stated. Later in the year the alliance was formally concluded at Hanover. 'We negotiated', wrote Dubois, describing the pace of business, 'in our dressing-gowns and our nightcaps.' One session took place after a dinner at which thirteen guests consumed seventy bottles of wine, and when the terms were settled Stanhope refused a present of 600,000 livres from his opposite number, who described his conduct as 'heroic'.[12]

Foreign policy in the new Europe suited Stanhope's temperament so well that he was inclined to leave domestic questions largely to his partner at the summit of politics, Charles, third Earl of Sunderland, and even conceded him the Treasury, keeping only a Secretaryship of State for himself. And in many ways Sunderland was well suited to administer a changing England. He was a child of the Revolution, in which his father had played so notable and ambiguous a part. Some of his most impressionable years—those from fourteen to seventeen—had been spent in Holland. He loved books, and was one of the greatest bibliophiles of his time; he was intelligent, with a strong turn for mathematics, and considered he had a talent for finance. Above all, he was not afraid of ideas, and as a young man his vociferous radicalism and anti-clericalism had embarrassed his Whig colleagues. But with all his gifts—

which had made a great impression on George I—his temperament was a bad one for a politician. Passion easily mastered his judgement. Disappointment or opposition had physical effects on him—he turned pale when he was excluded from the regency in 1714, and when Lord Midleton refused to back his plans to reform the House of Lords his nose bled. However rashly he had espoused a policy, it was not in him to retreat or bend; and there were few weapons to which he would not stoop in defending himself.

Stanhope and Sunderland drove Walpole and his followers into opposition and the estranged Court of the Prince of Wales at the time the Court of Directors were ordering the transhipment of their moth-eaten woollens from Cartagena to Portobello and deciding to call their new ship, just launched for the annual trade, *The Royal Prince*. The political changes were, as always, reflected in the election of directors for February 1718. Argyll and Horatio Townshend were eliminated. So were the veteran Sir Richard Hoare and George Pitt, both of them parliamentary business men of pronounced Tory principles and critics of the Bank. But the great displacement was that of the Prince himself, now living apart from his grumpy father and formally deprived of all official courtesies. In his place the King himself graciously agreed to the Company's humble request that he should be their Governor.

This unusual arrangement, which was authorized by Act of Parliament, set the seal on an association between Government and Company which was even more intimate than in Harley's time, and yet very different in character. Under Harley ministerial politicians had been strongly represented in the management, but the régime was not formally concerned with the Company. Under Stanhope no politicians were directors, but the King's Governorship, titular though it might be, made it impossible to dissociate the Company from the régime in the eyes of the public. The working connexion between the Company and the political world, moreover, lay at a lower, irresponsible level: with the four directors who were Members of Parliament and the six who held official posts connected with public money: notably Hawes, who acted as a financial go-between, not only for Aislabie, but for Walpole; and Harcourt Master, Receiver of the Land Tax for London and Middlesex, who knew everybody.

There was one constant factor—the Sword Blade. They had survived the vicissitudes of two elections, and of the six directors who had been with the South Sea Company since its foundation Blunt was one. Child, Tudman's old partner, had joined the Court in 1715, and so had Gibbon. Sawbridge was still a director, and was now an M.P. as well. Caswall only left the Court to concentrate on the banking business, which was thriving in spite of the Bank of England's return to favour after 1714. The Sword Blade was said—with the usual emphasis on fashionable clientele—to have the accounts of 'two or three blue ribbons and four or five cash keepers, who tell more money than they own'. Its notes, printed partly on marbled paper to prevent forgery, were widely accepted. Its power over the Company was demonstrated when in 1718 one of its most promising clerks, Robert Surman, was appointed to the growing South Sea bureaucracy, now thirty-five strong, as assistant to Knight. Like his senior, Surman was the offspring of country gentlemen and meant to make the business fortune on which to found a major landed family.[13]

In 1718, however, the Sword Blade were not undisputed masters of the South Sea Company. In the absence of an effective Governor (for King George never presided over the Court of Directors or over a General Court of Proprietors), its senior officers were Bateman, the Sub-Governor, and Shepheard, the Deputy Governor, both of them City veterans of immense experience and wealth who had weathered as many storms as Heathcote himself. Sub-Governor Bateman's estates straddled England from Herefordshire to Surrey. He was a knight, and had been Lord Mayor, and his suburban palace at Tooting had been decorated in the most fashionably opulent style by Thornhill. Two of his kinsmen were among the directors—Tillard, his cousin, who had once been President of Masulipatam, and Chaplin, from whom he had bought

Shobdon and to whose daughter he had married his younger son.

But in November 1718 Sub-Governor Bateman died at his town house in Soho, and three months later Deputy Governor Shepheard, Harley's old banker, 'the great Shepheard', as his obituarist called him, died also. The biggest financial institution in England, or, for the time being, in Europe, was deprived of its weightiest and wisest managers as Western Europe moved towards its great financial crisis. Their places were taken by far less gifted men. Sir John Fellowes, the new Sub-Governor, had been a director for seven years and was rich and ambitious; but he was youngish, and easily led, especially when things became difficult. Charles Joye, who took Shepheard's place, was a prosperous but undistinguished Baltic merchant from Southwark. Blunt dominated them both.

For some reason one of the vacancies in the Court left by these promotions remained unfilled. The other was accepted by Sir Theodore Janssen, who had given up his directorship in the previous February in exchange for one at the Bank. He was still a great name in the City—almost a synonym for financial grandeur; but he was no longer the shrewd Flemish business man he had once been. Thirst for even more wealth persuaded him, in an evil hour, to leave his books and his recently acquired country acres at Wimbledon, where he had planned to spend the rest of his life with the dignity of a baronet and a parliamentarian.

At this point the Company suffered a shock. A few years before, when the Italian adventurer, Alberoni, became the first minister of Spain, the Company, who were always thoughtful about matters of the kind, had presented him with a gold watch and their best wishes. In accordance with the spirit of the age, he had in the following years brought order, even vigour, into the drooping Spanish economy; and in 1718 his Mediterranean ambitions meshed with the diplomatic manœuvres of Stanhope and Dubois to bring about war between Great Britain and Spain. The newly launched *Royal Prince* with its carefully assembled cargo never sailed for

Spanish America. When war was formally declared towards the end of the year the Company's establishments there, with all their contents, valued at the possibly exaggerated figure of £300,000, were seized in defiance of the undertaking in the Asiento that eighteen months' warning would be given in such circumstances. James Puckle, the veteran projector, abandoned the promotion of fisheries to advertise his convincing-looking machine gun with its convenient attachment for firing either round or square bullets, according to whether the enemy were Christians or Turks.[14]

With its trade at a full stop for all to see, the Company became, from sheer necessity, a naked finance corporation; with its wisest heads removed, it was completely exposed to the financial manipulators who had played so large a part in its management from the first; its fortunes were linked, formally and informally, with those of the régime and the government. For Blunt and his syndicate there opened a truly tremendous field for the exercise of their professional skill; and in their moment of triumph their pride was stirred by the remarkable events then rising to their climax on the other side of the Channel under the direction of the greatest financier of the age.

CHAPTER V

The Two Cities

AMONG THE CONGRATULATIONS Harley had received in 1711 on his earldom and solution of Britain's financial difficulties was a letter from John Law. Law had travelled far since the killing of Wilson, and now, writing from Brussels, he hinted that if a pardon could be arranged he would willingly return to second Harley's efforts.[1] But Harley had never been a friend. As long ago as 1704 he had advised against allowing a similar appeal, addressed that time from Edinburgh, where Law had been seeking support for his financial schemes in a still independent Scotland. So instead of coming to England Law went to Turin, where he laid his plans unsuccessfully before the Duke Victor Amadeus. By 1712 he was at The Hague, and in the summer of 1713, on the morrow of the Peace of Utrecht, he arrived in Paris, where he immediately made contact with the finance minister of Louis XIV.

Law was not an ordinary adventurer, or even an ordinary financier: he was a man of destiny and deeply conscious of it. His travels, at any rate since 1708, had not been in search of personal fortune, for his golden fingers had already made him rich, with a fortune estimated in 1713 at a million and a half livres* and good credit all over the European business world. With the possible exception of Defoe, he had a stronger sense of the character of the Commercial Revolution than any man of his time. Behind his technical virtuosity lay a conviction, held with the true *perfervidum ingenium Scotorum*, that it was possible to release resources for man's service on a scale that had never

* At the usual rate of 14 livres to the £1, over £100,000 (contemporary) and over £1 million (modern).

77

before been dreamed of; and that the key for releasing them was a radical change in men's monetary habits.

Since both the change of habit he recommended and the release of material wealth he foresaw have come about, his leading theme seems simple and obvious to us; but to him the world seemed to be shackled to poverty by prejudice, and contemporary economists baffled by problems which were irrelevant. Chief among these prejudices was the habit, over which Locke and Lowndes had argued in the 1690s, of regarding metallic money as wealth; or at any rate as its safest, best, and ultimate representative. Law was by no means the only economist of his time to point out that metallic money was not the same thing as wealth: his originality consisted in showing that in an expanding economy it was not even convenient as a medium of exchange. It was troublesome to count, transport, or remit in any quantity; and its intrinsic value as metal was bound to vary with time and place from the exchange value assigned to it by mints. The lubricant and fuel of the economy should, Law considered, have no intrinsic value at all. It should consist of paper, which was easily handled and was capable of being given (as he thought) a stable value by the skill of financiers and the power of governments.

Paper currency, it is true, had been used for many years past, not only in England, but in Genoa, Venice, and Holland. But these paper currencies were unsystematic. They rested—even in the case of the Bank of England's notes—on the credit of individuals and institutions, and this introduced the variables Law felt it was his mission to remove. And on the whole even those who used paper as currency thought of it as representing money, rather than as money itself, which tended to limit each variety to the metropolis in which it was redeemable, and to professional business men who understood the complexities of European credit. Branch banks and a national paper currency were alike unknown.

This idea of a national paper currency which would be universally accepted because it was backed by the authority of the State and controlled through a network of local agencies was the heart of Law's plan for increasing the world's wealth. He was so sure such a currency would be preferred to metal that in his original pattern of the project he thought it necessary to set a limit to the premium paper should enjoy over gold and silver and provide that a debt of 100 should not require more than 110 in gold to discharge it.

By multiplying this centrally controlled and locally distributed paper currency, Law foresaw the possibility of building up capital which would correspond to, and so release, the latent wealth which surrounded mankind. He has been accused of believing that the wealth of a nation depended on the amount of money in circulation, and that one had only to add to the money to add to the wealth. But this was not what was meant by his dictum, 'Wealth depends on commerce, and commerce depends on circulation'. He may have had too high an idea of the exertions money could induce in eighteenth-century men, and he certainly underestimated the difficulty of changing their habits, but he was far too profound not to recognize that money should always correspond to accessible wealth:

> The strength of kingdoms [he wrote] is best judged of by their extent and the goodness of soil, by their situation for trade, by the number of inhabitants, and their inclination to industry, and by the coined specie which, being in more or less quantity gives means to the people to extend more or less their industry and trade.[2]

When he settled in France he was past forty, rich, and reputable. The dandified gambler had been replaced by a stately man in his prime whose charm and gifts of lucid explanation flattered and impressed all who met him. When he expounded his bold and subtle ideas quite ordinary people were delighted by the thought of how clearly they seemed to understand him. This remarkable compound of genius, egotism, and philanthropy asked only that the patrons to whom he applied should allow him personally to direct the currency experiment he recommended.[3]

On Louis XIV, whom he never appears to have met personally, Law could make no impression. The old King's long reign was ending in funereal gloom, but it was not yet quite over; and suitable though France, with its standing machinery and tradition of controls, was for Law's experiments, he still hankered after doing his work in England. France, he calculated, had the greater potential strength—he put it at three to one—but her economy was aground. England's was afloat, ready for the voyage. With the House of Hanover on the throne, the system established by the Revolution had been finally consolidated and public credit was on a secure parliamentary foundation. Law made one more effort, and turned from the government of Louis XIV to the British Embassy in Paris.

Throughout his wanderings, Law had kept in close touch with his father's old clientele among the Scots families which clustered round the House of Argyll and were now dominant in what they had made the northern part of Great Britain. They were now strongly represented in the new British régime's mission in France. The Secretary of Embassy was David Crawford, an historian and playwright, who had an acute insight in financial matters; the Military Attaché, Captain James Gardiner, who was long afterwards to fall trying to stem the rout at Prestonpans and provide the Rev. Philip Doddridge with a 'Christian Hero Animated and Crowned'; but was now living the fashionable life of a gay officer. The Ambassador himself was John Dalrymple, Earl of Stair, whose father had been William III's minister in Scotland and bears much of the responsibility for Glencoe. The Earl had commanded under Marlborough, and most of the leading figures in the new English Government were his personal friends, especially Stanhope and the younger Craggs; but his own financial position was weak. He owed £5,000 even after selling a considerable slice of his estates and accepting his embassy. On arriving in Paris his first business was an interview with Law.[4]

Stair at once saw what a good impression it would make for the new régime in England to mount an operation against the National Debt that would rival Harley's masterpiece, and wrote home recommending Law as the ideal instrument. 'I would not venture to speak thus', he wrote to Whitehall, 'had I not known him for a long time as a person of as good sense as I ever knew in my life, of very good solid sense and very useful, and in the matters he takes up with certainly the cleverest man that is.' The replies were polite but discouraging. Halifax was 'extream fond of having his assistance at the revenue . . . but there appears some difficulty in his case'. Stanhope wrote that he had put the matter to the King, who had expressed 'a disposition to comply with what your Lordship proposes though at the same time it has met and does meet with opposition'. The unnamed objections prevailed, and Law did not come to England. No doubt the voice of the murdered Wilson's relatives, who included the Townshends, was still important; but one may suspect that the jealousy of the Bank of England, now restored to favour, towards a rival whose abilities they well knew, weighed even more with the Government.[5]

★   ★   ★

In September 1715 Louis XIV died, and his great-grandchild reigned from his nursery. The period that so began is in almost every respect an aberration in the history of France. The Regent Philip of Orleans presided over an autocracy that lacked an autocrat; and both as man and Regent he was insecure. His personal insecurity showed itself in a compulsive search after pleasure and novelty that has made his court a byword for obscene gaiety and killed him before he was fifty. His two kinsmen, King Philip of Spain and the Duke of Maine, contested his right to be Regent. Both kinds of anxiety disposed him to depend on the bold and subtle economist who offered novelty to the jaded man and money to the needy prince.

Like everything else about the Regent, his administration had an experimental flavour. It was constructed on what were called 'presbysynodic' principles, involving numerous interlocking committees. Its first task was to tackle the financial and economic chaos the Sun King had left behind. Trade and production were at a low ebb, and the estimated expense of government for the coming year was over 200 million livres, a quarter of this sum being due as interest on the National Debt of over 700 million. Nearly the whole revenue for the year had already been anticipated, and the presbysynodic ministers saw no solution except default and bankruptcy.

Within six weeks of Louis XIV's death Law put his solution before them. He propounded it as a whole, for although in the event the celebrated 'System' was built up brick by brick, it was from the first an integrated conception. His proposal was for a bank whose functions would be fourfold: the issue of paper money backed by a guarantee of redemption on demand in gold or silver of a fineness specified in advance; the discounting of bills of exchange—in other words, financing future production; the operation of commercial monopolies; and the collection of the State's revenues. The committee of experts and officials before whom these proposals were placed rejected them. As one of them, the international banker, Samuel Bernard, told the Earl of Stair, it was impossible for a State bank to command the necessary confidence in a country where all depended on the will of the government. The Regent then plunged into the traditional remedies. Interest rates were forced down by decree, in spite of the exhausted state of the economy; state expenditure of all kinds was ruthlessly cut; and the coinage was debased.

Having been rebuffed in his frontal attack, Law resolved to advance by stages, making use of his continuing influence with the Regent and the Regent's old tutor and unofficial adviser, the Abbé Dubois. In the spring of 1716 he obtained permission to start a note-issuing bank as a private venture supported by well-publicized official goodwill. Law himself was the sole director and principal shareholder, untrammelled by cumbersome committees and pushing subordinates. So far as these last were concerned, he laid it down that no employee should hold more cash than the modest balance needed for his day-to-day duties. It is perhaps the most important difference between the 'System' and the South Sea that Law's promotion was throughout under the dictatorship of a single luminous mind whose object was not the making of money or the capture of political advantages, but the evocation of wealth.

Law was now committed to the service of France, for one of the conditions on which his Banque Générale opened its doors on 16 April (N.S.) 1716 was that its director should adopt French nationality; and the bank served France well. Its notes, with their promise of redemption on demand in coin of the fineness current at the date of issue, circulated freely both at home and on the European money markets; and when the government, in accordance with its programme, debased the coinage, the notes went to a premium as Law had expected. Few were presented for redemption. Trade began to revive, and taxes to come in more easily; and although the natural strength of the French economy and the return of peace no doubt had much to do with this, Law's bank reaped much of the credit. Within a year of its foundation it was one of the strongest financial institutions in Europe. When the Tsar Peter the Great came foraging for civilization in Paris in the summer of 1717, he paid particular attention to it; and in the same year it financed the Regent's purchase of the famous Pitt diamond, a stone the size of a greengage and the finest known in Europe, for 2 million livres. Branches—an essential part of the scheme —were established in the great provincial centres of Lyons, La Rochelle, Tours, Amiens, and Orleans.

It was much easier in centralized France than it would have been in England for a determined organizer to achieve nation-wide results by making a single strategic advance. Law's break-through came on 20 April (N.S.) 1717, when a decree was issued that local tax-collectors should make all their remittances to the Treasury in notes of the Banque Générale; and, what was more, that they should redeem for coin on the scale laid down by the bank any notes tendered to them for exchange by members of the public. The effect was to make the notes an official currency and to provide the bank with a network for circulating them throughout the country.

★   ★   ★

All this was followed with interest and a certain jealousy from the other side of the Channel. The younger Craggs, in particular, kept in the closest touch with Law's progress both through the official despatches which he and Stanhope, as Joint Secretaries of State, saw from 1718 onwards, and through a private correspondence with Stair which began before and continued after Craggs's promotion. A secondary series of despatches from Secretary of Embassy Crawford to his opposite number and fellow-author, Under-Secretary Tickell, supplemented the British Government's knowledge of the growing power of the country which was now formally their ally in the ambitious diplomatic scheme for dominating western Europe.[6]

Later, for his own reasons, Stair tried to convince Whitehall that Law was an enemy of Hanoverian Britain; but in fact, as Stanhope himself admitted, the arresting conception of an Anglo-French entente owed much to Law himself, who was already beginning to see his wealth-producing empire riding higher than even the biggest nation states. 'Je sais', Stanhope wrote to Dubois soon after negotiating the alliance, 'combien [Law] s'est interessé au traité qui devait affermir notre union, et qu'il a régardé l'union des deux couronnes comme la base de ses projets.'[7]

Naturally, all this political interest was accompanied by growing financial activity between London and Paris on the part of such men as Middleton, the Scotch banker in the Strand who did a great deal of Law's business in London, besides keeping the accounts of most of the Scotch nobility in the capital, and Sir John Lambert, the half-French South Sea director, who acted as London agent for Samuel Bernard and, with his French wife, was a regular visitor to Paris. The pace of these international dealings notably quickened after August 1717, when Law acquired a controlling interest in the Mississippi Company.

This Mississippi Company was a derelict concern with a charter going back to 1712, and so was almost the same age as the South Sea Company. Its sole asset of importance was the

PLATE V

THE RUE QUINCAMPOIX DURING THE BOOM: 1719

PLATE VI

A DIRECTOR'S GRANDEUR: THORNHILL'S DESIGN
FOR SUB-GOVERNOR BATEMAN'S STAIRCASE

monopoly of exploiting the French possessions in continental North America then known as Louisiana, but extending indefinitely north and west from the state now so called as far as the lakes in which the Mississippi rises. With characteristic flamboyance Law rechristened his new possession 'The Company of the West', but the old name stuck, and even when his enterprise stretched literally from China to Peru, Mississippi remained the word with which Law's name and talents were linked; and so it has been ever since.

The refloating of the Company of the West was accompanied by an operation which was very familiar to London financiers and politicians. Only a quarter of the newly authorized capital of 100 million livres (which was large, but not so large as that of the South Sea Company) was subscribed in cash and bank-notes. The rest of the purchase price of each 500-livre share was taken in State bonds, which were then at a discount of nearly 80 per cent. on the Stock Exchange in the rue Quincampoix. These *billets d'état* were accepted by the Company at their face value to make up the purchase price of the shares, so achieving a conversion which was similar in principle to those carried out by the Bank of England, the Sword Blade Company, and the South Sea; but more daring than any of these, because the market value of the securities taken in at par was much lower and the gap between the real and nominal value of the capital of the Company was in consequence much greater.

Bold as the capital operation might be, Louisiana at least belonged to France, and the profits of the Company depended on the exertions of the promoters, not the goodwill of an unfriendly foreign government. Law threw himself wholeheartedly into building up his new commercial front, and he was backed by the full weight of the government as well as the credit and resources of his private bank. Unlike the South Sea Company, he was able to insist on the prompt payment of the annuity due to his Company for relieving the government of a large slice of their indebtedness; and was strong-minded enough to tell the shareholders that if the new enterprise was to be got under way they must forgo any prospect of a dividend at least during the first year of operations. They had no ground to complain that the Company was idle. By May 1719 there were twenty-one ships in the Company's fleet; the foundations of a flourishing trade in furs and tobacco had been laid; and the capital of the colony, designated New Orleans in honour of Law's patron, was growing rapidly from the cargoes of voluntary and compulsory emigrants who were soon reaching it.

These were solid commercial steps, and Law took good care to extract the maximum publicity from them. Processions of emigrants, especially women, and massed marriages, made certain that Paris would become conscious of the Mississippi. Many of the colonists were recruited from prisons and brothels, and at some of the massed marriages the couples, for practical as well as symbolical reasons, were handcuffed together. Manon Lescaut bound for Louisiana under her guard of archers might not be a promising colonist, but she catches the imagination; but by no means all the recruits were bad characters. Bounties were successfully offered to respectable families. Couples paraded in garlands as well as chains. Law personally organized groups of pioneering Germans, who established themselves as far afield as Arkansas.

The secret of Law's success in this second stage of his advance lay in making the Mississippi fashionable among an aristocracy which lacked a focus of interest since the death of the King round whom it had revolved, yet was retained in ostentatious leisure at the capital by the tradition of fifty years. To the devout among them he stressed the vast opportunities his colony presented for missionary enterprise. The interest of the salons was captured by the specimen Indians brought back in his ships. And to gamblers and spenders he offered his shares, which, by special dispensation of the Regent, could be held by people of quality without loss of prestige.

Marching towards the completion of his system on both its financial and commercial fronts, Law now began to encounter the first serious opposition. Very much as the Sword Blade

86

and the South Sea had been opposed by the Bank of England, Law's progress was barred by the vested interest of the farmers of the revenue. In 1718 a change of finance ministers gave the opportunity for a new contract for the collection of a substantial part of the revenue, and the syndicate to whom it was awarded took the unusual course of forming a joint stock company to carry it out. This undertaking, nicknamed the 'Anti-System' because it was deliberately aimed at Law, made a great impression. Since the produce of the revenue seemed a more solid asset than Louisiana, the shares of the Anti-System were quoted at a premium, while those of the Company of the West, lacking the prospect of any immediate yield, ran steadily below par.

Subtle though Law was, he had a monopolist's temperament, and he could not tolerate the challenge or even the existence of the Anti-System. His first counter-moves were sober enough, and the main one, indeed, had always been part of his master plan. In the autumn of 1718 a decree was obtained from the Regent transforming the Banque Générale from a private company into a national bank. The joint stock was wound up and the shareholders repaid in cash. The Banque Royale, which opened in December 1718, was under the complete dictatorship of Law, and its power to issue notes was almost double its predecessor's. In practice, the Banque Générale had probably never circulated much more than a fifth of its authorized issue of 60 million livres: the new bank had an authorized issue of 110 millions, and they were not guaranteed in the same way as the old ones. Redeemable they remained, but only in current, and therefore debased coin, and steps were taken artificially to enforce their circulation. Notes were made compulsory for all remittances between towns where branches of the bank existed, and silver was declared not to be legal tender for payments in excess of 600 livres.

Law's next move showed that the Anti-System was driving him into dangerous courses, of which the consequences could not be accurately calculated. Early in 1719 he set himself deliberately to create a bull market in the shares of the Company of the West. This he did by personally making a celebrated wager. He offered to buy Mississippi at prices well above market rates for delivery in three months. But the most impressive part of his offer was to pay the seller his profit at once and forfeit it if, when the delivery date arrived, Law refused to take the shares on the ground that their value had not gone up enough. Expressing it in figures, Law offered to give 500 livres for a 500-livre share, then standing at 300; to hand over 200 livres of the advanced price; and to let the seller keep the 200 livres *and the share* if on delivery the share was not quoted at 500 or more. Although this ingenious arrangement, which was a complete novelty, did in fact limit the buyer's possible loss, to sellers it looked like an invitation to back a certainty, especially when the word went round that the great man would never have conceived such an offer if he were not fortified by inside knowledge. The ensuing boom was all, and more than all, that Law could have wished, and from it must be dated the beginning of the financial euphoria that swept over Europe.

Long afterwards, in a paper of typical bite and clarity, Law compared his management with the English imitation of it. In it he appeals to the underlying differences between the two economies—the English thriving and in no need of stimulation, the French semi-derelict and demanding a series of shocks to arouse its potentially greater strength. The stimulus he applied, he maintains, was well within the capacity of the French economy to absorb; and he calculates that whereas his combine, at its greatest extent, never undertook a dividend of more than $2\frac{2}{3}$ per cent. on a capital of £120 million, the corresponding figure for England, with a third of the economic strength, was 3 per cent. on a combined mercantile joint stock capital of £60 million.[8]

*   *   *

But his admiring rivals in England were not concerned with underlying economic realities. They were technicians in search of fortune, operating on the thirst for gain and the prejudice summed up in the expression 'National Debt'. The Sword Blade's strength lay in their position in Exchange Alley: in the mass of stock pledged with them, that had earned them the nickname of 'the City's pawnbrokers', and the 'fifty stock-jobbers and brokers bound hand and foot and laid in heaps at their doors'. Defoe had just turned from the completion of *Robinson Crusoe* to watch them: 'The truth is', he wrote of them, in 1719, 'that these men, by a mass of money, which they command of other people's as well as their own, will in time ruin the jobbing trade. But 'twill be only like a general visitation . . . like a common calamity . . . that drowns lesser grievances in the general deluge.'[9]

Remarkable as this prophecy was, it had more to justify it than mere suspicion. Law's conversion operation had already inspired Blunt and his colleagues to concoct a scheme for getting the war-becalmed South Sea Company out of the doldrums by converting part of the British funded Debt into South Sea stock. Their plan was recommended to the House of Commons by Secretary Craggs, who had been carefully briefed for his speech by the South Sea director, Gore, in February 1719, and was accepted.[10]

The satisfaction of the country gentlemen in Parliament was the greater because the new government was for the first time proposing to operate on the funded Debt, which was irredeemable, and not merely on the floating Debt, as Harley had done. The class of security chosen for conversion was a comparatively small slice of the whole, being the annuities arising from the Lottery Loan of 1710; and the choice was certainly deliberate, in that the original issue had been handled by, and was still serviced through, the Bank of England. By the Act of 1719 the Company was authorized to increase its capital by £1,150 for every £100 a year of annuity that was offered to them for conversion, up to a maximum of £2·5 million. The Exchequer was to pay the Company 5 per cent. on the new stock thus brought into existence, which would reduce the cost of servicing this particular item of the National Debt by nearly half if the conversion was complete. The Company's total authorized capital in that case would come to the impressive figure of £12·5 millions.[11]

In addition, the Company undertook to lend the government an amount proportionate to the annuities actually converted, and not exceeding three-quarters of a million, on which the interest would be 5 per cent. This attractive feature of the scheme was also the most dubious thing about it. The Company did not possess three-quarters of a million, nor could they borrow it readily; nor was there any question of asking the existing shareholders to forgo their dividend, as Law had done.

In this situation the promoters did not hasten to execute their scheme, but noted with satisfaction the signs of incipient boom in the increased numbers of patent applications and flotations on Exchange Alley; and made effective use of a timely intervention by the Old Pretender on the political scene. While the conversion was before Parliament in February, and South Sea stock stood approximately at par, James Edward was preparing, with Spanish support, the most inept of all the efforts his family made to recapture their throne. In the last days of March his main expedition, which was meant to land in the west of England, was dispersed by a storm, and the only force which arrived on British soil was a subsidiary one, directed at the Western Highlands. On 10 June this contingent, consisting of a few hundred Spanish regulars and the handful of Highlanders that had joined them, surrendered to the government forces, which were mainly Dutch and Swiss, after an obscure skirmish at Glenshiel in Moidart.[12]

The Pretender did not take part in this polyglot engagement, being at the time a guest of the King of Spain; but for a time it was believed in Exchange Alley—and the rumour was sedulously fostered by the Sword Blade organization—that he had not only been defeated, but taken prisoner. It had a tonic effect on the market, and when the books were opened for the conversion in July, South Sea, at 114, had gained nearly a dozen points over the February price.

It was represented as quite unreasonable that the prospective new shareholders should reap this capital gain. Although the Company, as the Act permitted, created enough stock to exchange the annuities at the agreed price at par, the annuitants had to accept the stock at 14 per cent. premium. This premium, retained by the Company in stock and afterwards marketed for their own benefit, raised a substantial sum in cash towards what was needed for the loan to the Government.

Although the operation was fairly modest in scope, and its success only partial (not more than two-thirds of the annuities were actually subscribed) the experience opened a magnificent vista to the Sword Blade partners for their future activities. 'Now', wrote Defoe, 'they stand ready, as occasion offers and profit presents, to stock-job the nation, cozen the Parliament, ruffle the Bank, run up and down stocks, and put the dice upon the whole town'.[13]

★   ★   ★

The energy of the boom on which they depended was now dancing to and fro across the Channel like a series of electric sparks. The summer and autumn in London saw patents for plywood, improvement in oils, drying malt by hot air. Sir Richard Steele, always short of money, and now attached to the wrong political faction, was concerned with the mathematician Gillmore in a venture which, as he told his patient wife, would certainly make their fortune. It depended on a scheme for bringing fresh fish to market in specially constructed tank ships, one of which was demonstrated that summer to two of the biggest tycoons in London—the Duke of Chandos, who had made his enormous fortune out of paying the army, and Tonson, the publisher, who had laid the foundation of his by buying up the copyright of *Paradise Lost* from Mrs. Milton. Though Steele was no business man, he grasped the international character of the new finance. In August 1719 he wrote trying to interest Robert Knight, Cashier of the South Sea, in his 'Fish-pool'; five days later, on the strength of having known him in the gay world of the early 'nineties, he wrote in the same vein to John Law.[14]

91

Law was now moving rapidly to the summit of his career. The sphinx-like seller of futures had not lacked his secret. In May 1719 the Company of the West, which had already added a monopoly of the tobacco trade to its privileges, had undergone a further transformation by absorbing every other oversea trading monopoly in France: the Companies of the East Indies, of China, and of Senegal. This new aggregate, which Law entitled the Company of the Indies, had an authorized capital of 100 million livres, and, by gathering into one huge monopoly the entire colonial trade of the most powerful nation on earth, was the most formidable commercial organization the world had yet seen.

From this position of strength, Law proceeded to crush the Anti-System. In July he secured from the State in return for a payment of 50 million livres the monopoly of coining money. In the same month he outbid the Anti-System for the farm of the revenues, and took it over. In August he placed the coping-stone on the System. An arrangement was concluded with the government by which the entire National Debt of France, capitalized for the purpose at 1,500 livres (over £100 million) should be converted into shares in the Company of the Indies. In return for relieving the government of this mountainous obligation, Law asked for a modest 3 per cent. on the capital figure. The necessary shares would be issued at whatever premium was appropriate in a quantity sufficient to carry out the operation. Even so, the par price of the shares required brought the total capital to the astonishing figure of 312 million livres, and the actual capital represented by them to no less than 1,797 million, or, in contemporary sterling, £130 million. In modern values this would be about £1,500 million, so that the Company of the Indies, even today, is still one of the largest capitalist enterprises that has ever existed.

Naturally all this, and the marketing of the successive issues of shares, was accomplished on a scene of mounting excitement. The premiums at which the shares were issued, though not designed, as Blunt's had been, to allow the Company to reap in stock the full difference between the market price and par, were quite enough to provide Law with what he needed to pay the government for the various concessions he had received. There was plenty of margin. The first issue came out in September at the relatively modest premium of 10 per cent.; the second at 100 per cent.; the third at 900 per cent., or 5,000 livres per 500-livre share.

Law did not rely entirely on the general euphoria, but employed two technical devices to gain these heights. First, payment for the shares was on the instalment plan, the instalments being the very easy ones of 10 per cent. on application and the rest in nineteen equal monthly payments. No doubt this was partly dictated by purely practical considerations, but the consequence was that as the market soared handsome profits could be made by trading in part-paid scrip; and it is profit in such scrip that is the key to the booms of 1719 and 1720. Secondly, as each enterprise was added to the combine and a further issue of shares was authorized to cover it, subscription to the new issue was admitted only on condition that the applicant held a certain number of shares in a previous one. The various issues were therefore collected like happy families, and were indeed nicknamed by the market 'mothers', 'daughters', and 'granddaughters'. Like so many of Law's devices, all this was as novel then as it is familiar now, and of course contributed notably to the advance of the shares, which touched 10,000 in November, 15,000 by the end of the year, and at their utmost peak, nearly, if not quite 20,000, or 4,000 per cent. on par.

These prices were, of course, buoyed up by a flood of bank-notes. In the latter half of 1719 the Banque Royale issued no less than 800 million livres worth of them in denominations of increasing size. There was no difficulty about circulating them. Coin from would-be speculators poured into the bank to get the notes which were so much more convenient for stock exchange transactions than metal money, and were the only currency the Company of the Indies would accept as instalments on the new issues. Nobody cared that now the notes had ceased to be redeemable in coin of any kind, fine or debased. To play the new game one had to have the counters. They even went to a premium, and at the end of the year Law prudently halted their issue in Paris altogether; but even then fresh measures were taken to encourage their circulation in the provinces, by forbidding major transactions there except in notes.

Some people did not share in the general rapture, and one of them was the Earl of Stair. When Law's conversion scheme was announced he was sceptical, and reported that it was 'more extravagant and ridiculous than anything that ever happened in any other country'. But scorn soon changed to jealousy and chagrin. 'You must henceforth', Craggs learned only a few days later, 'look upon Law as first Minister, whose daily discourse is that he will raise France to a greater height than ever she was, upon the ruins of England and Holland.' Stair added that he had high-mindedly declined a personal offer from Law of a private allocation of shares, holding that it would be inconsistent with his diplomatic status to hold them—a piece of selflessness which is equally inconsistent with Stair's own reputation as an active speculator on the Paris and London stock exchanges.[15]

The Ambassador's change of front about Law at the moment of his fellow-countryman's most dazzling success had two causes. Law could not resist patronizing his former patron as he now patronized almost the whole French aristocracy, and Highland pride was roused. But Stair had genuine official misgivings as well. His post-bag was full of letters from friends and relations in Scotland begging him to make their fortunes in Paris; and among the 30,000 foreigners who had flocked to Paris to speculate in person were many prominent people from Britain: Hutcheson, the economist M.P.; Lady Mary Wortley Montagu; Lambert, the South Sea director; a whole family of Campbells, including the Earl of Islay, whose intimacy with Law gained him instant admission through the crowd which always waited in the financier's outer room. Stair could not ignore this evidence of a flight of British capital to Paris, or its possible dangers to any further conversion schemes his own government might be contemplating. These fears and jealousies made him highly receptive to stories that Law was planning to extend his financial empire to the British economy; that he was opening a large bear account to depress British Government stocks; and that he meant to chain the East India and South Sea Companies to his chariot, and become the financial dictator of Europe.

As the autumn went on the British Embassy became almost hysterical on the subject of Law and the need to do something to compete with him. 'I wish to God', wrote Crawford to Under-secretary Tickell at the end of September, 'there may be something done quickly to put our affairs in order before it is too late, and that the great men of Britain would think of something else than merely of tripping up one another's heels.' Three weeks later Stair himself was even more specific in despatches to Stanhope and Craggs: 'By the success of Mr. Law's project the public debts of France are paid off at a stroke, and the French king remains master of an immense revenue and credit without bounds.' Britain must mount a scheme for discharging the National Debt at once if Law was not to 'raise the trade of France on the ruins of our trade'.[16]

*   *   *

The boom in the rue Quincampoix which Stair and Crawford were now witnessing is one of the most extraordinary scenes in the history of France. Stockbrokers had traded in this narrow street ever since Louis XIV's government had first issued paper to finance his wars, and there is a curious irony about the sordid and frantic struggles in the competing alleys of Paris and London over the paper ghosts of what had gone so gloriously into battle for the two nations during the past fifty years. As the successive issues of shares came out at the offices of the Company of the Indies in the rue Vivienne, the temperature steadily rose on the rue Quincampoix. The shares there—and it must be remembered that all dealings were now in the shares of a single great enterprise—advanced (with setbacks for profit-taking) on average ten points a day for seven consecutive months from July 1719 to January 1720. The booths of the brokers—for few had offices—were crowded with speculators from eight in the morning till dusk, when the street was cleared and the gates at either end were closed. The most extravagant stories went about and contributed to the excitement: fortunes gained at the turn of a day or two; humpbacks letting out their lucky humps as writing desks; huge gains by café proprietors and stationers for their trivial services. The avid, cosmopolitan, fashionable mob was the wonder of Europe.

Law regarded them with contempt, and the boom as a secondary phenomenon, a mere step in his much larger game. The time would come for it to be disciplined by monetary controls, but in the meantime he cheerfully paid out rope to it in the shape of bank-notes. His thoughts that autumn were on other matters. He was already finance minister in all but name, and the name itself was soon to follow. At his house in the Place Vendôme he studied the economic reports he had called for from every province of France, and drew up a stream of economic and administrative reforms covering every aspect of French life. To keep down retail prices hundreds of old-fashioned offices and practices in the Paris markets were summarily swept away and the internal duties on bread, grain, and flax were removed. An ambitious programme of public works, with particular emphasis on canals, bridges, and roads was drawn up. Even more far-reaching were his plans for a complete reform of the revenue and the poor law. All taxes were to be consolidated into a single 'denier royal' assessed on property, and without exemptions for privilege—a change which could have altered the course of French and European history if it had ever come into effect.* For the poor a national network of almshouses was to be created, financed by a local

* Law's *Memoire sur le Denier Royal* contains in its 14 points as succinct a statement of the principles of taxation as one could hope to find. Two of the metaphors he employs are especially striking. The government which levies taxes in excess of intended expenditure is like a farmer who hopes to reap without sowing; and the principle of taxation in accordance with capacity to pay is justified not as a matter of equity but by the example of the man and the boy trying to carry a load of 200 lb. Give each 100 lb. and the boy will collapse and the man will be left unable to carry the whole.

rate which would also be levied in accordance with capacity
to pay.

He was the greatest man in Europe, and had arrived at glory
by a path whose presence nobody had even suspected. His
personal fortune was enormous. He was a marquis by purchase,
a great landowner, and the possessor of a library of 45,000
volumes. Dubois is said to have suggested using his influence
with his friend Stanhope to get him an English dukedom and
the Garter; and the Emperor and the Bey of Tunis offered him
territories in which he could have been a sovereign prince.
But the only honours he accepted were the freedom of the
City of Edinburgh and a seat among the immortals of the
Academy.

In September he paid a visit to the rue Quincampoix. His
carriage drove slowly through the cheering, hysterical crowd.
Grave, serene, long-nosed, he scattered guineas—somebody
noticed that they bore the portrait of William III—from the
window as he went along. While the mob of punters and
jobbers scrambled for the metal whose magic it was his
ambition to destroy, men he had posted above for the purpose
emptied buckets of slops on them. It showed what he thought
of the stock exchange; but it took more than that to damp
their enthusiasm.[17]

CHAPTER VI

Selling the Bear's Skin

ON 23 NOVEMBER 1719 King George, freshly arrived
from Hanover, opened the new session of Parliament.
A Speech from the Throne can rarely have used more
confident language. It foreshadowed a five-point programme
which was both dynamic and far-reaching.

Abroad the war, skilfully limited in cost and physical effects,
was about to achieve its aim of compelling Spain to accept
British leadership in a European concert. 'All Europe', the
King said, 'as well as these Kingdoms, are on the point of being
delivered . . . by the influence of British arms and counsels.'
At home three important changes were hinted at in those parts
of the constitution which 'were most liable to abuse'. There
was to be a reform of the House of Lords which would at one
stroke rally the Whig magnates of Scotland permanently to
the régime by making twenty-five of them hereditary peers
of Parliament, and weaken the reversionary interest of the
Prince of Wales and the opposition Whigs by limiting future
creation of peerages. Secondly, the life of the existing House of
Commons might be prolonged beyond 1722, when its term
under the Septennial Act would end, with the possibility of a
return either to triennial Parliaments or even Parliaments of
indefinite duration. Thirdly, and hardly less important, the
tap-roots of the old Anglican order, the universities, were to be
subjected to radical reform. 'So far as Prudence can foretell', ran
the King's peroration, 'the Unanimity of this Session of Parliament must establish, with the Peace of all Europe, the Glory
and Trade of these Kingdoms, on a lasting foundation. I think
every Man may see the End of our Labours: all I have to ask of
you is, that you will agree to be a great and flourishing People.'

For over a century no government was to propose such a carefully concerted policy. It was designed to establish a lasting ascendancy for Stanhope and Sunderland. Both were still well under fifty, and power for a generation seemed to be within their grasp. Success depended on one thing: the good-will of the country proprietors whose votes, as ever, were decisive in the Commons and whose influence still pervaded the countryside. Only ten years had passed since Harley had risen to power on their shoulders, and although Stanhope and Sunderland were professed Whigs they were no less dependent on the country vote than Harley had been. Many of the country Members were the same men as in 1710, and the prejudices of the class had changed little in ten years.

The country gentleman still had the maximum prejudice with the minimum of comprehension about the National Debt. When he had nothing else to talk about, this was the topic to which he always returned. The modest South Sea conversion of 1719, though far from a complete success, had appealed very much to him. It had seemed to enable the government to raise half a million while at the same time achieving an actual reduction of interest on the Debt. It was true that the half-million had not been applied to paying off capital—it was needed for the war—but at least it had avoided the fresh borrowing and fresh taxation of Godolphin's time which had now become a political legend. As the King said in his speech, it was costing Parliament remarkably little to make Britain the arbiter of Europe. Nobody connected the multi-plication of company promotions in the City with what was, in fact, a mild dose of inflation.

The other item in the government's programme for establishing the country's and their own prosperity 'on a lasting foundation' was, therefore, the King told Parliament, a proposal for further reduction in the Debt. The plans, on which Blunt, Knight, and their colleagues had been working at least since the previous summer, had been laid before Stan-hope as soon as he returned from Hanover with the King on 14 November, which suggests that their authors were well aware of the government's political needs. Stair's urgent advice from Paris that something must be done to compete with Law reinforced the government's own assessment of the Parliamentary situation at home. On every count they were only too receptive to spectacular proposals.

We do not know the form of the original plan. Blunt is said to have declared that just as his original masterpiece, the Classis Lottery of 1711, had been improved upon by Law, so he would now improve on the Mississippi promotion. Aislabie, the Chancellor of the Exchequer, said afterwards that the scheme first offered was a copy of Law's—an amalgamation of the entire National Debt with the capitals of the three great corporations to form a single financial-cum-mercantile corporation of gigantic size, thus achieving at one stroke what had cost Law years of patient labour. This is doubtful. Aislabie had every reason, in retrospect, to magnify Blunt's ambition, and even Blunt, though his maxim was certainly to 'think big', would hardly have suggested anything so obviously unacceptable. Sunderland regarded the East India Company as being under his especial protection. Neither he nor Stanhope would have thought such an idea a safe basis for a reference in the King's speech and directions for detailed discussion with the Treasury which began early in December.

Sunderland, though the principal Treasury minister, took little part in these discussions, but both he and Stanhope were kept closely informed of their progress. The work was left to Chancellor Aislabie and Postmaster-General Craggs in his capacity as chief financial adviser to the government. The Chancellor well understood, and as a former October Club-man to a considerable extent shared, the prejudices of the country gentlemen on financial questions. He also had what seemed to him the advantage of a private contact with South Sea circles through his confidential man of business and financial shadow, Francis Hawes, who, as Cashier of the Customs, had an office conveniently situated in the City.

The other side of the negotiation was at first conducted by Blunt, Knight, and Knight's choleric confidential clerk,

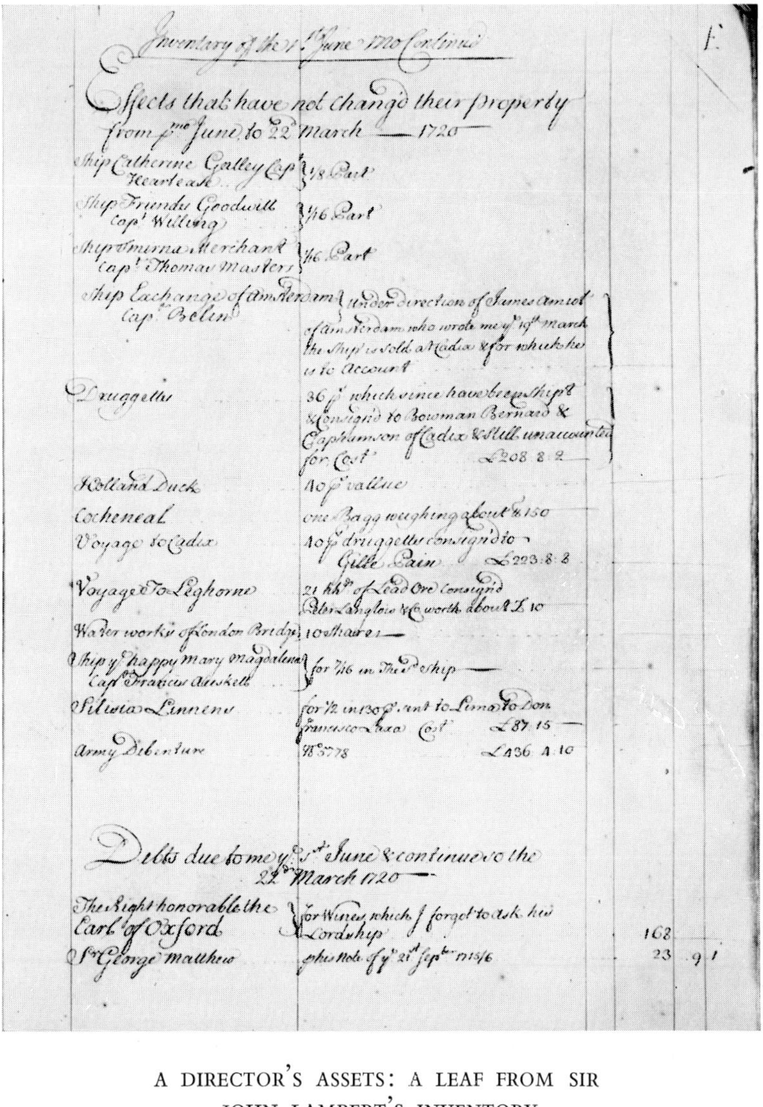

PLATE VII

A DIRECTOR'S ASSETS: A LEAF FROM SIR
JOHN LAMBERT'S INVENTORY

PLATE VIII

THE STOCK EXCHANGE HARLEQUINADE

Christopher Clayton. Soon afterwards they were joined by Caswall. He was no longer a South Sea director, but he was still a partner in the Sword Blade, which was the credit-creating agency behind the South Sea façade; and his two colleagues, Sawbridge and Turner, must also have been in the secret at this point, if not in the actual negotiations. The magnate Janssen, with his immense international interests, was also brought into confidence, as were the Sub-Governor and Deputy Governor of the Company, both of whom were completely under Blunt's influence. But the time had not yet arrived for bringing the impressive, cumbersome Company itself on the scene. The negotiation had been begun without any mandate from them, and their authority was not sought until the syndicate had reduced the proposals to what was intended to be their final form.[1]

The pressure on both Government and syndicate to achieve a spectacular coup increased sharply during the December negotiations.

Law's system was rising to its peak, and Paris had become the financial capital of Europe. Speculators and speculative capital were pouring into France, where Mississippi stock stood at 2,000 and the word 'millionaire' had just been invented. 'It is inconceivable what wealth there is in France now', wrote the Duchess of Orleans. 'Everybody speaks in millions. I don't understand it at all, but I see clearly that the god Mammon reigns an absolute monarch in Paris.' Joseph Gage, one of the most theatrical speculators of the century, was contemplating the purchase of a kingdom with his vast paper fortune, and Law himself was unwearying in his readiness to place funds subscribed by British aristocrats. During September 1719 the Duke of Chandos alone put £40,000 at the disposal of Drummond's Bank, to be invested under Law's personal direction. The Pay Office official, William Sloper, was said to have made £80,000.

Speculative fever was not the only stimulus coming from across the Channel. Profits were beginning to seep back into England to inflate the domestic boom, of which Secretary

Cragg's office had plain evidence in a steady flow of applications for patents. Two rival insurance subscriptions for capitals amounting to £3 million were opened on successive days, 22 and 23 December. The South Sea project was not to blame for these promotions. They presaged the tide on which it was possible to launch it. The anxiety of its promoters was that they might miss that tide, and that Law would yet prove a more powerful counter-attraction. It did not escape the notice of the market that when the great Chandos bought Mississippi he sold South Sea.

On the government there was another, yet stronger pressure. On 18 December their peerage proposals, which had been carried in the Lords, had to be withdrawn in the face of a heavy preliminary defeat in the Commons. Walpole had been the organizer, but the decisive votes had been those of the country gentlemen for whom Sir John Packington—the original of Sir Roger de Coverley—had spoken with the authentic English mixture of personal modesty and family pride: 'For my own part, I never desire to be a lord, but I have a son who one day may have that ambition.'[2] Only eighteen of the eighty county members voted for the government. Even squires sitting for government boroughs deserted their colours. Of the thirty members for his native Yorkshire, Aislabie could rally only eight; of the ninety-five baronets in the House, only twenty-four could bring themselves to vote against the possibility of promotion. Clearly a counterpoise was needed if the country vote was to be kept.

*　　　*　　　*

In the negotiations at the Treasury any idea of not only cutting out the Bank, but of absorbing it, had now been dropped. Nevertheless, the Chancellor, so he said afterwards, was still uneasy about a plan which left no room for the Bank's participation. He had in mind the House of Commons' strong feeling against financial monopoly, as well as the government's natural desire to see its credit spread as broadly as possible in the City.

The position before the negotiators was this. The Debt which the squirearchy so detested fell into two categories, costing roughly equal amounts. First were the *annuities*, most of them for ninety-nine or ninety-six years certain, which had been sold to finance the national struggle against Louis XIV. This was much the more objectionable portion politically. The annuities had been sold at a bad time, when interest rates were high. They could not be paid off or redeemed by lump-sum payments or through a sinking fund (except on terms acceptable to the annuitants), and it seemed to follow that these memorials of Blenheim and Ramillies would remain a burden on the taxpayer until nearly the end of a century which was still young. The annual charge for these so-called 'irredeemable' debts, guaranteed corporately by the House of Commons, was three-quarters of a million pounds, or, counting what was due on part of the 1710 Lottery not converted during the previous summer, just under £800,000.

The other category was the miscellany of obligations ranging from £52,754. 10s. a year for the Lottery of 1714 to £23. 8s. 3½d. a year due to Edward Clent, Esq., on an Army debenture mislaid by official carelessness and inserted in the National Debt by special Act of Parliament. Most of it was fairly recent in origin, though it included the veteran debt, Charles II's old score, for which his niece's government had reluctantly accepted service. But its common feature was that it could be, and actually was being progressively *redeemed* under Walpole's Sinking Fund. The total charge for this 'redeemable' debt was just under three-quarters of a million pounds a year. The bulk of it was held by the Bank of England either on its own account or as nominee.

The total service of the Debt, therefore, apart from charges of management and the amounts already 'engrafted' into the stocks of the three great companies, was rather over £1·5 million a year, and this was the amount negotiators at the Treasury were concerned to disguise as a single huge redeemable annuity to the South Sea Company. For this purpose it was necessary to represent the whole as a capital sum.

The need to do this was not merely technical. The astronomical and so bemusing figures produced by capitalization gave a desirable impression of bigness. It was Blunt's method, as it was Law's, to juggle with millions; a huge capital, even though it could not be employed otherwise than as a loan to the government, would give prestige to the Company; and in describing how he was relieving the nation of its burdens, the Chancellor would cut a much more dramatic figure in the Commons speaking in nine digits than merely in seven. To keep one's head in the maze of South Sea finance, it is important to lay firm hold on the fact that the capital figures were mere paper calculations.

It was easy to put a capital figure on the redeemables, since they represented actual sums lent at 4 or 5 per cent.—mostly 5. The figure was about £16 million.

The irredeemables, in the nature of things, had no automatic capital value related to money originally advanced. On an actuarial basis the capital value would have depended on the time each class still had to run—thus £100 a year taken out in 1704 for ninety-nine years would, at the ruling rate of 5 per cent., have been worth something like £1,900, or nineteen years' purchase. One of the great objects, however, was to cut down the cost of this particular type of Debt, and this was done by capitalizing all the annuities according to their original term of years, but without regard to the date they were issued. The number of years' purchase chosen—twenty for the ninety-nine- and ninety-six-year annuities and fourteen for the thirty-two-year and Lottery annuities—were such as to capitalize an annual charge of 5 per cent. for the former and just over 6 for the latter, making a global sum of about £15 million. The terms to be offered to the holders of the longest and most recent annuities were thus rather unfavourable.

The grand total of £31 million was a far bigger sum than had ever before appeared in the national accounts. Against it, an almost exactly equal amount of South Sea stock was to come into existence as fast as the holders of one responded,

during the space of one year, to an invitation to exchange it
for the other; for the conversion was to be voluntary. But how
much stock was to be issued for a given amount of Debt was,
as under the 1719 conversion, to be left to the movement of
the market, the wisdom of the Company, and the caution of
the Debt-holders.

Although the terms to be offered by the Company to the
public were thus designedly left vague, the bargain between
the Company and the government was quite specific. For
every pound of annual expenditure on Debt of which the
government was relieved, the Company was to receive a
pound a year from the government, except in the case of
certain irredeemable debts, for which they were to receive
only 14s. for each pound taken over. This concession was
worth about £40,000 a year immediately to the Exchequer.
Much more important—at any rate from the political point of
view—the Company was to undertake that after seven years
they would accept 4 per cent. from the government on all that
part of their annuity (including what was already in payment)
which was calculated on the basis of 5. In other words, if the
operation was a complete success, the service of the National
Debt would be reduced to a uniform 4 per cent. This would
save the government something like £400,000 a year, or
nearly the entire cost of the regular army. Moreover this
charge would be redeemable. The Chancellor would be able
to tell the Commons that in seven years' time the encumbrance on the national estate would be reduced by about one-
sixth; that the whole could be paid off as and when the nation
could afford it; and that if the savings were applied on sinking
fund principles, the Debt would be liquidated in twenty-five
years. As fast as this happened the resources of the Company
would be freed for profitable investment.

If, as one might say, this was a mere glittering prospect,
a more immediate benefit was to be offered as well. As soon as
the conversion year was over, the Company would make the
Exchequer a present of three millions in four quarterly instalments. This was not a loan, customary in previous conversions,

but an absolute gift to the nation. It was to be devoted to the sacred cause of paying off such redeemable debts incurred before 1716 as the cautious holders chose not to convert into South Sea stock; and to the extent that it was not required for this it would be at the unfettered disposal of the Exchequer. It could even be used for redeeming some of the Company's own annuity.

Of all the attractions which Blunt and Knight had thought of this, if the crudest, was also the most tempting. It was immediate, it was big, it was easily put over. Nor was it so crude as it looks, since besides being a bribe it was a kind of insurance for the whole operation. If the full amount of the redeemables was not subscribed into the Company, this additional resource would be there to pay off recalcitrants; while the mere threat of being paid off would encourage the holders—especially the Bank of England—to accept the Company's terms. If that happened, the whole sum would be available to strengthen the régime. This gigantic douceur to the public was, in fact, proportioned nicely to the enthusiasm with which the public would co-operate in the scheme.

Blunt and Knight well knew that the Company did not possess, and would not, in the ordinary course of business, ever accumulate spare cash amounting to three millions. Every penny of income, whether from the government annuity or from trading profits, would be needed to maintain even a 5 per cent. dividend on the giant capital. This did not worry them in the least. They were, in the language of the time, 'selling the bear's skin' before they had killed the bear.* It will, indeed, be convenient to refer to this three million, large thought it is, as the Little Bear.

Most bear operations are built on the hope that the stock dealt in will fall in value. In the South Sea promotion (as in the Mississippi deal in futures) the whole point of the bear operation was the hope and declared intention, that the value

---

* The present stock exchange term 'bear', i.e., one who sells for future delivery stock which he does not actually possess, in hope the price will fall, is, of course, directly descended from this usage: an interesting case of a displaced metaphor.

of the stock would rise. There was no mystery about where the Little Bear was coming from. Although the Company was to be allowed to create enough stock to convert at par, it by no means followed that the holder of £1 Debt would receive £1 stock in exchange. In the 1719 conversion the Company had exchanged in the market ratio of 100 stock to 114 Debt. Now the stock stood at 123 on the market while Debt was at par or below, and the rate of conversion would certainly not be below this. It followed that the Company would be entitled to create more stock than it needed for the conversion. If the conversion were at 125, this surplus would have a par value of more than £7 million and a market value of something like £9 million. This surplus could be sold for the benefit of the shareholders, who would, of course, include the former creditors of the nation. Through the Little Bear the government would take part in this profitable transaction.

It can now be seen clearly why Blunt and Knight calculated —as it proved rightly—that in boom conditions the holder of £100 a year annuity guaranteed by Parliament for eighty years and upwards would eagerly exchange it for stock in the Company worth at par £1,800, £1,600, or even £1,500 and yielding, on the Company's past dividend record, £90, £80, or £70 a year. First, the less stock he was given, the more the new stockholder could rejoice in the profit thereby accruing to the Company of which he was now a member, and the Company's consequent power to pay him a better dividend later on. Secondly, and still more important, the higher the price of the stock went, the greater would be the attraction of converting quickly and making a capital gain by promptly selling out. While one can say this was no more than a chain letter, a lifting of oneself up by one's own bootstraps, it was not wholly nonsensical. A conversion even on the terms of the previous summer would have amply yielded the Little Bear, a good dividend, and all other expenses. Given such restraint a serious crisis might have been avoided.

Restraint was, however, impossible, not merely because of the ambition and greed of the promoters, but for other, deeper reasons. The plan amounted to the injection into the economy which was already booming, of another £5 million or so of new money—ten times the injection of the previous year—with a simultaneous lowering of interest rates. The economy, as Law was acute enough to see from Paris, was in no condition to absorb such a sum in genuine production, and the South Sea Company was the least eligible of existing economic institutions to invest it usefully. Its trading prospects, which were in any case a dream, were unlikely to be brought any nearer realization by a policy which compelled the Company to devote all its resources to pushing its stock so as to show a large paper profit. As a finance minister Aislabie was committing a plain blunder in accepting the proposals. Strangely enough, though he was a thoroughly dishonest man, the blunder seems to have been an honest one. On 3 and 19 December he backed it by buying £22,000 stock in the South Sea Company at the market price of 123 and paying for it in cash.* This stock he got from Knight, who derived it from a source which will presently appear.

Such was the celebrated South Sea scheme in its original form. It suited the government so well that their judgement, warped by the prospect of dazzling political success, did not allow a moment's thought that the whole thing might be too good to be true. Aislabie, their principal agent, was a stupid and limited man, who saw for himself the prospect of gains which would make him one of the greatest men in Yorkshire. The motives of the projectors themselves are harder to penetrate. Even Knight was already rich. But the humble shoemaker's son, the cadet of the modest Warwickshire family, the small-town Baptist from Herefordshire and the rest, belonged to a self-made generation. They had the example of Law before them to show that through finance one could advance from nothing to overt power and dignity. Sir John Packington was not the only man in England who, in December 1719, thought his son might want to be a lord. In the great division

---

* But one cannot be sure. Receipts for this transaction were produced. Since they were signed by Knight, suspicion necessarily attaches to them.

against the Peerage Bill four of the five South Sea directors who were Members had voted against the government, and the other had abstained.

*　　　*　　　*

The main lines of the plan were agreed by Christmas, and Knight was beginning to drop hints to City contacts that 'something was to be done to mend the South Sea stock'. The object was to work the price gently upwards against the day when the proposals became public, if possible without at the same time forcing up the price of government securities as well. Now that matters were settled, alarm at the Bank seemed to matter less. Aislabie took a quick, modest profit on his £22,000.[3]

At the same time the London public were enabled to read a new edition of Law's masterpiece, *Money and Trade Considered*, with an enthusiastic preface contributed by Lord Islay from Paris, where the author had celebrated Christmas by a formal profession of Roman Catholicism. Although the treatise was more than ten years old, this was the first time it had reached a wide audience as the work of the man who was the wonder of the age. Even now it is a brilliant book, simple, subtle, and penetrating. As a contribution to economics as a science it can claim to be one of the first in the field. Unlike most contemporary writings on finance, its style seemed almost elementary; and yet it isolated two ideas which had never before reached men's minds in so succinct a form. One was that credit, if circulated, acted as money, just as if it were conventional currency. The other was that there was a direct relationship between what we call 'productivity' and the circulating medium. Lord Stair, who had now quarrelled so violently with Law as to verge on being declared *persona non grata*, commented that he was not surprised that a man who had proved gold could be turned into paper should be prepared to accept transubstantiation.

But in the last days of the year news arrived which did more than Knight's rumours or Law's economic theories to give a fair wind to the South Sea. King Philip of Spain dismissed Alberoni and announced his intention of accepting the Quadruple Alliance. There would be peace with Spain on English terms, and the way to the South American trade would at last be clear. On 30 December Stanhope set out into the storms for Paris to confer with Dubois about the triumph of their policy.

The time for publishing the proposals had clearly arrived, but before this could be done it was necessary that the Company should formally accept them. The Court of Directors, which throughout the negotiations had had no notice of what was intended in its name, was accordingly assembled on 20 January in an expectant atmosphere, for the news was already rustling through the City. Two adjournments were needed to secure the attendance of Blunt and Hawes, who for genuine or dramatic reasons were detained at the Treasury. It was not till the afternoon of the 21st that the Court learned of the proposals in the form of an invitation from the Chancellor of the Exchequer to make an offer on the lines agreed between the Treasury and the syndicate. Next day, before the directors had been able to do more than take formal note of this, the Chancellor unfolded the plan to the House of Commons on the basis that an offer would be forthcoming from the Company. Secretary Craggs followed him with a bland suggestion that the House should unanimously resolve to receive it.

The thing had been so deftly managed that the effect exceeded ministerial expectations. Craggs's speech was received in stunned silence, and for a quarter of an hour no Member rose to speak. Then Thomas Brodrick, an influential Anglo-Irish Whig of independent views who had been one of the chief opponents of the Peerage Bill, suggested that before closing with this particular offer the House should consider other tenders. The Chancellor, visibly shaken, urged that it was no time to hesitate—undertakings of this kind should be carried on 'with spirit'. After two hours' confused debate, the House adjourned without a vote; but having tacitly accepted there would be a scheme, and that the Bank would make a rival offer. Even Brodrick thought 'many a fair pound would be saved to the public' on the terms offered by the Company, let alone 'what might be got from the Bank'.[4]

The Bank's enthusiasm to compete with the Company was afterwards pleaded by Aislabie as a justification for embarking on a scheme whose principles seemed to be supported by the most orthodox and level-headed financiers in the country. This excuse is quite beside the point. No doubt the Bank directors, like everyone else, were by now infected with the fashionable doctrine of infinitely expanding credit; but their true motives in trying to outbid the South Sea offer were much more compelling, being defensive and political. Over the past ten years they had seen the annual payments from the government to the South Sea Company creep up to over £500,000 a year, so as to be within striking distance of the £750,000 which passed through their own hands on the same account. Now it was proposed to increase the South Sea annuity—*necessarily at the expense of the Bank's*—to nearly £2 million. Even the amounts of Debt not directly affected by the offer—the short-term borrowing on Exchequer bills and the annuity on the Bank's original loan of 1695—might be redeemed or transferred to the rival institution, and the Bank would become no more than an ordinary commercial banking house. Their old enemy, the Sword Blade Bank, would have succeeded at last in depriving them of their pre-eminence in the London money market at the very moment when stability at home and abroad seemed to promise lasting prosperity. For the Bank the devising of a counter-proposal seemed a matter of life and death.

They were not allowed much time. As soon as the debate ended on the 22nd the South Sea directors who were Members of Parliament had hurried to report to their colleagues assembled at South Sea House, where it was immediately resolved to make the agreed offer and to entrust its preparation to a committee consisting of those later known as 'the decemvirs': Blunt himself; the Sub- and Deputy Governors; Knight; Sawbridge of the Sword Blade; Hawes, and another Treasury office-holder, Houlditch; Chester, the prosperous banker;

Gibbon, the yet more prosperous bill-broker; and the gouty warlock, Grigsby.

At the Treasury, Ministers were divided about the latest turn of events. In conference with the decemvirs Sunderland and the Treasury Secretary Charles Stanhope suggested that the Company's offer should be baited with £4 million for the Exchequer instead of £3 million. Aislabie, whose heart was failing him, hinted that the Company should go shares with the Bank. Blunt, whose contempt for the Chancellor was steadily increasing, brushed him aside. 'No, sir,' he declared. 'We will never divide the child.'[5]

On the afternoon of 27 January two remarkable offers were laid before the Commons, both of them having been approved finally that very morning, one by a General Court of the South Sea Company and the other by the Bank directors meeting at Waghorn's coffee-house. The Company's Little Bear had grown by half a million to £3½ million. The Bank offered a Middle-sized Bear of £5½ million for the right to offer Bank stock to the holders of the National Debt. They added, significantly, that this was conditional on the Bank's being continued in 'the same powers and privileges that are already granted to them, with the addition of such further powers and privileges' as might be required for carrying out the conversion. Nothing was said in either proposal about the rate at which the conversion was to be carried out.

Blunt, who now had the whole machinery of the Company under his control, was not the man to be deterred by this; nor can there be any doubt that both Stanhope (who had returned from Paris on the 15th) and Sunderland were directly concerned in the last bids of this extraordinary auction. By manipulation of the South Sea Company's constitution, full authority to amend the Company's proposal had been delegated in turn by the General Court of Proprietors to the directors, and by them to the Sub- and Deputy Governors, leaving the negotiation still in the hands of the original syndicate. Over the last week-end in January an amended offer 'to outbid the Bank at any rate' was perfected by Blunt and his colleagues at a conference with Stanhope, and on Monday 1 February the directors, without being aware of its nature, authorized its presentation to the Commons Committee 'in the name of the General Court', which was done the same day. Next day the House of Commons, the directors, and the General Court, in this order, learned that the Company had raised the stakes to £4 million certain for the Exchequer, *plus a further sum*, which might be as much as £3½ million, depending on the amount of Debt actually converted. This Big Bear of £7½ million was accompanied by the hope that it would be favourably considered, 'since the Company are willing and do hereby declare they are ready to undertake the great work upon whatever terms may be offered by any other company'. For good measure, the offer also included a promise to throw open the whole annuity to redemption after four years instead of seven; to reduce the interest to a uniform 4 per cent. within the same period; and to circulate a million pounds' worth of Exchequer bills—formerly the prerogative of the Bank of England—without management charge or interest.

The Bank also made a revised offer, but it was not nearly so spectacular. No more than £5½ million was offered for the Exchequer. There was, however, one new feature which Blunt, for all his rhetoric, could not have included in his proposals. This was an undertaking to convert at a fixed rate of £170 Debt to £100 Bank stock. This, though above the current price of Bank stock by about twenty points, was at least some guarantee against the scheme bolting. But Blunt's offer carried the House by storm. Without a division, it resolved to accept the Company's offer, and what a journalist at once called 'the English Mississippi' had begun. Remitting the Bill to be drawn up by Aislabie, Craggs, Charles Stanhope, and two other ministers, the Commons turned with relief to measures for making the River Douglas navigable and the troubles of the straw hat industry. In Exchange Alley South Sea stock rose thirty-one points, from 129 to 160.[6]

A day or two afterwards James Milner, the merchant and M.P., called at the Bank. In a little parlour he found 'a parcel of her old servants, who under her auspicious reign had raised themselves to be worth two, three, or four Plumbs a man. I could hear only a few broken words: "buy long annuities, lock up our cash, distress, upstarts, revenge and ruin, &c."' Everyone considered the long reign of the Bank was over. Its stock fell sharply. Erasmus Lewis, as acute an observer as any, thought 'the least discerning eye can discover that a body of men, with a stock of forty-three millions, and credit for as much more acting by united counsels, must fill the House of Commons, and rule this little world. . . . What occasion will there be for Parliaments hereafter?'[7]

When they met on 5 February, the General Court of the South Sea Company showed no resentment against the way the directors had acted in their name, but unanimously passed a vote of thanks to them for their 'great care, prudence, and secrecy'. The directors left the meeting with authority to 'act and do all such matters and things as they shall think convenient for the most effectual execution of the said proposals'. In particular they were given a completely free hand to decide in the light of events the crucial question of the rate at which the conversion should be carried out. Cheered by these expressions of confidence, they approved warrants for nearly £5,000 in payment of directors' fees, and certain payments to the press. The enthusiasm of the General Court showed only slight abatement when it was announced, a few days later, that to strengthen the Company's position in discharging its patriotic task, payment of the dividend due at Christmas, 1719, would be deferred for twelve months.

Sub-Governor Fellowes now, owing to what he afterwards called confusion of mind, retired to the country on medical advice, leaving the other decemvirs to embark on the most delicate of all the transactions in the affair. This was the gratification and acquisition of 'friends'. The initiative undoubtedly came, in most cases, from the 'friends' themselves, for although spirits needed to be sustained in the vigorous pamphleteering which now raged over the merits of the scheme, the promoters could be reasonably sure of a majority for their Bill on the strength of the £7½ million alone. The method of gratification was in all cases the same, and had been made familiar by Law. It consisted of 'transferring' a certain amount of stock to the 'friend' at or near the current market price. He did not pay for it, but was entitled to 'sell' it back to the Company whenever he chose, and receive as 'profit' the increase in the market price. The size of these bribes on credit was thus proportioned to the success of the Company in pushing the value of its shares. Knight acted as registrar, undertaking in each case to transfer the agreed number of shares in his own name, either directly or through intermediaries. The fact that neither he nor the Company held sufficient shares at this time was of no importance, since no actual transfers took place, and by the time they did take place the Company would have the surplus stock to cover them. They were, however, scrupulously entered by Knight in a private ledger with green covers.

During February Knight handled twelve applications of this kind, including those from the Craggs, father and son, and Sunderland, who made his through Postmaster Craggs. Sunderland, rather to the concern of Deputy Governor Joye, received the right to make a 'profit' on £50,000 stock at 175— in other words he was to be allowed £500 for every point the stock rose above that figure. Postmaster Craggs received £30,000 on the same terms. The request of Secretary Craggs was more altruistic. He really thought—so he told several of the decemvirs who came to see him in Westminster Hall— that it would be an advantage for the Company to have friends in the Royal Family, and suggested a distribution between George I's mistress, the newly created Duchess of Kendal, her two 'nieces' (actually her daughters by the King) and his own patroness, Countess von Platen. After some haggling, during which Craggs beat the syndicate down to a figure well below the current market price for the stock, it was settled that these ladies should be allowed £120 each for every point the stock went above 154. Aislabie, who was now determined to play the market for all he was worth, collected the right to £200 for every point above 130—a bargain struck on 12 February, when the market price was already 180. Through the director Gibbon, Lords Gower and Lansdowne were also introduced early to this select circle, which was completed by four Members of Parliament, Sir Robert Chaplin, the South Sea director, being one of them.* £25,000 public money in the hands of Hampden, the Treasurer to the Navy (whose cashier was the ubiquitous Hawes), was also laid out in stock on behalf of this unworthy descendant of the great opponent of ship money.[8]

The drafting of the Bill was going steadily forward, and the regular presence of Knight at Westminster suggested to increasing numbers of the privileged that there was a chance of early and profitable entry into the South Sea. A Member named Travers, finding himself next to the great Janssen in the House, asked him in a whisper what he thought of the stock. Janssen said diplomatically he was sure he did not know, but that Knight, whom he had sighted 'on the steps of the Speaker's chamber', would certainly sell some to Travers 'to oblige a friend' if Travers wished; and there, in the lobby, a bargain for £2,000 worth was struck.[9]

*   *   *

In this atmosphere, on 22 February, the House of Commons passed a resolution expressing concern about the number of mushroom flotations in the City and the improper use of charters for objects outside the scope for which they were originally granted. The person responsible for this, and the chairman of the Committee the Commons set up to go into the question, was John Hungerford, the Member for Scarborough and standing counsel to the East India Company. His political reputation was Tory, and not unspotted, for he had once, long ago, been expelled from the House for bribery.

* Gower was one of the biggest gainers in the whole affair. He 'sold' out at the end of May, and duly received his 'profit' of £64,000. The other three M.P.'s were Thomas Wynn, Lieutenant-General Pepper, and Lord Chetwynd.

As a young barrister, his noisy parties and fierce dogs had annoyed the benchers of Lincoln's Inn; but he was now a bencher himself, and on financial questions was heard with respect.

Although Hungerford had at one point in his career promoted a Bill against gambling it is difficult to believe that this intervention was disinterested, or meant to be anything but helpful to the South Sea Company, of which he was a little later one of the most enthusiastic defenders. His purpose in drawing attention to upwards of a score of recently floated bubbles aiming at a total capital of £40 millions, and the attempted use of the Royal Lustring and Mines Royal charters (the latter dated back to Queen Elizabeth) to carry marine insurance undertakings was not to discourage the South Sea but to clear the field for it. The promoters had Law's monopoly of the Paris stock market before them, and meant to do the same in Exchange Alley if they could.

Hungerford's inquiry uncovered a great deal of scandal about every quarter of the City except South Sea House. All this was as planned. But it had one other result which the promoters had not foreseen, and found very embarrassing. If charters for mining and fancy fabrics were inappropriate for insurance, charters for making sword blades were inappropriate for banking; and the Sword Blade Charter was therefore one of the first to be sent for by the Committee. This move had to be defeated by an injection of ministerialists into the Committee—which was not a 'secret' one in which only named Members could vote—who crushed it by a division of 75 to 25.[10]

About the same time Charles Stanhope, Secretary of the Treasury and one of the ministerial members of Hungerford's Committee, decided, after some hesitation, to accept from Sawbridge, one of the Sword Blade partners, a promise of £50,000 South Sea stock which Sawbridge did not at that time possess. This, together with £10,000 'transferred' to Stanhope at the same time by Knight, was the largest single purchase of friendship made by the decemvirs. The bargain that Stanhope should have £500 for every point above 250 and £100 more for every point above 270 was punctiliously kept. It is difficult to resist the suspicion that this was partly extorted by the threat to the Sword Blade charter.

*   *   *

During the negotiation of the South Sea scheme the speculative funds on which the promoters relied to float their own stock were still eagerly flowing towards Law. Sir John Lambert had been in Paris since August 1719—an absence which should under the Company's rules have vacated his directorship, though he afterwards pleaded it as an alibi. Lord Belhaven, a member of the Prince of Wales's court, had been sent over in January to speculate on his master's behalf. As late as 15 February Lord Strafford, for whom Law had laid out £20,000, was preparing to visit Paris incognito. He had sold out of South Sea at 125 and professed not to care in the least that it now stood at 178, so great was his admiration for his 'old friend Mr. Law, the greatest subject in Europe'.

But there were ominous signs. Already in the middle of January Lord Islay, who was in close touch with Law, considered the market was breaking. In February Lord Strafford's agent was writing home for two pairs of good leather shoes to keep out the winter damp in the rue Quincampoix, where he was in attendance from dawn to dusk, 'so faint without eating that I have been ready to drop'. In Paris ordinary things like shoes had grown fantastically dear.[11]

Law was faced with a serious inflation. Although he considered that the actual and potential wealth of France was ample to support the paper money he had so far put into circulation, the holders of the currency took a shorter view. To them paper was still a promise of wealth, not its guarantee, and they now scrambled to act on this engrained habit by turning their paper into what they considered solid values—bullion, land, and durable goods. When argument failed, Law took to stronger measures. On 14 February the Company of the Indies and the Banque Royale were amalgamated and all dealings in the

Company's shares were stopped. The issue of further paper money was halted. The purchase, circulation, and import of bullion was prohibited. It was a determined effort to establish a permanent, stable paper currency.

The Earl of Stair reported the vigorous reaction of the public on 18 February. The price of the shares sank like a stone, as Law had intended. 'Tous les Juifs ont déserté et les Français commencent à se pendre.' Law was in a truculent, anti-British mood, saying that France, not the South Sea Company, would obtain the privileges arising from peace with Spain, and ostentatiously buying herrings in Holland instead of at Yarmouth. But his attempt to turn the inflationary tide lasted only a fortnight. The fashionable and possessing world whom he had so successfully interested in his shares saw no reason to make the sacrifices Law was demanding to save the currency, and they had the upper hand. The force that had raised him now began to push him on to the downward path. On 26 February Law was compelled not only to agree to the reopening of the stock market, but to support the price of shares with a note issue which now became unlimited. Tentative speculation began again, but the English investor had had enough of the Paris market. Among those who left was Sir John Lambert, whose departure seems to have been hastened by the French official view that he was 'damned sharp and no good character here'. The robust Huguenot rejoined his colleagues on the South Sea board on 8 February, and did not respond to an invitation to advise in Lisbon on the projected Portuguese Brazil Company. This was wise of him, since the Archbishop of Oporto had suggested privately that any subscriptions to that company by Jews and heretics should be forfeited for the company's benefit.[12]

*　　　*　　　*

While Law was struggling with the inflation which was finally to submerge him, a violent public controversy about the South Sea scheme was going on in London. On one thing both supporters and adversaries of the proposal were agreed:

the buying of the annuities could not possibly be accomplished
without a spectacular advance in the price of stock. This was
indisputable, because annuities were already commanding
inflated prices in the expectation that such an advance in the
stock for which they would be exchanged would take place—
long annuities were being bought for as much as twenty-five
years' purchase when the maximum price on a 5 per cent.
interest basis would have been twenty. This much weakened
the arguments of those who opposed the scheme, and wished
to insist on the Company guaranteeing the terms of the conversion in advance. The invariable reply to them was that only
by giving the freest rein to the Company's capacity to make a
profit could it be expected to execute a scheme which was
likely to be so profitable to everyone else. Indeed, so the
Company's apologists argued, the rise in the price of stock
which would certainly follow the passage of the Bill without
a limiting clause on the rate of conversion, was indispensable
for the scheme's success. Only one controversialist on the
other side managed to free himself from the apparent dilemma.
'The additional rise of this stock above the true capital', he
wrote, 'will be only imaginary; one added to one, by any rules
of vulgar arithmetic, will never make three and a half; consequently, all the fictitious value must be a loss to some persons
or other, first or last. The only way to prevent it to oneself
must be to sell out betimes, and so let the Devil take the hind-
most.' This advice, though not disregarded, was ineffective in
stopping those who were now fascinated by the prospect of
capital gains in a market where the stock shot from 218 to 320 in
three days (19-21 March) on reports from Paris that Law was
having nightmares and had been dressed down by the Regent
himself, sitting on his close-stool.[13]

The private preparations for the Bill continued in parallel
with the public controversy. During the first three weeks of
March, up to the day the South Sea Bill was read for a second
time in the Commons, twelve Members of Parliament* were

* John Roberts, Edward Rolt, Samuel Tufnell, John Burridge, Colonel James Scott,
William Chetwynd, Sir Copelston Bampfield, John Bland, Thomas Seabright, Henry
Drax, Colonel Graham, and John Bampfield.

credited in Knight's green book, after conversations in taverns and coaches, with £39,000 stock at prices varying from 175 to 200. Most of these were introduced by the director Chester.

There was a great deal of hypocrisy afterwards about this largesse. It was on a huge scale, and only the most superficial attempts were made to hide it. It would not have served its purpose if it had been wholly secret. The promoters rightly reckoned that the best advertisement for the stock was the number of public men known to have faith and interest in it. Penetration of the governing class, not stock exchange rumour, was, and remained, the technique by which Blunt and Knight like Law, achieved their most spectacular successes.

The certainty of profit by investing in the South Sea in advance of final acceptance of the Bill was the talk of all the drawing-rooms in London during the early weeks of March, when the Earl of Sunderland's daughter Anne was married with great pomp to William Bateman, son of the late Sub-Governor. The great Duke of Chandos himself had decided to cut his losses in the Mississippi and go in for what he called 'one of the best funds in Europe'. Three days before the Bill was published on 17 March, the Earl of Halifax, Auditor of the Receipt of the Exchequer, laid out £4,000 at 184½. The Duchess of Rutland wrote about the same time to her stockbroker:

> . . . this comes to good Mr. Warner, to lett him know that I am allmost sure, I can mack an advantage by bying today in the South Seas with the hundred and four score pounds is still in your hands . . . so I would bye as much as that will bye today, and sell it out agane next week, for tho I have no oppinion of the South Sea to contineue in it I am allmost certine thus to mack sum litell advantage to her that is good Mr. Warner's reaell freind. . . .

Hoare's Bank, which had been buying steadily since early February, increased its buying tempo right up to the 22nd, when it brought its total holding of South Sea stock to £17,000, acquired for an average price of about 160.[14]

The Bank of England, however, did not mean to go down without a final struggle. In the markets of Europe brokers who had connexions with them were doing their best to discredit South Sea stock—an activity which was noticed in Amsterdam. But Westminster was the serious battle-ground. No very strong challenge was mounted at the Second Reading of the Bill on 21 March, which was carried by 201 to 131, but every ounce of strength was thrown behind the motion, debated two days later, to compel the Company to fix its terms of conversion in advance and write them into the statute. The ground had been prepared beforehand with petitions from the three chief seaports of the kingdom against the proposed financial monopoly, which were presented to the crowded House immediately before the debate began. The lobbies were filled with agents and observers who carried reports of the debate by water to the City, where South Sea stock oscillated wildly over no less than 110 points, between 270 and 380, as contrary news arrived and spread through the market. The debate lasted for six hours. Walpole, who had sold the last of his South Sea holdings three days before at $194\frac{1}{4}$, cogently exposed the dangers of unlimited advances in the stock, and was supported by his brother Horatio, George Pitt, and Steele, who, besides writing pamphlets against the South Sea, had produced a scheme of his own to liquidate the Debt with a series of ten-member tontines. Chancellor Aislabie, who had been fortified on 1 March with another £20,000 stock at 170 in Knight's green book, replied with the now familiar arguments, and was seconded by Yonge, who a few days later was to be credited in the same place with £3,000 stock at 350. Both the opposition tellers were Bank directors. The unusually large number of 384 Members voted, and the government won by a majority of 96.[15]

When the news reached Exchange Alley South Sea struck 400 for a few hours, and then settled down round 330. Hoare's promptly sold out £10,000 of their holding at a price high enough to cover their total outlay and leave £7,000 stock in hand as profit. Among the sellers that day at 350 was the

fashionable broker Warner, acting for the Marquess of Hart-
ington. A further distribution covering ten Members of
Parliament and four peers* was made by Knight and his
associates a day or two later, on 25 March.[16]

25 March, Lady Day, was also appointed for the final
humiliation of the Bank. The Speaker announced to the
Commons that he had given formal notice for the whole Debt
held by the Bank, in so far as it was not being taken over
by the South Sea Company, to be redeemed in a year's time.
The amount was £3¾ million, and its disappearance meant
that the Bank would cease to be a national institution. Its stock,
which had touched 176 on the day of the debate, fell steadily
away to a mere 130. The Third Reading of the Bill, which took
place only three days later, showed how little fight was left in
the opposition, who mustered only 55 votes. Knight was prudently closing his purse-strings, and on the day of the Third
Reading only two more M.P.s—Colonel Monroe and Patrick
Haldane—were entered in the green book. Walpole and his
followers, for reasons which will presently appear, had abandoned the Bank's cause as lost, and turned to other projects. They
had never, indeed, been entirely convinced by the arguments
with which the Bank had briefed them.

The passage of the Bill through the Lords, which was
handled by Stanhope and Sunderland personally, is chiefly
interesting for the only surviving document which proves
beyond all doubt the close liaison kept up between the South
Sea syndicate and the government. On the night before the
debate, Aislabie wrote to his confidant Hawes:

> I do not know whether Sir John Fellowes be in towne, and
> therefore I write to you to desire you to speak to them to
> be at Lord Stanhope's tomorrow morning to meet Lord
> Sunderland and myself, who want to talk about the annuities
> before they go to the House. Be pleased to speak to Sir John

* Sir William Gordon, Commissioner of Army Accounts, William Forrester,
Joseph Bankes, Colonel Montgomery, Thomas Poultney, Sir Montague Blundell, Sir
Wilfred Lawson, Charles Longueville, William Younge, Sir William Carew, the Earls
of Rothes, Essex, and Haddington, the Marquess of Winchester.

Fellowes, Mr. Joye, Mr. Blunt, Mr. Gibbon, Mr. Chester, and any other two.[17]

Briefed that morning by the decemvirs, Sunderland was easily able to dispose of the last remnants of opposition. The octogenarian Duke of Buckingham and the wayward Duke of Wharton were hardly serious adversaries. Lord North and Grey's old-fashioned invective about the evils of stock-jobbing, which diverted 'the Genius of the people' from honest industry, was not worth replying to. Lord Cowper had been more effective, comparing the scheme to a Trojan horse 'received with acclamations, but contrived for destruction', and lecturing the House about the responsibilities of government. 'In all public bargains', he had urged, 'it is a duty on them who are entrusted with the administration to take care that the same be more advantageous to the state than to private persons.' Sunderland's reply concentrated on this point. Of course, the Company had the hope of profit, otherwise they would never have undertaken the task; but whether they gained or not, their undertaking would stand. Nobody could have foreseen in February that the stocks would have advanced so much, and surely the Company was entitled to the profits secured by 'the wise management and industry of its directors'. The Bill was passed by 83 votes to 17. Two days later, on 7 April, it received the Royal Assent.[18]

*   *   *

In the first days of April Knight, with the help of his deputy, Surman, prepared for the quarterly audit of the Company's cash in his private room at South Sea House. The debate in the Lords had not then taken place, but so far as he was concerned the parliamentary campaign was over. The details of it, entered in his green ledger, had necessarily to be reflected, though in disguised form, in the Company's cashbook, which consequently showed the bogus sales to peers and politicians as a series of parcels of stock 'sold to sundry', and amounting in all to £574,500 stock. These entries, which were needed to justify the payments of 'profit' later to be made out of the Company's cash, had already been objected to as insufficiently informative by the committee of directors who last inspected the cashbook. Knight had hinted then that the entries concealed great names; but not, of course, that the names had not made any payment.

The consideration shown as having been paid by the anonymous 'sundry' was £1,259,325, which Knight should have been able to produce in cash to the auditors. Explaining to his deputy that a 'transaction of a private nature' was concerned, and that most of the stock in question 'had been disposed of to persons of distinction', Knight made balancing entries in the cashbook purporting to show '*loans* to sundry' on the security of £574,500 South Sea stock deposited with the Company. One may doubt if this imposed on the auditors, but it allowed them to turn a blind eye.[19]

It is possible to account with some confidence for more than half of this £574,500. £15,000 represented a genuine (though favourable) conversion of annuities for the Duke of Portland, and £32,000, which may have been paid for, went to foreign financiers, mostly Dutch. Much more can be identified as having gone in political distributions: £216,000, or nearly half the total, to ministers and courtiers; £81,000 to the twenty-seven Members of the House of Commons; and £38,100 to six peers; so that altogether identifiable 'persons of distinction' took £335,000 stock on credit. The dimension of these bribes, i.e. the difference between the 'purchase' price and the market value if measured at the time Knight made up his book, was about £400,000.

More than a third of the fictitious stock cannot be accounted for in this way. This amount—£191,900—corresponds closely to the total of three of Knight's bogus entries in the Company's cashbook: £113,000 in the last week of February; £12,000 on 4 March; and £68,000 on 21 March.

It is quite possible that these allocations had simply been used during the previous three months to prime the market. Then there were the decemvirs themselves. Why should they have hesitated to take what they bestowed so open-handedly on others? But they had other ways of enriching themselves.

For instance on 18 February, when Knight was distributing parcels of (as yet uncreated) *stock* to politicians, he advanced to the Sword Blade Company £105,000 from the South Sea Company's *cash* against a deposit of £70,000 stock which was no doubt as hypothetical as the rest of the stock in which he was dealing. If politicians were let in on the ground floor, the Sword Blade was admitted to the bargain basement.

There remains one other possible explanation. The King himself, and the Prince of Wales, must have known about the allocations, and the King at any rate had a powerful claim to be included. As head of the government and Governor of the Company, he symbolized the happy union of the two parties in the great undertaking, and he certainly did not hesitate, at a later stage, to take a hand in the market on his own account. Aislabie acted for him, and surrendered the record of the royal dealings to the King personally on ceasing to be Chancellor. Knight always said that of all the secrets he knew there was one which, if revealed, would amaze the world. If this was a private allocation of South Sea stock to the King and the Prince of Wales in March—a possibility which cannot by any means be excluded—it would have a most important bearing on the sudden change in the relations between father and son which revolutionized the political scene early in April.

The City was now poised for the boom. Few had the wisdom of the Earl of Halifax, who at this point sold out a parcel of stock he had bought a few days before the price soared on 23 March, and almost doubled his outlay of £4,000. The news was spreading feverishly to the provinces. 'South Sea is all the talk and fashion', wrote Mrs. Windham to her relatives in Norfolk. 'The ladies sell their jewels to bye, and hapy are they that are in. . . . But first the dealers are the greatest gainers. Jemy [her son, who was in the Salt Duty Office, under the director Ingram] is so pleased . . . he can't look at you without a simper. . . . Mr. Whitworth . . . gave me 200 guineas for refusal of South Sea Stock at 500 in two months for 1,000 stock. . . . Never was such a time to get money as now.'[20]

If Knight had drawn up a statement of the liabilities for next year already incurred by the Company against the profits of the conversion, it would have run as follows:

£ million

To the Exchequer, for the privilege of convert-
ing the Debt . . . . . . 7·5
To the Exchequer, for Exchequer bills . . 1·0
Fictitious stock, 'sold to sundry' . . . 0·6
Dividend on existing capital at Christmas, 1719,
and deferred to Christmas, 1720 . . . 0·3
Dividend on existing and advanced capital—say,
at 5 per cent. . . . . . . 2·0

Total 11·4

On strict arithmetic this sum could have been raised if the conversion took place at 140. On 7 April, when the King and Governor gave his assent to the South Sea Bill, the stock stood at 335. Was there not every reason for confidence?

CHAPTER VII

Spring

LORD STANHOPE HAD spent the last three weeks of March in Paris conferring with Dubois. No doubt he had noted Law's increasing difficulties with satisfaction, but he had left the parliamentary handling of the South Sea Bill entirely to Sunderland, Aislabie, and Craggs. He arrived in London only just in time to be briefed and take part in the final stages in the House of Lords; so he can hardly have been party to the opening of the great intrigue, about which rumours began to circulate early in April, to reconcile the King with the Prince of Wales and reunite the two wings of the Whigs.

There were formidable obstacles to such a plan: the King's own stubborn malignity towards his son and all those connected with him; and the natural reluctance of some ministers, especially Sunderland, to share office with men who had tried, sometimes successfully, to thwart their favourite plans—the peerage scheme, for instance, would have to be finally abandoned if Walpole was to be brought in. With the financial scheme and the peace both going so well, there was no obvious need to buy outside support with costly concessions.

One minister, however, Secretary Craggs, was particularly suited to the task of reuniting Court and party. Craggs was a conciliator by training and temperament, and a perfect contrast to his disagreeable, scuffling master, the King, who seems to have liked him, or at any rate tolerated him, rather better than most of his ministers. Craggs specialized in confidential dynastic negotiations, the last of which had no doubt bought him the goodwill of the Duchess of Kendal and Madame von Platen, whose South Sea shares allocated in February were now worth double what they had not yet paid for them.

Craggs, too, had to consider that the King was growing old. In May he would be sixty, and Craggs, at thirty-five, looked forward to a long career crowned by peerage in the next reign. 'After I have continued some two or three years more where I am', he had written complacently to Stair, soon after becoming Secretary of State, 'I should be glad to rise higher. At present nothing could move me to put myself in a more glaring light.'[1] Moreover, even in this reign the influence of the Prince of Wales as Duke of Cornwall was particularly important to the Craggs family, most of whose parliamentary interest lay in that county. Craggs thus had reason to press the advantages of a royal reconciliation on his colleagues: namely the increment of electoral interest from the opposition Whigs; and the end of a royal quarrel which had done great harm to the dynasty in the eyes of ordinary people. What better spring-board for general confidence could there be than a public scene of forgiveness and reunion in the Royal Family? On 9 April, a week after Stanhope's return to London, Countess Cowper, Lady-in-Waiting to the Princess of Wales, noted in her diary the first news of the offer of reconciliation to reach Leicester House. The initiative, she recorded, came from Craggs, and was received by Walpole.[2]

Walpole would not have been attracted by the idea of a coalition so long as the Bank of England was still in the running against the South Sea Company and the Leicester House faction could still bask in their triumph over the government on the peerage question. But these battles were all over now, and the alternative to reconciliation might be an unlimited stay in the political wilderness. Even before the struggle with the Company was finally lost he had taken some steps of reinsurance against failure. Shortly before the great March debate he had personally demonstrated his confidence in the Bank's cause by selling completely out of South Sea; but at the same time he had induced the Prince and Princess to enter South Sea at prices, and on terms which strongly suggest entries in Knight's green book. The date Lady Cowper gives for this transaction—23 March—tallies closely with Knight's entry of 21 March of £68,000 fictitious stock sold 'to sundry'. From entries in Deputy Cashier Surman's private banking account with T. and J. Martin, it is clear that the Prince later received 'differences' from the Company. This could hardly have been achieved without an influential intermediary, and here again the name which suggests itself is Craggs.[3]

Walpole was also aware that the King himself had an important financial interest in a reconciliation. More than half a million was needed to clear accumulated arrears on the Civil List. It was impossible to apply private gains from the South Sea to this debt, and the King would have to appeal to Parliament unless some other expedient could be found. Between them, Walpole and Craggs had discovered an expedient for dealing with this problem.

A meeting of the minds of Craggs and Walpole is not usually quoted as the origin of the reconciliation. It is more often said that it arose from Sunderland's alarm at learning of a plot the King was supposed to be considering, to replace him and Stanhope by the Walpole faction—if need be, with the help of Austrian troops. The evidence for this is a mysterious letter,* said to be from the King's private German adviser, Bernstorff, to the Emperor Charles's Vice-Foreign Minister, which was shown to Sunderland in translation by an anonymous business man. Other copies of the translation—all, perhaps significantly, undated—seem to have circulated to important people at the end of April. But, if, as one account suggests, this letter led to a three-day conference between Stanhope, Sunderland, and Craggs, which culminated in the decision to treat with Walpole's faction, that decision must have been mooted and taken between 2 April, when Stanhope arrived in London and the 9th, when news of the offer reached Leicester House. The time seems hardly adequate.[4]

There was no question that with the country poised on the edge of adventure every political group was effervescing vigorously. Lady Cowper, listing four 'little schemes' she

---

* The original, which should be in the Imperial Archives in Vienna, is not there.

heard of afterwards, concluded that 'there was not a rogue in town was not engaged in some scheme or project to undo his country'. Bernstorff's was one. But whether his letter was genuine or not—and it is hard to believe King George would readily have committed himself to his son's political advisers—its probable role was to impress Sunderland into joining the project which Craggs and Walpole had already developed; and from Stanhope's particular point of view, to discredit the King's German camarilla, which he resented as a parallel foreign office.[5]

*   *   *

While the politicians were negotiating the details of reunion in the privacy of Horatio Walpole's lodgings and overcoming the *amour propre* of their respective masters, the South Sea Scheme, now invested with full Parliamentary authority, was setting out on its public career.

Someone is said to have asked Newton what he thought of the prospects of the stock, and received the reply that he could calculate the motions of the heavenly bodies, but not the madness of the people. He practised what he preached, for on 20 April he signed a power of attorney disposing of his £7,000 stock at the solid profit of 100 per cent. Nor was he the only one. Under the impact of profit-taking, the stock fell away noticeably in the first fortnight of April, and for a time actually dipped below 300. There was a shortage of cash in the market, and if the terms of conversion, which depended on the current price of stock, were to be favourable to the Company, an immediate remedy was needed.

Reinforcement was on the way, because in the wake of the main South Sea Bill the promoters had secured a second statute authorizing the government to create £1 million of Exchequer bills, which were the equivalent of cash, and lend them to the Company for a year. By a clear understanding between Blunt and Aislabie it was intended that these bills should be lent by the Company to such members of the public as were willing to buy stock with them, so supporting the market. The news that this Bill had received Royal Assent on 12 April probably helped the stock in its climb back above the 300 mark; and in the meantime some assistance was got from the circulation of rumours that the peace with Spain would include the exchange of the unprofitable rock of Gibraltar for territorial concessions in South America, and the removal of all the former quota restrictions on ships to be sent there by the Company. In fact, as the Court books show, the Company's negotiator at Madrid had scarcely begun his approaches to the Spanish government.[6]

But possibly the most helpful influence of all at this difficult moment for the promoters was the hostile activity of Law. From Paris he was watching the advance of the South Sea with increasing anxiety. Early in April he began heavy forward buying of their stock in Amsterdam, and even, according to the Earl of Stair, sent funds to England for the purpose of building up a big enough holding to carry out crushing 'bear' operations in May.[7]

Blunt, however, was not the man to rely on mere favourable influences. He had far more positive proposals in mind for advancing the stock, and on 14 April he announced the first of them, which he had cleared with the directors only on the previous day. This was an offer of £2 million new stock at 300, of which £60 was to be paid on application and the rest in eight two-monthly instalments. Adding more stock to a market which already seemed to be sagging was not only bold: it was hardly legal, since no new stock was supposed to be created until the conversion of the Debt had begun.* In effect he was proposing—as he frankly told his fellow-directors—to realize part of the Company's profit before operations had begun, and this topsy-turvy thought made 'The First Money Subscription' an outstanding success. Blunt's judgement that

---

* Though Scott stigmatizes this as plainly illegal, the Act was ambiguous on the point. It provided that the Company, for the purpose of carrying out the Act, should be entitled to 'make calls of money from their members, or may open books or subscriptions . . . or by any other method they shall think fit in a General Court'. Nevertheless, it was expected that the conversion would precede the sale of the stock it was to create.

132

the market was pining to be deluged in stock was entirely vindicated. A million is said to have been subscribed for in an hour after the books opened at 9 a.m. on 14 April. Among the subscribers was the King himself, put down by Chancellor Aislabie for no less than £100,000 stock. In a matter of days the books were filled to overflowing, for the promoters covertly expanded the issue by £250,000. When this came to light soon afterwards, it was attributed to the confusion which necessarily surrounded the Company's operations. It was, however, deliberate, as will be seen.*

The price of the old stock at once went to 325, with a corresponding premium on the part-paid new stock, so that a cautious subscriber was in a position to make a capital gain of 8 per cent. by immediate resale of his subscription. This cheered everyone, but even more important was the sight of the Company for the first time flushed with cash and its equivalent to the tune of something like £1¼ million. Not all of it was cash, because Sword Blade and East India (but not Bank) notes were also accepted. The syndicate were thus able to redeem a good deal of Sword Blade paper which had been pumped in to support the market during February and March. Surman's account with the Sword Blade suggests that this had been done at the rate of at least £100,000 a month ever since January.[8]

The torrent of cash at the Sword Blade, where much of the subscription was taken, did, however, have one untoward effect. A clerk called Davis, who was suffering severely from toothache and had been gambling privately in the stocks, absconded by boat with £4,000 in the company of one of the bank's porters named Crook, 'a middle-sized man of a thin, pale, complexion, thin-bodied but large legs', and a corn-cutter called Eustace. At first the Sword Blade, who in their own interest were good employers, let it be known that if Davis would return, all would be forgiven. But when there was no response to this, Sir George Caswall exerted the

---

* The actual amount subscribed proved later to be £2,720,930 (*Notebook in possession of Mrs. Asher*).

influence of the syndicate in a direct approach to Secretary Craggs. A messenger from the Secretary of State's office caught up with the fugitives at Dover, where they were easily identified by the bandages in which the wretched clerk had wrapped his jaw.[9]

Meanwhile the curtain rose on the second part of Blunt's scheme of promotion. On 21 April the first General Court of Proprietors since the Act was passed was graced by 'the greatest appearance of nobility and gentry that was ever seen on such an occasion'. The time to announce the terms of the conversion had not yet arrived, but the assembly were told that, subject to their approval, the midsummer dividend would be 10 per cent., that the new, partly paid stock would participate, as would any other issue before Midsummer Day, and that the directors had no doubt that future dividends would be equally satisfactory. True, the dividend would not be in cash. It would take the form of a bonus distribution of stock; and it was not generally known that Grigsby, acting for the decemvirs, had bought up a large number of options on this dividend (which had till then been about 3 per cent.) during January and February.

This rousing news was by no means all. The cash position of the Company, Sub-Governor Fellowes explained, was so healthy that they were in a position to lend to the proprietors on the security of their stock. It was in the interest of the proprietors that they should do so, since 'attempts may be made to depreciate the stock at the times of the execution of the Act' (i.e., the conversion itself), 'the profitability of which does chiefly depend on the price of the stock'. The amount to be lent was announced as half a million and the interest as 5 per cent. No applicant was to have a loan of more than £3,000. For an advance of £250 the deposit of £100 stock would be required. It would be necessary to repeal a by-law forbidding the Company to lend on security of its own stock. The Court concluded with a vote thanking the directors for their 'great care and prudent management of the Company's affairs' and conferring on them plenary power to 'do all such matters and things as they shall judge for the good of the Company', including the proposed and any future loan. It was the last meeting the proprietors were to have for some months. Next day the stock was marked at 350.[10]

So Blunt completed the first cycle of his design. Like Law, he had constructed a financial pump, each spurt of stock being accompanied by a draught of cash to suck it up again, leaving the level higher than before. As fast as stock issued—and it was Grigsby's most important task to see it did not in practice issue too quickly—the money received for it was returned to the market to support the prices and take up fresh issues at the higher price. The reciprocal nature of the operation can clearly be seen in the fact that the first loan, though formally limited to half a million, actually ran to over a million and a half, or just about the amount of cash at the company's disposal from the First Money Subscription.*

But besides completing the circuit for boosting the price of stock the loan and its successors served other important purposes. It will be remembered that the First Money Subscription had been secretly expanded by £250,000. Since this did not yet appear as capital which had to be accounted for, it enabled Knight, once the deposited stock had begun to flow into his hands, to cover a great part of his earlier bogus 'loans to sundry'. In other words, under the disguise of 'loans' on security of stock they had never possessed or paid for, a great part of the bribes to politicians could be discharged in cash collected from the public. All that happened was that the politician reminded Knight of the dimensions of his bribe in terms of stock, and received a cash payment. The net effect was to transfer to politicians, in this and succeeding loans, a sum of between £1 million and £2 million cash which came from the pockets of the money subscribers. The loan ledgers (about which there was considerable scandal later on) show at

* Innumerable further instances of the method employed can be found by comparing the lists of borrowers with the lists of subscribers to the subsequent subscription. One will suffice. Twenty men of title were advanced sums in excess of the authorized amounts between 10 and 22 June. Eighteen of them appear as subscribers to the Third Money Subscription, which opened on 15 June.

least twenty-one of the lesser names which figured in the green book depositing stock and receiving nearly £400,000 cash in exchange. Natural discretion and the limit of £3,000 for each borrower* no doubt prevented the appearance of the more important personages in the lists, but they were certainly concealed by groups of fictitious names. When the whole matter was investigated afterwards the deficiency of stock against loan was found to correspond almost exactly to the amount of fictitious stock 'deposited by sundry'. Against it the Company had 'lent' over £2 million.

The valuation of the old stock at 250 for purposes of the loan while marketing the new stock at 300 made for economy in redeeming these bribes, which would have cost the promoters far more if they had been paid off at market prices. It also served a purpose which was much less in the interest of the Company. Since all stock deposited as security was formally transferred to Knight, the Company and its cashier had become possessed of a fund of stock, acquired at relatively low cost, on which it was a standing temptation to trade for capital gains, relying on being able to replace the pledged stock when the loan was returned. Since Blunt's whole system depended on the price of the stock never encountering a serious setback, it is obvious that by trading in pawned stock the Company ran a serious risk of getting 'caught short'. Worse still, from the point of view of the promotion's success, the return of this stock once more to market naturally acted as a clog on the price. This and other profit-taking operations were responsible for the comparative gentleness of the upward trend for nearly a month after the new loan was announced.

The demonstrations of confidence on 21 April did not extend to at any rate one of those who, if he was not present at the General Court, had every right to be. The sagacious old stationer and former M.P. for Tamworth, Thomas Guy, held no less than £54,040 in South Sea stock, then worth on the

---

* The limit, like all other rules laid down for the loan, was repeatedly broken. Among the most flagrant breaches was a loan of no less than £97,576 to John Gumley, Muster-master-General, who deposited £41,200 stock as security on 25 April. In the next Parliament he appeared as an M.P.

market well over £150,000. He had had the bulk of it ever since he had subscribed holdings of Debt into Harley's venture in 1711, so that some of it probably went back to those distant days in the early 'nineties, when he had bought up seamen's pay-tickets at a discount in riverside taverns. Many years, too, had passed since Guy had endowed his first charity, the free library of his native town; and now, at the end of his life, he was contemplating greater benefactions. The day after the General Court, 22 April, Guy began systematically to sell out. Spreading his sales over six weeks, and never selling in larger parcels than £1,000, he cleared the whole £54,000 in just over six weeks on a rising market. It is a heartening exhibition of steadiness of purpose,* and his reward of £234,000 was in proportion to his sagacity. It was the largest honest fortune made out of the Bubble, and the hospital it built is the best memorial the Bubble has left behind it.[11]

*　　　　*　　　　*

The moment had now come for the royal reconciliation to be staged with the maximum propaganda effect. Two days after the enthusiastic South Sea General Court, the news quickly spread that the King, after receiving a letter from the Prince (its terms had been arranged by Walpole and the Ministry), had sent a message inviting his son to come to St. James's. Craggs's leading part as peacemaker was recognized by his being its bearer. After a private interview with his father, the forgiven Prince was carried through cheering crowds back to Leicester House, his chair attended once more by the escort of guards and beefeaters which marked his return to favour.

The two chief actors had gone through the ordeal of renewing friendship with the worst possible grace. The King had been at his most bear-like during the negotiations, and had allowed his fury to explode on three of his chairmen, whom he

---

* Guy's steadiness is the more remarkable in that he was an intimate friend of Deputy Governor Joye (whom he made a trustee of his hospital) and therefore had ample opportunities to trade with inside information if he had wished. There is no sign that he did so and, once out of the market in mid-June, Guy stayed out.

sacked for jolting him on the way to the theatre. At the actual interview he hardly managed to utter more than the first words of the French speech he had prepared. The Prince, on his return home, refused to see anyone for several hours, and it was noticed that his face was grim and bleary, 'as one has seen him before upon occasions when mightily ruffled'. But 'the whole town was feignedly or unfeignedly transported'. Ordinary people were sincerely glad the quarrel was over. The rival groups of politicians embraced and shook one another by the hand at all public gatherings. The dissident Whigs were formally received by the King, and their titular chief, Devonshire, carried the sword of state before the King and his heir to chapel. Sunderland entertained his late enemies at a well-advertised dinner, and discussed the new arrangements by which Townshend was to become Lord President instead of Mary Wortley Montagu's father, the Duke of Kingston, and Walpole would replace Newcastle's brother-in-law, the Earl of Lincoln (who was awarded the Garter soon afterwards), as Paymaster-General. This office was particularly well sited to take advantage of the coming boom, and incidentally brought its holder into financial contact with the brother of Aislabie's friend, the decemvir Hawes, who was cashier at the Pay Office.[12]

There were other reasons, which intimately concerned the private interests of Walpole and Craggs, for timing the reconciliation at this particular moment. The report of Hungerford's Committee on mushroom promotions had been printed and would soon be debated, and among the twenty-two schemes for fisheries, funeral furnishing, finance, and trade which it dealt with were the two big marine insurance undertakings familiarly known as Onslow's and Chetwynd's Bubbles, one being presided over by Lord Onslow and the other by Lord Chetwynd. Both these groups had for some time been making energetic attempts to get the privileges of incorporation which were regarded as essential for the success of large-scale insurance of ships and cargoes. Their manœuvres were exposed by the Hungerford Committee in such telling detail that both the Attorney- and Solicitor-General, who were deeply implicated, were superseded; but in spite of the mud through which the syndicates had waded, incorporation still eluded them.[13]

Changing tactics, the two groups had now decided that if the market could be captured from the Dutch, who till then had a virtual monopoly of marine insurance, it was big enough for both of them. But they still had to face the opposition of the South Sea syndicate, whose policy it was to destroy all competition for investment and prevent any further incorporation of joint stocks: a policy that on 27 April received the timely aid of the Hungerford Committee's report, whose recommendation of a statutory ban on all joint stocks not authorized by royal charter was at once accepted by the Commons and led directly to the so-called Bubble Act; which was imposed, contrary to the impression usually given by economic histories, to protect the South Sea's rise, and not in consequence of its fall. The leading South Sea men's support for this narrow-minded policy does not seem to have been affected in the least by the fact that several of their fellow-directors—Walpole's friend Sir William Chapman, Sir Jacob Jacobsen the steelmaster, Raymond, and Chester—were among the directors of Chetwynd's insurance;* or even by the large amount of South Sea stock that had found its way into the insurance company portfolios. The promoters never showed much tenderness for the interests of the other men on the South Sea board.

Politics, however, saved the insurances from the jealousy of the South Sea. Both Walpole and Craggs were deeply interested in them. According to Lady Cowper, both men had bought large blocks of shares at bargain prices early in the year, and this is confirmed by entries in Walpole's account with his brokers.† From the very beginning of the peace

---

* Both Assurances had significant interlocking directorates—Chetwynd's with the South Sea, Onslow's with the Africa Company. Of the twenty-three directors of Chetwynd's five were South Sea directors or their relatives; the board of Onslow's included Decker and three Royal Africa directors.

† Lady Cowper speaks of large purchases at 4½—the price of Onslow's early in February. Walpole's account with Gibson and Jacomb (Plumb, 291) shows payment on 26 April for blocks in both Assurances which correspond to purchases at this price and the concurrent price of Chetwynd's.

negotiations between Leicester House and St. James's these
companies were designated as playing a vital part in the
settlement, and they therefore had to be exempted, in the teeth
of the South Sea, from any restrictions on bubbles. The
arrangement was that as the price of incorporation each insurance company was to pay £300,000 towards clearing the
King's Civil List arrears. The King was certainly not to be
persuaded with anything less, and even with it he was hardly
satisfied. 'Did you not always promise me,' he said grumpily to
Sunderland, 'to bring me the Prince bound hand and foot—
and what's become of all the money you promised me?'[14]

As a result, Onslow's and Chetwynd's insurances survive
today as the Royal Exchange and London Assurances, the only
major promotions of the period to escape the jealousy of the
South Sea. On 4 May their incorporation was recommended
in a royal message to the House of Commons, and the House
ordered the necessary legislation to be tacked to the Bill they
had commissioned on receiving Hungerford's report, for
slaughtering all promotions, present or future, which should
interfere with the great golden calf. Walpole moved the
address of thanks to the King for finding this way of avoiding
further calls on Parliament. With considerable skill he had
managed to scramble on board the balloon just as it was rising.

On the day the insurance question was settled he was seen
strolling in Westminster ostentatiously arm in arm with
Sunderland and Craggs. Even the Jacobite Atterbury, writing
to the Pretender's agent in Paris, thought 'the seeming reconciliation will by next winter grow real and the grand money
schemes here projected of late will settle and fix themselves
in such a manner that it will not be easy to shake them'.[15]

*　　　　*　　　　*

The scent of money was in the air like the breath of spring.
The pleasure grounds of Belsize Park were on the point of
opening, with special facilities for ladies, a raffle room 'just
as at Tunbridge Wells', a bowling green of unsurpassed
evenness, and coursing in the neighbouring woods. On

Newmarket Heath Charles Stanhope, Secretary to the Treasury, had just won the King's Plate. But there was no question that the true centre of fashion was now in the City, where the ladies 'of the other end of the town' had rented a shop a few doors away from Blunt's office in Birchin Lane, and had turned it into a club for tea-drinking and playing on the stock exchange. 'At leisure times, while their agents are abroad, they game for china.' William Chetwood was turning out a stream of farces like *The Stock Jobber*, making fun of it all:

Bubble: First, an insurance of ships to the spacious world of the moon—a project for building a fleet of flying ships of the greatest burden ... noses insured from fire... to furnish rods to flog the universities abroad ... to make hoop petticoats ... to show bears, monkeys and monsters ... to make hempen halters—I think this is an ample list of projects Mr. Cheat-all.
Cheat-all: You're right; but what will be the certain depending profit from these mighty schemes?
Bubble: Only as much as we can genteely get by subscription——
Cheat-all: What will that amount to?
Bubble: About four or five millions—a sum which will make three or four persons very easy in their circumstances. ... They'll deposit their cash with eagerness, and, like the dog in the fable, catching at the shadow, willingly resign the substance.

It was hardly an exaggeration. The rising whirlwind of speculation was catching up innumerable projects, old and new, possible and visionary, sound and unsound. It is impossible to reckon the exact number, because the same subscription was often advertised under different names at the different coffee-houses and taverns where it was necessary to open books, and many had no existence apart from their titles and pretensions. But from about five a month in December, advertised promotions rose to over twenty in February, and to nearly thirty in April. Insurances, fisheries, and finance companies of all kinds had been the first favourites, and some of these were genuine; but, as the fever rose, came many others for exploiting services, inventions, and new trades: improvement in the coaling trade from Newcastle; large-scale funeral furnishing; chains of pawnbrokers; mines and exploitation in 'Argin' for gum arabic, ambergris and ostrich feathers, in 'The Isle of May' for salt, and in every part of discovered and undiscovered America. There was the company for carrying on the patent for heat-resisting paint, and for trading in wool with Barbary and 'preserving our countrymen from being carried into slavery'. Puckle added to the machine gun he already had on the market a patent sword he had invented, which, he wrote to Stanhope, was 'worth a victory to the army first has it'.[16]

Towards the end of April the lunatic note of the 'nitvender' —or selling of nothing—was already sounding clearly. It becomes hard to distinguish between advertisements intended to impose on contemporaries, like the gold mines in 'New Britannia' and those, inserted as pure jokes, which have imposed only on historians, such as this:

> In a few days a book will be opened for taking in a subscription of 2 millions sterling, as a joint stock, for the immediate, expeditious, and cleanly manner of emptying necessary houses throughout England, whereby very great advantages will accrue to the Company in general, by making large quantities of salt-petre with the soil, besides other conveniences for the benefit of the Projectors (not proper here to be mentioned) and as the Projection is entirely new . . . 'tis not to be doubted that a charter will speedily be granted for the same.[17]

Nor were the takers of even the most bizarre offers always foolish people who had faith in the profitability of machine guns or the settlement and exploitation of North America. The punter's aim, often achieved, was to part with his subscription, as soon as bought, to someone perhaps as level-headed as himself, who had the same idea. This was the central tragedy of the South Sea year. Whatever promise of material progress there was in human ingenuity, was blighted by the determination not to invest, but to make capital gains.

The jeering spirit of scepticism ran alongside speculative zeal every step of the way. It was, on the whole, a popular, rather than an aristocratic or moneyed scepticism. People of quality were ready enough—far more ready than they would have been later in the century—to welcome the humble who made their fortunes, and to jostle to improve their own. Even that epitome of landed gentility, Sir John Packington, advertised a 10 per cent. commission for anyone who would discover a lead-mine on his estate. But the rabble pelted the new equipages rolling in the spring sunshine in St. James's Park with hoots of 'South Sea' and 'Stock-jobber'. They were delighted when a broker called Snow was hanged at Tyburn for highway robbery, and very cross when his friends managed to rescue his body before it could be suspended in chains. Steele captured the mood in his weekly, *The Theatre*, with a fable about a Prince who committed his fortune to projectors and was saved by the loyalty and good sense of the common people. 'Princes may be poor; but when they have to do with projectors, they cease to be Princes to avoid being poor.' The shot was well-aimed, though it hardly became Steele, with his fishpools and his tontines, to fire it. There were even some seditious broadsheets hawked about, hinting that the royal reconciliation was a sham. The vendors were whipped.[18]

But is it possible to be more precise about who the speculators were—to distinguish groups in the throng? So far—though this soon changed—the English boom was confined to London. And to London that spring were coming a great many of those who, only a few months before, had been crowding the rue Quincampoix: such people as the Counts Bareta and Constansana and the Abbot of St. Agnes, the three sons of the Governor of the Austrian Netherlands; and 'Beau Gage', who had gained and lost a huge fortune in the Mississippi, made a tender for two European crowns, and was to finish his career as a Spanish general and grandee. Typical of the arrivals were the Campbell brothers, John and Peter, relations of the Duke of Argyll. Just as the Scottish Whig nobility had been among Law's most fervent supporters, so now they were an unmistakable group in the South Sea. Several had been in Knight's green book—the Earl of Rothes, for instance, whose appointment as Lord High Commissioner to the Church of Scotland was announced on 16 April, a few days before he cleared his profit of £18,500 on fictitious stock allotted in March; the Earl of Haddington; and the Duke of Montrose. Lords Dunmore, Hyndford, and Rothes all took huge sums from the Company by way of loan, which they promptly reinvested. Another distinguishable group, to which the Campbell brothers also incidentally belonged, was Army officers. Thirteen large advances to colonels and brigadiers were made in the first loan, and in later loans many more.

Scottish noblemen and Army officers were two segments of the upper class in particular need of money. The ministerial Scottish peer had found it hard, since the Union, to keep up the state in London and the Home Counties which competition with the English peerage demanded of him. The senior Army officer was faced not only with the prospect of prolonged peace, but with new financial hurdles across his peacetime advancement. Among the other events of the spring of 1720 was the issue of the first formal warrant laying down the tariff of purchase for commissions: £4,000 for a troop in the Horse Guards, £7,000 for a colonelcy in the Dragoons, £1,000 for even a captaincy in a marching regiment.

Then there were women. For a brief moment fashion and the existence of a market in which women could deal legally because the law had never thought of it, gave great married women prominence and wealth in their own right. The ladies of the Princess of Wales's Court, the daughters of Earl Ferrers, the Duchess of Rutland, the Countess of Gainsborough, and, in her own way, the Duchess of Marlborough, were only a few of those who, with or without their husbands, dealt in stock. Like other signs of emancipation of manners which are characteristic of the period leading up to the Bubble, such demonstrations of feminine independence did not survive it.

Blunt and his colleagues surveyed the eager, fashionable crowd and the subsidiary bubbles with divided feelings. The speculative fever suited their plans, but interfered with their technique. With each stroke of their financial pump some of the cash that primed it was escaping into other channels. The cash poured out on the first loan, which had been meant to support a Second Money Subscription, they now saw soaking away into the pockets of other projectors. Politics had preserved the two insurance projects in spite of all they could do, but they were resolved to see that competition was put down before the time came for the conversion itself.

Meanwhile, with the aim of carrying the stock to 400, which was the approximate price at which Blunt already thought he might fix the conversion of the National Debt, there was a further money subscription. This second subscription was opened on 30 April, the offer being £1 million new stock at 400, payable in instalments and secretly expanded (to £1½ million), as the previous subscription had been. It was marketed by allocating a quota of £26,000 to each director, for which he in turn made up a list. The balance of nearly a quarter of a million was marketed by the Sub- and Deputy Governors, who 'had a great many to oblige'; and as the best possible advertisement the books were carried in state, the day before the subcription formally opened, to both St. James's and Leicester House, where the King and his heir each put himself down for a well-publicized sum. The subscription was announced as a success, but in fact appears to have fallen short of the target by nearly £300,000.[19]

*   *

This was the last stroke on the pump before the conversion terms were due to be announced. While the method had resembled Law's, Blunt's greed and the activity of the private enterprise bubbles produced a remarkable difference between London and Paris in boom conditions. Law, who took the whole economy for the scope of his management, and was backed by the whole power of the French autocracy, aimed at stimulating real economic activity by expansion of liquid credit. Hence the part that bank-notes played in his system, and the hideous inflation which ultimately overtook and destroyed him. Blunt had no such economic objective, and his aims were purely financial. He did all he could to prevent the credit he had created from escaping his control, whether to genuine enterprises or to rival financial schemes. Law's pump fed an open spray, which watered, and eventually drowned, the economy. Blunt's was meant to be a closed circuit. It is one of the ironies of the whole story that England should have been saved from a general paper inflation mainly by the greed and narrow-mindedness of her financial masters.

The exceptions to this comparative absence of inflation were two. Luxurious and showy spending rose sharply. The accepted signs of wealth—coaches, jewellery, new clothes—were all in strong demand and their prices rose. But more important was the demand for the other great symbol of personal status—land. The City man and the impoverished Scottish peer, the climbing government official and the modest Member of Parliament—all saw within reach the chance of realizing the traditional ambition of broad acres, a great house, a name handed down from one generation to another. Estates—particularly estates within easy reach of London—went to increasingly high premiums. It was probably the most serious leak in Blunt's system, and it grew steadily graver.

The directors and officers of the Company themselves were among the leaders of this scramble for land. Gibbon and Chaplin spent nearly £20,000 between June and September in acquiring estates; Houlditch almost doubled that figure. Sir Lambert Blackwell laid out another £10,000 adding to his already enormous estates in Norfolk. The most spectacular buyer of all was Deputy Cashier Surman. In March 1720 his real property consisted of a field near his native Tewkesbury in reversion, some tenements in Bear Lane, and one-fifth of the office of Marshal of the Marshalsea Prison. His purchases during the summer and autumn—not all of them completed —came to £180,000, relating to twenty-seven properties in nine different counties. The grant of arms which he sought and secured in August was supported by as many acres as the crests of most peers.[20]

As the South Sea scheme gathered momentum the news from Paris was both serious and satisfactory. In the second week of May, Craggs received from Stair a copy of what the covering despatch described as 'the most extraordinary decree that has ever appeared in any country'. It was the last despairing effort by the great economist to stem inflation. He was no longer the urbane, imperturbable manipulator of a year before. He could not sleep, and one night a startled officer of the guard found him dancing frantically round two chairs (perhaps they symbolized the inconsistent interests of the shares and the notes) which he had placed in the middle of his bedroom. Despondency and stress are the only explanations for the violent jar he now gave to his managed economy.

This new decree—the celebrated Arrêt du 21 Mai—simply cut the value of all notes in circulation, and the fixed price of shares by one-quarter, with immediate effect, and provided for their further reduction by stages until they would be worth precisely half their face value. As an academic remedy for inflation there is perhaps something to be said for this crude piece of internal devaluation; but Law's mind had moved too rapidly for the psychology of the people. They had perhaps just begun to believe that paper could have a real, not just a representative value as currency, and many of them had not even advanced so far. They simply saw their wealth reduced by half; as indeed, it must be admitted, it had been, for bargains made during the inflation had still to be met in the deflated currency. Paris, Stair reported, was like a town taken by storm, and he put the loss to British subjects alone at £3 million. Troops appeared in the streets and the Parlement refused to register the edict, which after a few agonizing days was revoked. Again the inflation was resumed, but with shattered confidence. The System, though it was to struggle on a few months longer, never recovered its magnetism.[21]

The way was now clear for the London syndicate to

dominate the markets, not only of England, but of a Europe caught in the paper frenzy from Denmark to Portugal. In Copenhagen the Government was engaged in a debt-conversion operation. Geneva and Berne, where the financial brothers Rudolph and Isaac Faesch operated; Amsterdam, with its great brokers, Pieter Schabaalje and Abraham Tzerwen; Sythov and Favon of The Hague; were all turning to the rising sun in London. Dutch East India stock, which had stood at 800 on the Amsterdam stock exchange in the Kalverstraat in January, stood at 1,000 in May; Dutch West Indies had doubled. Buying orders for South Sea stock poured into London from Holland, 200,000 pistoles arriving in one consignment from Amsterdam towards the end of April; and private expresses scuttled to and fro across the North Sea with market intelligence in the favourable winds. 'It is certain', wrote one observant broker in Amsterdam on 19 April, 'that so long as the wind continues E.S.E. South Sea stock will sell at Amsterdam at 325'. As spring turned into summer the London papers no longer troubled to quote the price of Mississippi stock. As he drove to business from his modest but comfortable home in Stratford to his office in Birchin Lane, Blunt basked in a following breeze.[22]

CHAPTER VIII

Summer

A T THE MOMENT of launching, the mastery of Blunt
and his immediate associates over the whole enterprise
was absolute. The Act had provided that the Treasury
would appoint managers who would handle the actual transaction between the Debt-holders and the Company. On 6 May
a Treasury warrant signed by Sunderland and Aislabie constituted the directors of the Company as managers of the
scheme; and the new managers promptly appointed Knight's
confidential clerk, Christopher Clayton, their secretary.[1]

Nor, though they were all managers, had the directors
themselves, as a body, any continuing influence over policy.
Many of the more enterprising and wealthy of them, such as
Chapman, Lambert, and Janssen, had their own affairs to
attend to as the boom got under way; and the smaller men
were content to be well placed for the inevitable pickings.
From now on, if the Court of Directors was formally consulted
at all, the consultation was only on the eve of action. Even the
Court's Committee of Treasury, which was a more business-
like body than the full Court, was reduced to impotence. Its
days of meeting were deliberately changed at short notice to
prevent the more inquisitive members turning up, then it was
packed with Blunt's nominees, and finally it was ignored
altogether.

Stripped of its façade, the South Sea machine in action
consisted of a strategic triangle, with Blunt at its apex and
Knight and Grigsby respectively in control of the outgo and
intake of cash. Knight, seconded by Surman, held in his hands
the innumerable threads leading to brokers and go-betweens,
from the company's official broker, Matthew Wymondesold,

to Joseph Shaw, who admitted later that he never kept a cash-book in his life. Knight also had access to the credit reservoir of the Sword Blade Bank, where a bottomless current account was operated in Surman's name. It shows a turnover of more than a million between the middle of April and the middle of May; and in the following four weeks nearly four millions.[2]

Grigsby's office, which issued stock and recorded transfers, was the weakest part of the machine, and a source of anxiety from the start. The former coffee-merchant was growing old and infirm, and his staff was always having to be reinforced and cheered on with extra pay. Chronic overwork in all departments at South Sea House was the rule and probably the deliberate policy, since it created the desired atmosphere of urgency; and considering the pressure put on the clerks, it is astonishing how well they managed. But with all that could be done for them—and the simplification of the transfer procedure was a constant preoccupation of the organizers— Grigsby's staff very soon found it impossible to keep abreast of the transfers of stock reported to them on the three days a week appointed for settlements. This sheer physical inability to register changes of ownership in the stock naturally encouraged credit trading and speculative forward sales, particularly when, as happened from time to time, the transfer office had to close in order to catch up with existing arrears, and bargains could only be made 'for the opening of the books'.[3]

Once the cycle of loan and subscription had got under way in April, an invitation had been issued to the annuitants to deposit their annuities at South Sea House in readiness for a decision about what they should receive for them. No fewer than 70 clerks and 28 subordinate staff were assigned to meet the expected rush; and the numbers were fully justified. Within a few days at the end of April a quarter of the annuities had been deposited 'blind'.[4]

Up to this moment the excitement and speculation had been mainly metropolitan and international; but with the approach of the conversion itself interest spread all over the British Isles, and to all classes save the humblest. Dublin, Edinburgh, Bristol, and Norwich became as expectant as London, Berne, Basle, Paris, and Amsterdam already were; and the expectancy filtered rapidly down to the smaller cathedral and market towns and the modest seats of the squirearchy. Quotations of the South Sea stock began to appear in such local sheets as the *Plymouth Weekly Journal*; and in the first fortnight in May the rumour that every £100 a year of annuity would be exchanged for £1,000 South Sea stock ran through the whole country. Since the stock stood on the market at 350, and the natural value of the long annuity, considered as a fixed interest security, was sixteen times the annual income, the conversion looked as if it would give the annuitant a capital worth thirty-five times the annual yield.

Some of the directors, who did not know that nearly the whole of the £2 million or so already raised in the money subscriptions had been poured back to the politicians and market operators, were for paying off a large part of the annuities in cash. Blunt smothered these suggestions in his grandest manner, declaring 'he was for following the humour of the people, who are fond of the stock at any rate. There is no other way to please them but by giving them stock for their annuities.'[5]

He was perfectly right. The ripples of disappointment which greeted the Company's offer when it was promulgated on 19 May were largely due to part of the exchange price not being expressed in stock. For each £100 a year of a long annuity, the holder was offered £700 stock, £500 in 4 per cent. South Sea bonds, repayable in ten months at par, and £75 cash. This the Company described as thirty-two years' purchase, because they valued the £700 stock at 375 (i.e., £2,625), or slightly below the highest market levels. The same technique was used to represent the offer for the 'short' annuities as seventeen years' purchase.* As additional inducements, all the

* The exact terms for the various categories of debt apart from the long annuities were: 14 per cent. annuities—£700 stock, £500 bonds, £11 cash for each £98 a year; prizes in the 1710 Lottery—£400 stock, £200 bonds for each £100 a year; blanks in the 1710 Lottery—£350 stock, £300 bonds, £53. 10s. cash for each £98 a year; 9 per cent. annuities—£350 stock, £200 bonds, £17 cash for each £90 a year.

stock offered was to rank for the midsummer bonus distribution of more stock, and the bonds (making their first shy
appearance in the system) would be accepted from 1 December
onwards as the equivalent of cash if tendered towards instalments already undertaken on the money subscriptions. The
offer would be open for one week only.[6]

The skill with which Blunt had made his dispositions now
appeared. With the annuitants wavering in face of what looked
like an underbid, he threw in his financial reinforcements in
the shape of the £1 million Exchequer bills which had just,
under statute, been lent to the Company. The day after the
offer was announced these, along with all the Company's
spare cash and Sword Blade credit were thrown into the market
in the shape of a second loan on stock on terms even more
generous than the first. The interest was 4 per cent. instead of
5, and the Company would advance £300 for every £100
stock deposited. The pump-handle, which had been skilfully
left in its upward position, was driven down with maximum
effect. As the money poured out of Knight's office the price
of stock soared. On the third day of the offer the annuitants
saw the stock the Company was dangling before them at 375
being sold in the Alley at 460, and on the fifth day at 495.
By the end of the week something like five-eighths of the
annuities had been surrendered to the Company in exchange
for the promise of about £3¼ million stock.

The paper profit of the Company was, of course, enormous,
since they were entitled by the Act to bring into existence over
three times as much stock as was needed to convert at this rate,
and the balance left in their hands was worth, at market prices,
more than £20 million. Admittedly a good deal of this had
been committed in one way or another already (i.e., to the
money subscribers and the names in the green book), and the
increase in cash income from the government for relieving it
of this slice of indebtedness was only £50,000 a year. Nor,
in the general atmosphere of confidence, did the Company feel
obliged to issue stock certificates, let alone the cash and bonds
promised, to their lucky new proprietors at once. This was

regarded as a purely clerical operation, to be settled at leisure.

Well-concerted strategy was the secret of the conversion's success. But direct propaganda, though it played only a subsidiary part, was not neglected. Encouraging stories about the Company's American concessions and huge gains by lucky investors made a well-timed appearance in the newspapers. During the conversion week itself, Knight and Surman were seen everywhere about the coffee-houses, dropping hints about large foreign buying orders, which would certainly maintain the price of stock. There was some truth in what they said, and the rumours prevented at least one cautious operator, John Martin, the banker, from taking his profit. Hoare's bank did not sell a single parcel, and actually began buying again cautiously on 27 May.[7]

The truth was that the annuitants, making all allowances for the salesmanship to which they were subjected, did not get a bad bargain. They had been persuaded to exchange gilt-edged for a leading equity by an illusion about capital values —namely, that the market value of holdings (in the case of a long annuity) were more than doubled. But this meant the long annuitant could not lose even if the capital value of his equity was halved by the fluctuations of the market.* The short annuitant had a smaller safety margin, since on the rational value of his fixed interest security (which was nine years' purchase) he stood to lose if the market price of South Sea stock went below 220. But this was only a protection if the annuitant held on to his stock, and that was just what Blunt's methods tempted him not to do. Nor, given the circumstances, did it follow that the person who subscribed an annuity had paid a rational price for it. Often, in expectation of good terms, he had paid an inflated one.

Blunt understood finance but not the intoxicating consequences of imaginary wealth. Throughout the country he had set in train an inflation, not, it is true, of currency, but of credit. James Windham, of the Salt Office, was a typical

* Technically, this can be expressed by saying he held his stock at 150, although he thought he was paying 375 for it.

carrier of the infection when he wrote to his Norfolk relatives that he had grown so rich he would soon be buying an estate. Soon the relations, in their turn, were writing back begging him to stake their fortunes as well, and getting credit down in Norfolk on the strength of their luck.[8]

Fortunes already 'made' were beginning to break out in spectacular displays as the fashionable London season ran to its climax. In the middle of the conversion week itself Sunderland was installed at Windsor as Knight of the Garter, and the customary feast is said to have cost him £2,000. Four days later the biggest crowd Lady Cowper had ever seen at Court celebrated the King's birthday at St. James's. A hundred dozen of claret were drunk, and the bulky Duchess of Kendal far outshone the Duchess of Bolton by appearing in a dress covered with jewels valued at £5,000. The congratulatory ode offered to the King by the Reverend Laurence Eusden boldly referred to the source of it all:

> *Hence (for in his peculiar reign were laid*
> *Schemes, that produc'd the sure increase of trade)*
> *Shall generations, yet unborn, be told,*
> *Who gifted them with silver mines and gold;*
> *Who gave them all the commerce of the Main,*
> *And made* South Seas *send home the wealth of* Spain.[9]

The directors, fresh from their triumph, made a gala appearance at their Governor's birthday, and 'had much more court paid to them than the ministers themselves'. One was said to have made £3 million in three months. Janssen, whose South Sea holding was valued at a million, was presented with a diamond ring by the Prince of Wales. He was knocking down the old Tudor mansion at Wimbledon, which had once belonged to the Cecils, to build afresh, and even his housekeeper had compiled a dowry of £8,000 in the South Sea. Grigsby, who had just bought a country house in fashionable Wanstead and was said to be worth £50,000, was helped out of his coach on arrival by the now senile master of Blenheim. Both the Marlboroughs had been early in the market, and this was the moment the Duchess had decided to sell out and put her money into Bank and insurance shares.[10]

The boom in insurance had been even more spectacular than in the South Sea. When Walpole and Craggs had been buying them back in February Chetwynd's insurance could be had for as little as 4, and at the beginning of May could still be had for 20. By the end of May they had gone to 50. Onslow's too more than doubled in price during May. The new equipages in the Park were labelled 'Insurance' or 'South Sea' by the crowds, and there were as many of one as of the other. Secretary Craggs, with typical kindliness, had distributed the proceeds of well-sold parcels to his servants and his clerks, tipped his old tutor £1,000, and was acquiring a row of houses at the bottom of Whitehall, which he proposed to demolish and replace with an impressive mansion. Walpole was systematically buying land down in Norfolk.[11]

The crowd in Exchange Alley was as thick, and almost as aristocratic, as it was at St. James's. More than one sword was drawn there—a thing almost unknown. A Scotch peer had his pocket picked in Garraways, and an Irish earl lost his wallet coming out of South Sea House. Jonathan Wild's lost property office at the Old Bailey throve on retrieving missing portfolios containing papers said to be 'of no value to any but the owner' —4,000 shares in the Sail Cloth Company, 3,000 in Shales's Insurance, 6,000 in Baker's Annuities, 2,000 in Salter's Hall Remittances, 1,000 Wyersdale's Turnpike, 2,000 in the Company for Insuring Seamen's Wages, Sword Blade notes of large denominations, and 1,000 in Arthur Moore's Royal Fishery 'to be transferred to a Lady of Quality'.[12]

Although several South Sea directors—notably Sir John Lambert—were individually concerned in these 'Lower Alley' bubbles, those in control of the Company watched their spawning with growing alarm. More than 100 were advertised in May and the first fortnight of June, despite the steady progress of Hungerford's Bill designed to suppress them. The newspapers doubled in size to carry the notices—twenty-three on 7 June, twenty-four on the 9th, fifteen on the 10th. There was the Company for trading in hair, the Company for improving and trading in the truly national commodity of woad; a Company for purchasing disputed titles to land, and one for manufacturing hats and caps; companies for importing broomsticks from Germany, for fixing quicksilver, for extracting silver from lead, and for 'settling the country on a desolate river more than seventy miles up the main continent in Acadia'.[13]

Almost more than the South Sea itself, this tail to the comet has caught the historical imagination. Swindles, in the sense of being primarily money-getters, most of these companies undoubtedly were; but they illustrate far more than the gullibility of the age. They sprang from a vision of material progress in advance of the technical capacity to achieve it. The 'desolate river' was the gateway to North America, and the site proposed for settlement was Montreal. There really were gold-mines in Terra Australis, which the irrepressible Captain Welbe was again raising a subscription to discover. The 'Grand Dispensary' designed to 'serve all families, shipping and poor in Great Britain with medicine at reasonable rates and the constant advice of able physicians' was not always to be a chimera.*

When the Bubble Bill passed the Commons at the end of May there was a slight hesitation in the Lower Alley, but it was only a matter of a few days. Early in June the news broke that there was to be yet another South Sea loan. It was to be unlimited in size, £100 stock was to be taken as security for £400 (instead of £300), and any individual could get an advance of up to £4,000, which was consequently available to anyone who could produce £1,000 stock.

This prospect of another money bath sent the market into ecstasies. South Sea stock made its most sensational leap yet—

---

* I have found no evidence for the most celebrated of all—the company for a project which shall hereafter be revealed; but perhaps its prototype is the 'Proposal for raising the sum of Six Millions sterling to carry on a design of more general advantage . . . and of more certain profit . . . than any undertaking yet set on foot' advertised in the *Daily Post* for 21 May. No complete and accurate list of the Lower Alley bubbles exists. The best is in *Scott. iii.*

from 610 to 870—in the first two days of June. Royal African nearly doubled in sympathy (105 to 190) and two further projects, one for insurance against robbery and embezzlement and the other for establishing simultaneously a coral fishery and a calico factory, were announced. On the day before the loan opened no fewer than twenty-four projects were advertised.[14]

But it will be noticed that for the first time Blunt had departed from his pattern of alternating loans with subscriptions, of first flooding, then mopping up. This was the second successive loan and was purely an addition to the speculative money in the market. It was the most dangerous stimulant he had yet dispensed.

Time, however, was still working on his side, and against his competitors. Two days after the loan opened on 9 June, Royal Assent was given to the Bubble Bill, and a proclamation was instantly issued bringing it into force on Midsummer Day. For more than 100 years thereafter the unauthorized joint stock company was to be a common nuisance and its promoters subject to the penalties of Praemunire—infinite fine and perpetual imprisonment. The effect was all that Blunt could have desired. Soon after Midsummer Day one newspaper rejoiced that at last a man could walk through the Alley without having to insure his pockets. 'The South Sea mongers', wrote another, 'have extended their lines from Garraways Coffee House to the Lower Alley, and taken possession of the Bubblers' camp.' Mother Jones, the newspaper-seller outside Jonathan's who had been crowded out by the hurly-burly, got her pitch back. It looked as if Blunt had beaten the Alley cheapjacks, as he had beaten the Bank.[15]

King George chose the day the Bubble Act became law to publish a spectacular honours list. It contained two new dukes, seven other new peers, and two baronets. One of these last was Walpole's friend, Chapman, who served on the boards of both Chetwynd's and the South Sea. The other was Blunt, honoured 'for his extraordinary services in raising public credit to a height not known before'. The City trumpeters and drummers paraded in honour of the two new baronets outside their houses, and at the other end of town, south of the Park, a grand new square was planned for the new fortunes. It was to be called South Sea Square, and was to stand on the site of what is now St. James's Park Underground Station.[16]

The son of Joseph Bankes, M.P., met Blunt at the summit of his glory on 15 June. His business with the new baronet was to present a promissory note for delivery of £1,000 stock which had been given to Joseph Bankes during the spring—a part, one suspects, of the bear's skin. Now he wanted £4,000 for it under the terms of the loan. At South Sea House, where Blunt was holding court in a reception-room at the bottom of the main staircase, the crowd was so thick, and Blunt so busy, that it was some time before the young man could get him to pay any attention at all. Testily saying he had no time to do more, Blunt took the promissory note and scribbled out another, this time promising in his own name to transfer the same amount of stock to Knight, and gave it back to Bankes, telling him to take it to the Cashier. Knight, in complete contrast to Blunt, was discovered in a quiet room upstairs, where with the greatest courtesy he counted out £4,000 cash in return for what was, in effect, Blunt's cheque on the Company.[17]

This particular £4,000 returned safely enough to its masters only a few days later in the Third Money Subscription, which, of course, was planned to follow in the immediate wake of the third loan. But, in spite of the victory over the cheapjack bubbles, there were other dangerous leaks in the system, for the higher Blunt forced his prices, the greater was the temptation to get out with a profit. On 10 June Thomas Guy sold the last of his holding at 600—well below market rates, but he probably insisted on cash. Next day Charles Stanhope, Secretary to the Treasury, collected his share of the bear's skin in the shape of two enormous Sword Blade notes, one for £47,000 and the other for £202,230, representing the 'difference' between the £60,000 stock at the prices credited to him in the green book and its current market value.[18]

The most ominous sign was in the property market. Land near London was now fetching up to forty-five times the annual rent, and the correspondence of property prices with South Sea quotations was so close that it was publicly referred to in the auction rooms to encourage bidders. The newspapers' loss of advertising revenue from bubble promotions was more than made up by the notices of estates for sale, and more than one bubble-monger transformed himself overnight into an estate agent. It was reported that a speculator, brought to his death-bed by sheer over-exertion, had declared he died happy, 'for though I have lost my life, I have got an estate'.[19]

The urgent need to get loose money back was the main reason for the unprecedented scale of the Third Money Subscription, which marks the high tide of South Sea finance. The market was asked for no less than £50 million, the offer being £5 million stock at the resounding figure of 1,000 per cent.— or well above the current quotation, which after the rush to over 800 had hovered between 715 and 780. The bait was an excessively generous easy-payments plan. Only a tenth of purchase price was asked for at once, and the next instalment— also 10 per cent.—would not fall due for more than a year. After that there would be eight more instalments spread over four years. The books opened on 15 June.

Apart from the urgent need for fresh cash and the equally urgent need to mop up the market, there was a new reason for haste. The London season was coming to an end, and the fashionable world was preparing to leave the Alley. Secretary Craggs's splendid diplomatic reception on 4 June was in the nature of a farewell. Next day the King made his last festive appearance of the season (in the costume of a Venetian nobleman) at a masked ball in the Haymarket. His heavy luggage was already on its way across the North Sea to Hanover, whither the whole diplomatic corps and much of the political and smart world had to follow him. Bills were being settled on all sides, and elaborate equipages organized out of market gains. The King's own stock account was not the least important of the settlements which called for attention as a result. Aislabie dealt with it the day before his master left on the 14th, selling part-paid scrip in the First Money Subscription (on which the royal outlay had been £20,000) for no less than £106,400. Three days later he laid out this huge sum (under the alias of Vernon) partly in the purchase of fully paid stock from Knight and Hawes, partly in the Third Money Subscription, and partly, with a prudence for which the King was later to be very glad, in nearly £40,000 worth of Land Tax tallies. Altogether the King had every reason to be gratified at the message of farewell and thanks which the directors, on the eve of his departure, voted should be sent to their Governor.[20]

The subscription lists for the Third Money Subscription are the fullest record we have for any South Sea operation and read like a directory of contemporary England. Half the House of Lords and more than half the House of Commons were included. As was now customary, the greater part of the stock offered—in this case four-fifths—was allotted entirely on the nomination of directors and of four favoured politicians—Sunderland, Aislabie, Charles Stanhope, and Secretary Craggs. Only a million was left to be scrambled for by the general public, and it was devoured in a single day. As soon as the books closed the receipts were fetching 60 per cent. premium in the Alley.[21]

The lists submitted by the various directors speak very clearly of each individual's field of influence and energy as a canvasser. The Sub- and Deputy Governors, who disposed of nearly a fifth of the total issue, assembled nearly 100 peers and more than fifty members of the House of Commons. They also covered the daughters of the Prince of Wales, their governess (the Countess of Portland), their sub-governess, and preceptor; six nominees of Sir Robert Walpole; the entire East India Board; and all the Commissioners of Excise. Blunt's list, which topped the £100,000 mark, was notable for the number of officials from the Treasury and other government departments it contained; Janssen's for an impressive international collection from Geneva, Paris, Amsterdam, and The Hague, and for repayment of his obligation to the Prince of Wales in the form of allocations of £10,000 each to him and the Princess. Gibbon and Chester also provided spectacular lists; Lambert a list with a high proportion of French names.

Far the largest and most glittering collection was produced by the sociable Craggs. It allocated nearly £700,000 stock. Twenty-one peers (including three dukes) and no less than 154 Members of Parliament (including the Speaker) subscribed to it. Nor had he restricted himself to his political acquaintance. His friendships in the world of art and letters brought in Pope, Kneller, and Vanbrugh, to whom he added the Prince of Wales's *valet de chambre*.

No influential corner was neglected in the lists: Black Rod, the doorkeeper of the House of Lords, the Commissioners of Victualling and the Commissioners of Customs. Lord Chancellor Parker appeared on no less than four lists, for a total of £23,000 stock, indicating a prospective outlay of a quarter of a million over the next five years. When the subscription books closed it was plain that once more boldness and energy had brought success. The cautious as well as the excited fell in behind the band. Martin, the banker, had taken £500 and made the first payment on the nail, 'though I believe if you had been in town you would scarce have had the courage to have ventured, but when the rest of the world are mad we must imitate them in some measure'.[22]

Cash was sorely needed, and it went out almost as soon as it came in. By now the Company had lent something like £5 million, but the instalments so far due on the earlier money subscriptions (even assuming them all faithfully paid, which was by no means the case) plus the Company's other revenue since April, had not been more than £3½ million. The balance had been drawings on the Sword Blade. But it was impossible now to stop lending, even though the return in terms of raising the price of stock was diminishing. Up to the beginning of June the lending of about £4¼ million had brought the stock up 430 points, but even with additional lending on the part-paid stock represented by the subscription receipts (for which there was no formal authority) the creation of fresh credit was now hardly keeping the price steady.

The price, particularly at this moment, had not only to be maintained, but to be advanced still further for the second phase of the conversion itself. The whole field of the redeemable debts remained to be conquered, and there were still irredeemable annuities which had not been subscribed in May, which were now, of course, changing hands at fancy prices. Blunt was determined the conversion should be done at the figure of 1,000 he had already used for the Third Money Subscription—and indeed he dared not do otherwise. 'The advancing by all means, of the price of the stock,' he truthfully told his colleagues, 'is the only way to promote the good of the Company.'[23]

Other means were at hand besides the now worn-out process of lending. Early in June it had been announced that the transfer books would be closed at midsummer for at least a month to allow the stock bonus to be worked out, and this had helped to depress the price by imposing a settlement on bulls. But once the closing had taken place the rebound was startling. Freed for an appreciable period from any necessity to comply with their bargains, the speculators went completely wild, and market quotations 'for the opening of the books' shot to 1,000. This, the zenith, when stock was actually changing hands at different prices at the two ends of Garraways, lasted only for a few days, but the new wave of speculative credit kept quotations comfortably above 900 for several weeks.

During this veritable silly season the foremost figure in the market was Edmund Waller, a descendant of the poet who had once praised Sunderland's grandmother 'Sacharissa' in verses which were still fashionable. He was also Aislabie's son-in-law as well as a director of the Royal Africa Company, and there is ground for suspecting that his speculations included a good deal of business for the Chancellor of the Exchequer. He brought hardly any money to the market himself, but during the whole boom his drawings on the Sword Blade Bank came to over three-quarters of a million, and his turnover with six stockbrokers whose accounts survive, to £300,000. Practically all his business was on credit. His prices were the most bullish in the market—often 100 points and more above the newspaper quotations—and have the doubtful distinction of including the highest price at which South Sea was ever offered: 1,100, on 10 July. He found no buyer.*[24]

The ladies who had caused so much interest in the Alley in May were out of town by the end of June. At Axminster Mrs. Molesworth, 'still almost South Sea mad', was rejoicing that the allocation she had got from Lady Sunderland in the Third Money Subscription had almost doubled in value. But even the £50 she had found for the first instalment on it had been borrowed, and rates of interest were too high for her to venture more—a significant straw in the wind. Mrs. Campbell, the maid of honour who had made the marriage of the year with Colonel John Campbell, was at Bath, though her husband was still in London, 'bowing', her correspondent assured her, 'to no other altars than those erected in 'Change Alley'.[25]

In London the Sword Blade Bank and its affairs were much in the public eye. Sir George Caswall fought and won a boisterous election for Sheriff of London and Middlesex as the government's candidate; and the defaulting Sword Blade clerk, Davis, was hanged. To the last he had expected his old employers to get him a reprieve, and at Tyburn, to which he rode in a coach, he blamed his downfall on intolerable pressure of business. Since his time the pressure must have increased still further if one is to judge by Surman's account with the Sword Blade, which had a turnover of more than £3½ million between 20 May and 24 June.[26]

In the haven of stable prices created by the closing of the books, Blunt and his colleagues were laying further plans. There were already rumours of a further money subscription—

* A great many of Waller's clients were connexions of Aislabie's in Yorkshire, and there is one receipt from Aislabie himself 'for the profits made by him for me', which proves that the Chancellor was taking a personal hand in the market through his son-in-law.

the fourth—at a figure some said would be 1,500; but for the moment this was more than the decemvirs dared suggest to the Court of Directors. The serious item was the issue on 9 July of an invitation to the remaining holders of National Debt, whether in the form of annuities not subscribed in May, or of the as yet untouched 'redeemables', to deposit their titles at South Sea House in readiness for the terms of conversion the Company would offer. There were comparatively few annuitants left now, but more than half of those there were came forward. The response from the holders of the redeemable Debt was even better. The orders for this class of Debt had to be given at the Bank of England, who held the securities and paid the interest, and so great was the throng there that extra tables had to be set up for the clerks in the street outside. Altogether more than seven-eighths of the redeemable Debt was thus put at the Company's disposal—over £14 million— £6 million being subscribed, it was said, in a single day. Especially satisfactory was the Bank's humble request to be allowed to subscribe their own holding of redeemables up to an amount not exceeding £300,000.[27]

*   *   *

If Blunt had considered the European scene at the beginning of July, he might have found in it a pattern which would have made him doubt whether the prosperity of the London bubble was likely to hold. It had always been one of his favourite ways of rallying his colleagues to tell them the eyes of Europe were upon them; but the truth was that the eyes of Europe were now moving elsewhere. For the past three months the paper tornado first roused by Law had been centred over London. Now it had crossed the North Sea and settled over Holland and Germany.

Ever since the spring the traffic to the Dutch ports in market news had been brisk, and a regular item of note had been the arrival and departure of Dutch 'scoots' at Harwich. During June any ship bound for Holland had found it worthwhile to advertise an agent on 'Change who could be 'spoken to' during the week before sailing, and by July there was a regular twelve-hourly relay of messengers between Harwich and Helvoetsluys. The characteristic speculating crowd of fashionables had established itself in the Kalverstraat at Amsterdam: the Princess Dowager of Orange Nassau; Prince George of Hesse-Cassel; the Tsar's envoys, Princes Kourakine and Dolgoroucki; and the agents of the Queen Mother of Spain. Alongside them were more business-like traders.*

This market was not content to deal exclusively in South Sea stock, and in spite of discouragement from the authorities in some towns, notably Amsterdam, June and July saw a crop of native promotions in Holland. Nearly all were finance companies of one kind or another, especially insurance, and whatever may be thought of their origins, some of them were far from frivolous. The Maatschappij van Assurantie, Disconteering en Beleening, for instance, which survives today as a great insurance house, was advertised by anonymous handbills left in Rotterdam coffee-houses, and started with a subscription of only 1 per cent. of the proposed capital. English specialists in insurance flotations came to Holland to advise on its foundation. Civic pride alone made it popular to have a local subscription, and insurances were started at Schiedam, Utrecht, Harlem, Delft, Gouda, The Hague, and many other places—all beyond the reach of Blunt's Bubble Act and its penalties of Praemunire. Their shares were even quoted on the London market. On 16 July it was reported that eighty Jews, Presbyterians, and Anabaptists, till then denizens of the Alley, were on their way to Holland to mend their fortunes in Dutch insurance, and they were soon followed by Sir John Cook, the ecclesiastical lawyer of Doctor's Commons.

Holland was not the only place of pilgrimage. Others were on the way to Hamburg, where the Exchange was crowded from morning till night, and nothing the magistrates could do seemed to stop the multiplication of insurance companies and the soaring of their stock to 1,000 and higher.

*The *Financial Times* for 5 May 1958 contains an advertisement of R. Mees & Sons, bankers and insurance brokers, founded 1720.

Across the North Sea, inaccessible rivals; across the Channel, ominous ruin—this was the picture. In Paris once precious paper was being publicly shovelled into bonfires to show the government was in earnest about inflation. Law was not beaten yet, and he imperturbably told Crawford, who had now decided to settle in France with his Mississippi fortune, that he would yet bring things under control. He had sixty-two ships at sea (two more were building for him at Limehouse) and high hopes of capturing a lion's share of the India trade. But in fact matters were desperate. The stream of currency decrees had produced bewilderment and paralysis. The Duke of Berwick, taking leave of the Regent for the holidays, said he hoped Law would not have lost the kingdom at picquet by the time he got back; and the Regent himself was reported to have said, with the petulance of a king in a fairy tale, that he had put the nation into Law's hands 'mais pardieu, s'il ne fait pas fleurir le Royaume, je l'enverrai au diable avec son système'. On 7 July there were ugly scenes when a crowd rushed the bank, trying to exchange paper money, and some were bayoneted by the guard. Law's coach was mobbed, and he had to take refuge in the Palais Royal.

At least one international investor read the signs correctly. Early in July the Canton of Berne ordered their London agent to sell their entire South Sea holding of £200,000, and cleared the better part of £2 million.[29]

The Alley itself wore the confused, choppy look of a tide that neither runs nor ebbs. The midsummer shock administered by the Bubble Act had already begun to wear off, and although one or two of the lesser bubbles were actually offering the subscribers their money back, a much greater number were making a gingerly return to daylight. Certainly the possessors of such improbable shares as Captain Welbe's Australian plan, still set some store by them. Even the government's carefully publicized disallowance of nearly a score of quite well-supported applications for patents early in July, including Arthur Moore's Fishery, Sir John Lambert's Greenland scheme, and Sir Alexander Cairn's trading company with Germany, failed to check the recrudescence.*

A more circuitous device for removing speculators from the market was the order given in mid-July for all Army officers to return immediately to their posts. This was not justified by any operational requirements, and had at least one unfortunate result when a certain Colonel Smith, dissatisfied about the final settlement with his stockbroker, waylaid the wretched man at night and, with help of two lackeys, broke his head open and cut off one of his ears.

But so far as Blunt was concerned, the 'lower Alley' in its second wind was not more than a nuisance. He was far more concerned at the appearance of a new syndicate, manipulated by a man whose training was the same, and whose intelligence was as great, as his own.

Case Billingsley was a City solicitor and a remote connexion of the new Solicitor-General, Philip Yorke. He had been deeply concerned in the marine insurance scheme which ultimately became the Royal Exchange Assurance; and in the murky legal battles about it in 1718 and 1719 which had caused a sensation when brought to light before the Hungerford Committee, and bespattered the name of Attorney-General Lechmere. Billingsley had not been daunted by the hard things that had been said about his acquisition of the Charter of the Mines Royal to cover the insurance project. In 1719, when the York Buildings Company had advertised their waterworks and goodwill, he had promptly bought them, with the frank intention of using the landholding powers of the charter (which were intended to enable the laying of pipes) to acquire land forfeited by Scottish Jacobites after 1715. It was, in fact, precisely the same manœuvre as Blunt's long ago in Irish real estate. By July 1720 Billingsley had added a third to his string of companies by obtaining a charter of incorporation to exploit the mineral wealth of Wales; and possibly a fourth, in the Royal Lustring Company which, having long ceased to make lustrings and alamodes, was now covering the Sun Fire Office.

* To this phase belong the Bubble playing cards, of which specimens are preserved in the library of Worcester College, Oxford. Each card is devoted to a particular promotion, and bears a satirical epigram.

Billingsley and his associates considered that with these charters they could defy the Bubble Act; and when their shares began to appear on the market during July there was an immediate boom in them. The Prince of Wales himself, who was reputed to have a large holding in Billingsley's Welsh Copper Company, accepted the Governorship of it against the urgent advice of Walpole and Spencer Compton.

Blunt might be anxious, but the ministers hardly saw a cloud in the sky. Those of them who were still in London in the middle of July 'got some very drunk, and others very merry' at yet another dinner-party given by Sunderland. Stanhope, in Hanover, was playing the part of the year's leading European statesman, organizing peace between Sweden and Denmark, and simultaneously acting as host to two kings—his own and Prussia's.[32]

It is difficult to find a parallel to the infatuation of the ministers during the high summer. One by one they left London to enjoy themselves in the provinces. Newcastle settled for his holidays near Nottingham, where he was said to be living at the rate of £2,000 a week, and tipping £100 to the servants after a week-end visit to a neighbouring peer. For the anniversary of the King's accession he spread thirty-six tables for the gentry alone at the banquet he offered to all comers. In a vainglorious letter to Charles Stanhope, he enclosed a list he had compiled against the possibility of another money subscription, and in his fussy determination not to be overlooked, sent a duplicate of it to Sunderland:

> I really believe I shall by this get quite clear, and by that means I shall be the better able to serve my friends and the good Old Cause, neither of which will I forsake while I live.[33]

Secretary Craggs too was relying on the South Sea to cement his political future. 'All the world', he wrote to the country Tory George Clark, whom he tried in vain to inveigle into the fresh list he was compiling, 'is thriving by this South Sea.' His own influence with the directors, he declared 'has reached so far that I have been able I wont say to oblige, but to serve incredible numbers. . . . It is what nobody Whig or Tory has made any difficulty not only to accept but to desire. It costs me nothing.' When Clark declined Craggs grew quite cross at this 'pother about such a trifle which costs me nothing, and in truth is an obligation to me'; and on the refusal being repeated he grew positively malicious—'the profit will of course fall to some rich director who will not know how much he is obliged to you'; no friend would attribute an ill motive to Clark 'but a certain race of envious and ill-natured men' would not hesitate to do that very thing.[34]

He was in the highest of spirits, and delighted at being in virtual charge of affairs in London during the dead season. 'We are in a perfect tranquillity here', he wrote gaily to Newcastle on 28 July, 'and without the least scrap of domestic news.' Sunderland and Charles Stanhope were on the point of setting out to join the King and Stanhope at Hanover; Walpole had already gone to Norfolk. The elder Craggs was 'out of order'. 'I am at last settled at Twickenham, where we had a mighty handsome entertainment . . . a bonfire at night, barrels of ale and illuminations. The night concluded with the ringing of bells, when the King's and Royal Family's and other loyal healths were drunk, to the great content of the town of Twickenham, which I hope will prove well affected to the present happy establishment.' By the first week of August only the Lord Chancellor, Townshend, and the Duke of Grafton remained on the scene to act with the Secretary as a regency for the absent King.[35]

Sir John Blunt was also on holiday by the end of July, but he had not gone far, nor without misgivings. Before going to Tunbridge Wells, he had made arrangements for supporting the market on a larger scale than before, both by lending and by direct purchase of stock through the Company.* For lending purposes the Sword Blade was employed to make advances on the strength of subscription receipts—a device

* Between 8 April and 21 November the Company (contrary to its by-laws) bought £332,250 of its own stock for more than £2 million through its official broker, Wymondesold. Most of this was bought in August and September.

which had the double advantage of maintaining the premium at which these circulated and extracting instalments for the Company from the numerous subscribers who had shown more readiness to put down their names than pay cash.

The Sword Blade machine—which was being openly employed for the first time in the Company's work—did not work quickly enough for Blunt, and an ugly drop in market prices below 900 during the first few days of August brought him rushing back to town to transfer the operation on his own authority from the bank to Knight's machine at South Sea House. An unpleasant scene took place when some of the directors tried to stop him on the ground that confusion would be caused by altering the arrangements. 'The more confusion the better,' roared Blunt. 'People must not know what they do. The execution of the scheme is our business. The eyes of all Europe are upon us. Both Houses of Parliament expect to have it done before Christmas.'[36]

And indeed he was about to put the last story on his house of cards. The books for taking the names of the holders of the outstanding redeemables and the rest of the irredeemables had already been filled in July, and it only remained for the Company to announce the terms on which this crowning conversion was to be carried out. This was done in a resolution dated 3 August. On paper these Debt-holders were to get even better terms than those who had converted in May, since they were conceded what was called thirty-six years' purchase for the long annuities instead of thirty-two, and the price of the stock given in exchange was fixed considerably below the rates being quoted in the newspapers.

But the holder of a long annuity for which £700 stock, £500 bonds, and £75 cash per £100 a year had been offered in May, was now to get only £400 stock, £400 bonds and no cash. The difference arose simply from the fact that the stock was now valued at 800 instead of 375. The holders of the redeemables, whether at 4 per cent. or 5, were to get £12. 18s. South Sea stock for every £100 a year surrendered.

This decision, though celebrated by a clergyman in an ode

for which the Company gave him a handsome fee, made a most unfavourable impression on the Debt-holders and the market generally. The annuitants saw at once that far from getting better terms by holding out (or by buying their annuities at inflated prices) they were to be treated much worse than the May subscribers. They not only got less stock, but a much smaller hedge against a collapse of the market. Whereas the annuitant who converted in May had basked in a great capital gain and was safe so long as the price kept above 150 (if he were a 'long' annuitant) or 220 (if a 'short' one), those who converted in August stood to lose as soon as market prices went below 300 in one case and 500 in the other. The owners of the redeemables (the most considerable of whom was the Bank of England) were even more exposed, since they exchanged at almost eight to one, and a fall of as little as 5 per cent. below 800 meant a loss. True, there was a prospect of capital gain on immediate sale, but with the books closed completion of any such bargain was highly speculative. When they had worked this out a number of annuitants asked for their securities back, only to learn for the first time that each page of the subscription books had been headed by a preamble which had the effect of transferring the holdings of all who had subscribed to the Company's own nominees, with authority for them to accept whatever terms the Company should offer. Blunt was not a scrivener for nothing.

This was the moment Blunt chose to carry out a direct assault on the Billingsley promotions, and disastrous as this was to prove, it is difficult to blame him. The time was approaching when the transfer books would have to open once more, and he knew the speculative credit in the market was already above danger level. Over the month since the middle of July the bulls had turned to Billingsley's ventures with a will, bidding York Buildings and Lustrings up by no less than 300 per cent. and Welsh Copper by 200. On 18 August the regency announced that on the motion of the Treasury proceedings were to be opened under the Bubble Act against the Billingsley companies, and the Law Officers were to apply for writs of Scire Facias so that their charters could be subjected to scrutiny. The Prince of Wales was induced to relinquish his Governorship of Welsh Copper. Messengers from Craggs's office appeared in the Alley and some subscription touts were arrested. But although the Billingsley shares were marked down sharply and the South Sea Company, who made no secret about the initiative having come from them, piously applauded 'this seasonable Interposition of their Excellencies', Billingsley and his colleagues were not so easily beaten. Fortified by legal advice they announced that they would contest every step of the proceedings against the charters.[37]

The boom was now playing havoc with even the most respectable concerns, who were having to stoop to the same despised practices as the bubblers to maintain the attractiveness of their shares. The East India Company was reported to have contracted with a clergyman who would guide an expedition to Ophir, the source of Solomon's riches. Even more serious, the Bank of England itself was reduced to lending money on the security of its own stock to keep its place in the market.[38]

In the third week of August the Chancellor of the Exchequer, who had lingered in London to make up King George's account (sent to Hanover on 18 August) and play the market for himself, called on Blunt at South Sea House before setting out for Yorkshire, and timidly asked 'if he had any commands for the Treasury'. Blunt told him abruptly to mind his own business. Much was said afterwards about Blunt's high-handedness at this crisis in the Company's affairs, and it is true that both his oppression of the annuitants and his attack on Billingsley mark steps in what, retrospectively, one can see was the downward path. Just as in May all had worked out for the best, now all was for the worst. Blunt was a narrow-minded man, but it is hard to believe a more imaginative one could have done better. Nor was he entirely unimaginative, for he chose this moment to disclose a plan which constitutes his one serious claim to stand beside Law as an economist. He proposed that London should become a free port, open to cargoes of all origins carried under all flags. Customs duties would be charged only on goods actually released for sale in England. The plan, which contains the germ of the 'bonded warehouse', was transmitted to Hanover, with the intention that it would come before the next session of Parliament.[39]

The extent of trade which might be brought to London could be seen in the Dutch East India fleet which had just docked at The Hague, eighteen ships strong, with a cargo valued (at cost price) at 7 million guilders. On board were 1,000 tons of pepper and nearly 300 tons of saltpetre. From France, along with the encouraging news of Law's financial troubles, came alarming accounts of plans to expand French overseas trade. Among the most unsettling of these was the rumour that one of Law's confidential emissaries was on his way to Madrid to negotiate a share in the South Sea trade itself.

This was not the only, or the worst, news from France. At Marseilles on 31 July two dockers unloading wool from a ship from Sidon were overcome by dizziness. It was the plague. In a few days the town was ringed with a cordon and fugitives were shot on sight. Quarantine regulations began to appear in the newspapers all over Western Europe alongside the financial reports. Craggs's mail from Paris enclosed the forms of intercession to be used in churches with the latest decrees regulating the paper currency.[40]

The plague, which seems to have been a particularly virulent form of smallpox, spread rapidly, defying measures to check it. It may have been helped by the undernourishment of the poor in the South of France, which arose from the inflationary prices of food. Ordinary human alarm at its approach was heightened by a superstitious fear that it had been sent as a judgement on human materialism, and much was made of its having apparently been delivered through commercial channels. Altogether the news had a disheartening effect in markets and on confidence generally.

On 22 August Grigsby opened the enlarged and redecorated Transfer Office at South Sea House to enable changes in the ownership of stock during the previous two months to be registered.

CHAPTER IX

Fall (1)

THE DAY OF reckoning came in London rather as a huge, long-heated cauldron comes silently to the boil. The town was on the point of being given over to the great annual carnival of Bartholomew Fair, and on the Monday the transfer books opened, workmen were tearing up the paving-stones of Smithfield to drive in the stakes for the stalls and show-booths. The City was already full of freaks, fencers, play-actors, and mountebanks. As the week passed the streets were choked, day and night, with a roaring mob, drinking, gambling and gaping. Entwined with it all this year, was the oriental pageant of a fashionable Jewish wedding, to which all the smart people still in town, including the Prince and Princess of Wales, were invited. The exotic rabbinical ceremonies and public feasting for the marriage of the Cornels lasted three full days, and lent a curious exotic tinge to this particular repetition of Merry England.

Craggs was still congratulating himself over the success of the operation against the Billingsley companies. However crude the instrument he had used (the writs of Scire Facias were not even drafted for more than a month after the announcement, and nobody was sure if they could be made good), he had ruined the market for Lustrings, Welsh Copper, and York Buildings shares. The Attorney-General, Craggs wrote to Stanhope, was 'admirable, sensible and diligent', and Solicitor-General Yorke was 'a pretty fellow'. It never seems to have crossed his mind that by pricking these bubbles he had made it even more difficult than it otherwise would have been for those who had made speculative bargains in the last two months to meet their commitments without selling South Sea

itself. He was equally unimpressed by the dismal despatches
reaching him from Paris about the desolation of the paper
economy there, with big notes fetching hardly a tenth of their
face value in small change on the black market at the Hôtel
de Soissons. He even asked Sir Robert Sutton, who had replaced Stair as British Ambassador and was finding Paris
almost impossible to live in, whether he should take an
opportunity which had come his way of writing Law a
patronizing letter.[1]

Down in Norfolk Walpole was no more percipient than
Craggs, in spite of the uneasy hints he was now getting from
his more wary financial advisers about the future. On 22
August—the day the books opened—he was planning to sell
out his holding of the Third Money Subscription, of which he
had £6,500, at a quite unrealistic premium, and use the profit
for the next money subscription. On the same day Pope, in
London, urged Lady Mary Wortley Montagu to buy with the
prospect of certain profit.[2]

And yet the signs were clear enough. The size of the impend-
ing settlement could be measured by the fact that in the week
before the books opened the Stamp Office sold £6,000 worth
of stamped paper for use in stock transfers. Blunt and his
closest associates were well aware of the peril they faced, but at
this critical moment, caught between the demands of pride
and self-preservation, they were unable to decide whether
to concentrate on saving the Company or themselves.

* * *

They had made some preparations for riding the rapids
ahead. Throughout August ever-increasing sums had been laid
out in lending to the market, and, more recently, in surreptiti-
ous buying of stock on the Company's account. Drawings
on the Sword Blade for these purposes during the month up
to 9 September came to no less than £2½ millions. The
directors also agreed to forgo the next instalments on the
earlier money subscriptions as they fell due, and to treat them
instead as lent to the subscribers—a piece of recklessness which

deprived the Company's cash-box, which was already almost empty, of any prospect of early replenishment.[3]

The culmination of this policy was the extraordinary episode of the Fourth Money Subscription. The idea of a further money subscription following the spectacular success of the Third, had been mooted as long ago as the middle of July, and had set the Duke of Newcastle eagerly to work at Claremont compiling more lists of people he was anxious to oblige. On hearing from Craggs that the directors had decided to restrict the next subscription to existing shareholders, 'which has quite demolished all our Court lists', the Duke had been quite crestfallen. The reason for this decision had been the quite simple one that the directors had found the nobility and their clients better at promising than at paying their instalments. They meant the next subscription to be a City one, with some real security behind it.[4]

In the end the Fourth Subscription had been put off altogether for the time being, but this new-found caution in the Court of Directors had neither pleased the ministers (who were inundated with requests for inclusion in new lists), nor satisfied Blunt, who knew better than the other directors how important it was to keep the system flushed with money. As the settlement day approached he had become quite offensively insistent that, short as money might now be on the market, this subscription must be taken, and taken at 1,000 like its predecessors. Sub-Governor Fellowes and the main body of directors, who were now thoroughly alarmed, had protested in vain. Blunt had got his way, and on St. Bartholomew's Day itself the subscription was opened for £1 million.

The terms were unexpectedly stiff. £200 per cent. was asked for on application and the rest in equal instalments over the coming two years. There were the usual crowds, and an elaborate entertainment was given at South Sea House to celebrate the occasion, with Hoadly the Whig bishop, who was a large shareholder, as the guest of honour. But the old fire was missing. The books were filled, but the more observant noticed that the sober clothes of merchants and bankers were scarce in the throng, and that the subsequent trade in scrip was anything but brisk, the premium, where available, not exceeding 20 per cent. Although ministerial lists were excluded, the main body of the subscribers was fashionable or military. Walpole sent an order, which luckily for him arrived too late. 'We did not subscribe anything for ourselves', his bankers told him consolingly, 'not thinking it worth the bustle.' He was in good company. The subscription list from the court in Hanover, amounting to £300,000 was also turned down.[5]

Each director had undertaken to subscribe £3,000, but Blunt limited his stake to £500. He had been buying land busily since 1 June, and in August had entered into contracts for even more. More discreditable still, he was milking the Company it was his duty to save by unloading on it his own holdings of stock, getting 'loans' in cash from the depleted coffers at South Sea House instead.

*   *   *

The crowd at South Sea House on St. Bartholomew's Day had not been the first crowd there that week. The rush to register stock transfers had begun the moment the books opened on the Monday, and had so appalled the directors that they had closed the transfer office next day. This bought hard-pressed speculators a short respite, and when the books were opened again on Friday it was announced that they would be closed again on the last day of the month.

Blunt must have known that so far as the Company was concerned he now had his back to the wall. The cash paid in for the last subscription—and as usual there were promises to pay among the cash—came to something like a quarter of a million, but this was by no means enough for immediate needs, let alone further support of the sagging market. The immediate needs were for the cash payments to the annuitants who had converted in May. The general shortage of ready money everywhere was now making them impatient for what a month ago they would willingly have forgone for stock.

Though his heart must have been sinking, Blunt put as bold

a face on things as ever. With supreme effrontery, he urged yet another money subscription on his fellow-directors, and for a few days actually got it accepted. With the connivance of Knight and Grigsby, but unknown to the other directors, he arranged for an issue of £1·2 million worth of bonds, which was halted in mid-career by the personal intervention of the Sub-Governor. His other expedient was also not a new one, for Craggs had mentioned it to Stanhope as early as the beginning of the month. On 30 August the Court of Directors announced their intention of recommending a dividend of 30 per cent. for the current year and a guaranteed dividend of 50 per cent. for the next ten years.

Extraordinary as this announcement was, it was not quite so grotesque as it seems at first sight. The aim was to stabilize the market at something like the existing level of stock prices, and to halt dangerous speculation by encouraging stockholders to keep their holdings in the knowledge that even at the advanced prices they had paid they would get a reasonable yield. But for this purpose it not only came too late: it was hardly bold enough. Those who had paid ten times face value for their shares saw quickly that they would be lucky to get 5 per cent. on their money.

Nobody had given a thought to yields back in May and June, when capital gains had been the only cry. Now, ironically, they were brought face to face with the realities of investment by the very step which has been denounced as the most outrageous deception in the Company's career. Perhaps this is why Blunt had hesitated to use the weapon a month earlier, and now it recoiled with fearful effect. People suddenly became aware that to earn the dividend proposed on the stock it had created, the Company would require a profit of something like £15 million a year; and that although something like a third of the surplus stock (which constituted the only profit so far) had not yet been disposed of, prospects of its profitable disposal looked much less impressive than they had done a month ago. As for the Company's trading profits in South America, these depended on the Court of Madrid, and at this moment the news leaked out that King Philip was insisting on the return of Gibraltar before agreeing to any concessions whatsoever. The government's decision to put Gibraltar on a war footing, which was made early in September, seemed an unhopeful beginning for any negotiation about commercial concessions.

An unhealthy concentration on the real value of South Sea stock in terms of yield and prospects was to characterize that autumn. Innumerable pamphlets of the most baffling complexity appeared on the subject. Among the most cogent was the calculation of the economist M. P., Hutcheson, who wound up his analysis by pointing to the many unknowns which prevented any satisfactory value being assigned. Among them he listed the Company's loss by trade on the original capital, which he called 'Y', through lending on their own stock, 'Z'; in getting the Act passed, 'Q'; through defaulters on instalments, 'R'; through buying its own stock, 'S'. Against this he put 'the profits or advantages accrued to the Company by their trade, for several years past, remaining to be found out. I shall call it "O" '.[6]

*   *   *

Craggs, to judge by his reports to Stanhope in Hanover, did not even yet see the abyss that was opening. His letter of 2 September cheerfully referred to the postponement of what would have been the Fifth Subscription, and did not utter a word about the slump which had now carried the price of South Sea from 830 on the day the books opened to 755 on the day he wrote. But those, and they were not a few, who had contracted to accept stock at 1,000 or even more were far from being so comfortable.[7]

Blunt had always seen his project as a European one, and now Europe was fast withdrawing its confidence. Every week brought reports of gold being exported. In Paris the orthodox bankers were regaining control of financial policy from Law, and their London representative, Bernard, working in close contact with the South Sea director Blackwell, began selling

South Sea heavily early in September to raise bullion for repatriation to France. In Holland operators like Pieter Schabaalje, who had been involved against their judgement in their own local boom and saw it too was overblown, were telling their London agents to sell out.

When Craggs wrote to Stanhope on 6 September, he excused the brevity of his letter by saying 'there is no earthly thing here worth mentioning': but now even he, let alone his experienced old father, the Postmaster, could hardly have deluded himself into thinking this was a mere passing phase. Walpole's bankers were positive the market had collapsed; and for those who were bemused by the stock exchange reports there was even more convincing evidence of how the strain was beginning to tell. Two days before Craggs had written to Stanhope, Charles Blunt, Sir John's nephew, and probably the son of the Charles with whom he had shared his earliest triumphs in public finance, had gone into an upstairs room and cut his throat with a razor.[8]

The General Court of Proprietors of the South Sea Company which now had to be held, was organized with the utmost care to preserve an impression of continued confidence. Although the proceedings were not due to begin till midday, the hall was filled at nine in the morning of 8 September with a reliable crowd, so that hostile groups arriving later could not get in. Apart from endorsing the proposed dividend for the next ten years, the main business was a vote of confidence in the directors, which was proposed by Postmaster-General Craggs and seconded in a long speech by Hungerford, the promoter of the Bubble Act, who assured the meeting that in all his experience he had never known such wonderful results to be produced in so short a time. The universal wealth flowing from the original scheme had washed away all party differences, and the country was at peace with itself for the first time in a generation. Town, country, and Church had all benefited—'not a few of the reverend clergy having got great sums'—and he only hoped the directors had done as well for themselves as they had done for the nation.

At this point an interruption by some August annuitants was howled down and a motion that they should be allowed to withdraw from their disastrous bargain defeated. The concluding speech was made by the Duke of Portland, who said he could not understand what reason anyone had to be dissatisfied. This impressed everybody, for the Duke's holding was known to be large, and much of it* had been bought at long prices.[9]

This sort of thing could not save the stock now. The day Charles Blunt cut his throat 'upon some discontent', as the papers put it, the price was verging on 750: when Craggs wrote that there was nothing worth reporting it was barely 700; the day after the packed General Court it sank to 575, and the receipts for the Fourth Money Subscription went to 20 per cent. discount. With the stock went Blunt's reputation and his power over his fellow directors. He was deserted even by the decemvirs with whom he had 'sold the bear' in the spring. The day the stock went below 600 he was handed an illiterate note signed with receipt numbers 'F.4, C.6, K.93' warning him that unless he let the August annuitants withdraw his life was in danger. This was no joke, for not long afterwards he was shot at in the street by an exasperated speculator.[10]

Applebee's Weekly Journal reported that even when the transfer books were closed 'light skirmishes happen every day between the two nations called the Transferrers and Accepters'. It was thought that the transferrers, being for the most part professional operators, would get their money from the noble, political, and military amateurs who made up the bulk of the accepters and were used, by their code, to honour gambling debts. But this was an inadequate generalization about a completely chaotic state of affairs. Not all accepters were amateurs. Two big bankers in Cornhill were known to have accepted £14,000 South Sea for delivery in October at 1,100, for which they would have to raise £154,000. Bargains like this could be complied with, if at all, only by unloading

---

* Not all of it. In March he had been allowed by the Company to convert a substantial annuity into South Sea stock on highly favourable terms.

stock and scrip in increasingly ruinous quantities on the collapsing market.[11]

When the books opened again in 12 September paper fortunes were being demolished on every side. An attempt had been made to prepare for this reopening by a relaxation of the austere terms of the last subscription and doubling the time allowed to pay the instalments—a last feeble gesture of Blunt's policy. But this issue remained obstinately at a discount, and from now onwards affairs were out of Blunt's hands. In little over a fortnight he had sunk from being the most courted to being the most despised and hated man in London.

In the only course now open to the Company, he could have been nothing but an embarrassment.

This only course was an appeal to the Bank of England, which the Company, under Blunt's guidance, had outbid, affronted, and done their best to supplant. Even without him the approach had to be indirect, and was only achieved by the mediation of a group from the East India Company, with whom Fellowes, Joye, Janssen, and Chester had a meeting on 15 September. Next day the two groups had a conference with three Bank directors, Delmé, Gould, and Heathcote.[12]

Sir Gilbert Heathcote, the personification, though no longer the Governor, of the Bank, was now in his seventieth year. He was reputed the richest commoner in England and was probably the most seasoned man of business in Europe. On 17 September the old man who had defied Harley and bullied Queen Anne was summoned before the regency to report on the conversations with the Company and advise on the rescue of public credit. It cannot but have given him a sense of triumph and grim satisfaction.

He was a man on whom emotional appeals and stories of bad luck made no impression, and he had his lifelong rival at his mercy. The only hope was that as a lifelong Whig he would be prepared to rescue the régime from the political bankruptcy which, as Craggs now saw, loomed beyond the financial calamity.

Two days after Heathcote's meeting with the Regency

there was a conference at the General Post Office between the Company, the ministers, and the Bank. Apart from Postmaster-General Craggs, who presided, there were five representatives from each. Those from the Government were Secretary Craggs, Chancellor Aislabie, the Duke of Kent, Townshend, and Walpole, who had dashed up from Norfolk to attend to his own and the nation's financial affairs in the previous week. The Bank's team was led by Heathcote and Governor Hanger. The South Sea party was the same as before, with the addition of the banker Gore, and did not include either Blunt or any of the Sword Blade partners.

The discussion started at nine in the evening, and at the end of six hours Heathcote was still refusing to commit himself to anything. 'I can by no means be so hasty,' he is reported to have said at one point, 'for old men cannot walk so fast as the young.' The most he would concede was that the Bank would consider an arrangement of which Walpole then and there made a memorandum. Whether the arrangement was of Walpole's devising it is impossible to say.

The drowning Company was eager to represent even this as a commitment, and largely because of this the document drawn up by Walpole in the small hours of 20 September has come to be known as the 'Bank Contract'. It was not formally a contract at all, but contained three proposals:

1. The Bank to raise £3 million from the market on its own credit, and by an appeal to national sentiment.
2. This £3 million to be lent to the Company by the Bank for one year.
3. The debt of £3·75 million due from the government to the Bank, of which notice of redemption had already been given, to be redeemed forthwith by a transfer of South Sea stock from the Company to the Bank at a rate which remained to be agreed.

By this arrangement the Company would be able to lay its hands on some cash, and have the price of its stock underpinned at whatever figure the Bank was prepared to offer for the block of shares it was to take: but even so the reversal of fortunes was dramatically illustrated by the third point. The debt in question represented the original capital (plus some later accretions) which Heathcote himself had helped to raise for the government a quarter of a century before. When the intended redemption had been announced the gesture had been held to mark the end of the Bank's peculiar predominance in government finance. Now the rival concern was only too glad to hand over a great part of its only asset—surplus stock—at the Bank's valuation, so that the Bank could become South Sea's biggest shareholder.

On one further point which was raised Heathcote was adamant. He would consider saving the South Sea—for the Bank's sake and on the Bank's own terms: but he would not lift a finger to save the Sword Blade from the consequences of dishonesty and folly. 'If the South Sea Company is to be wedded to the Bank,' he declared, 'it cannot be allowed to keep a mistress.' It was the end of the duel between the Sword Blade and the Bank of England. The importance of the midnight meeting at the Post Office lies not in any agreement about the South Sea crisis, but in the fact that never thereafter was the pre-eminence of the Bank of England to be effectively challenged. This stand of Heathcote's was enshrined in the concluding words of Walpole's note: 'That the cash of the South Sea Company be kept at the Bank.'[13]

If Heathcote vindicated the Bank's pre-eminence on 20 September, he also, by the means he took, precipitated the nationwide financial panic which began when the Sword Blade opened its doors on the following Monday.

The inflationary paper they had issued over the previous six months poured in from all sides and they were reduced to ordering up wagon-loads of silver to pay out slowly in small change. One lucky note-holder got no less than £8,000 paid out to him in shillings and sixpences. But it could not last. On Saturday, 24 September, a notice appeared on the closed doors of the Sword Blade announcing that all obligations would be met in due course at 5 per cent. interest, and that in the meantime creditors could have South Sea stock valued at 400 per cent. if they preferred. On the same day a curt note appeared in the margin of the Court Book of the Bank of England: 'Sword Blade Comp. don't pay.'

Since the current price of South Sea stock was 370, and this virtual insolvency of the Company's bank sent it skimming down to 180 by the end of the month, the terms the Sword Blade suggested were hardly acceptable to its creditors. These might have even been more angry if they had known of the precautions that Turner, Caswall, and Sawbridge had taken to safeguard their retreat. As far back as 25 June the partners had formed a new banking firm in which the ostensible partners were Robinson Knight and Henry Blunt, the nephew of Robert Knight and the son of Sir John Blunt. To this new firm the old partners had paid over in cash the substantial sum of £1,166,875. 4s. 1d. The collaboration of Blunt and Knight in this transaction not only underlines the intimacy between the directing spirits of the Company and the Sword Blade partnership, but suggests that even at the height of their success Blunt and Knight were not the complete dupes of their own pretensions. Suspicion is redoubled when it is noticed that Charles Stanhope, Secretary of the Treasury, on realizing his gigantic holding of fictitious stock for £250,000 at the Sword Blade on 11 June, received it in notes signed by Henry Blunt, and not by the senior partners; which notes were in due course honoured by the new firm.[14]

$$\star \qquad \star \qquad \star$$

Meanwhile, on the morrow of the Post Office meeting, the South Sea directors, with their varying degrees of guilty knowledge, had to face a General Court very different in temper from the packed assembly of 8 September. Sir John Fellowes, who can have had little sleep, managed after an apologetic speech* to extract authority to continue negotiations

* 'The affairs of your Company in relation to the price of their stock and subscriptions having taken an unexpected turn to the disadvantage of the Proprietors (although your Court of Directors have not been wanting in their best endeavours to preserve the same) . . . they have used their utmost care to accomplish [an agreement

with the Bank, to whose generosity he made fulsome references. Pulteney was put up to allay the disturbing rumours about tension with Spain over Gibraltar. Then the Sub-Governor announced what the meeting had really been waiting for. The directors were considering what relief could be given to the annuitants and subscribers who had taken their stock at 1,000. Weight was added to this—though it had been expressed in the vaguest of terms—by speeches from the East India magnate Decker, and Postmaster-General Craggs.

Even to mention this possibility was a most painful thing for the directors. It meant writing down assets by more than 50 per cent. If the terms for the Third and Fourth Subscriptions and the August conversion were reduced from 1,000 to 400, the Company would be surrendering £28 million stock that would otherwise be surplus, and £37 million future cash income from subscribed instalments. After allowing for the bold midsummer bonus of stock and the transfer to the Bank, the net surplus of stock from the whole vast operation would come to only about £20 million instead of more than £50 million; and out of this £10 million had already been pledged to the money subscribers while £8 million would shortly be due to the Exchequer. In other words, the Company's income might, with luck, cover a 15 per cent. dividend over the next five years.

There was, however, no alternative. Among the innumerable creditors' meetings which had formed since the beginning of September, like crystals in a sudden frost far the most vocal was that of the annuitants and subscribers at 1,000. Their spokesman, struggling for this moment into the prominence for which he had always pined, was Eustace Budgell, who at this meeting made a scathing attack on the directors. He is an unsympathetic yet in some ways sorrowful figure, the ineffective shadow of his notoriously successful cousin Addison. First as a journalist, then as a climbing politician, he had clung

with the Bank] which they have reason to believe they shall be able to effect.' To be fair, it must be admitted that Fellowes did not yet represent the agreement as achieved. He spared the Sword Blade any reference to the approaching transfer of the Company's account.

to Addison's coat-tails, devilling *Spectators* and making himself useful in the official world of Dublin. But Addison had died too soon, and Budgell had none of his cousin's power to ingratiate himself with influential men. He had alienated Sunderland, lost the Irish jobs Addison had got for him, and had at last ventured his fortune in the South Sea in a desperate attempt to achieve the foundations of political independence. At thirty-five he had already crossed the line which divides promise and failure. This embittered journalist who in the end, consumed by paranoia, was to leap into the Thames with his pockets full of stones,* was a fitting leader for men made desperate by disappointment, and on 20 September only one director, Chester, had the courage to reply to his charges.[15]

Ten days later, however, when they faced another General Court—the third since the beginning of September—the directors were more confident. Since the original Post Office conference, they had had three more meetings with the Bank, two of them with ministers present, and they had brought themselves to believe that agreement had now been reached on all major points. The vital evening had been that of 23 September, which had resulted in a further document, also drawn up by Walpole, stating that the price for the £3·75 million of Bank capital to be transformed into South Sea stock should be 400. This second part of the 'Bank Contract', which was ambiguously described as 'minutes or agreement' by the Company and as 'proposal' by the Bank, had been agreed to, in their respective understandings of it, by the two governing bodies. The Bank had already opened their rescue subscription, Sir Gilbert Heathcote was now present all ready to make a heartening speech about having seen many storms and weathered them all; and Sub-Governor Fellowes felt able to open the proceedings with the encouraging news that 'the directors had come to the following agreement', of which he then gave the terms. No doubt it meant the end of the

---

* Addison and the Addisonian success, which had eluded him, tormented Budgell to the bitter end. After his suicide a slip of paper was found on his desk saying
What Cato did, and Addison approved
Cannot be wrong.

Company's independence, but with the market price of the stock at 200 the Bank's readiness to pay 400 seemed plain salvation. For the unfortunate Fellowes himself, with a holding of £86,436 South Sea stock, the difference meant £172,872.

Budgell, who that day, by an interesting coincidence, received a loan of £500 from Sub-Governor Fellowes, welcomed the news of a firm agreement, but signs of dissension began to appear among the directors when he went on to demand that all speculative transfers of the receipts for the later subscriptions should be revalued in the same way as the later subscriptions themselves.* Although the Sub-Governor had already explained that this was not the policy of the directors and was in any case impossible, several of them, including Master, Janssen, Ingram, Houlditch, and Blunt himself, openly declared that it was the only fair thing to do. The meeting grew more and more disorderly, demands were made for an inquiry 'to bring to justice the betrayers of their country', and a certain Captain Maggot denounced the director Page by name for having nominated himself to £50,000 in the Third Money Subscription and then selling the receipts at 250 per cent. premium—a transaction which, if it took place, would have netted Page a profit of £6,500 for an outlay of £10,000.

Postmaster-General Craggs recalled the meeting to order with an energetic appeal that the Bank's subscription should be supported by those who had gained in the summer. They would fail now at their peril, 'for 'tis not locking up our monies that can now give security. No, every man in England is concerned: and for my part I would not be seen at such a time as this to have more money by me than would pay for a week's expenses.' The more general attitude, however, was expressed by Walpole, who at that moment was on his way back to Norfolk with as much gold as his bankers could lay their hands on.[16]

*　　　*　　　*

* *Scott* (iii. 328), by a curious oversight, attributes Budgell's speech on this occasion to Sub-Governor Fellowes. He also misdates the General Court.

Far away in Hanover, King George had only just heard from his regents about the calamities which had overtaken the country and Company he had left behind so prosperous. They had put off writing until 21 September—no doubt so as to include what comfort he got from the Post Office conference —and only then had Secretary Craggs and his colleagues screwed up the courage to lay before their master 'the very extraordinary case which hath happened in the last fortnight'. Having done so, they gave full rein to their despondency. The exchange was about to turn against the country; despair and bankruptcy were everywhere apparent; an obvious oppor- tunity was presented to His Majesty's enemies, both at home and abroad. They concluded that 'the only secure remedy against the many dangerous consequences of this accident are to be found in an early meeting of Parliament, animated by Your Majesty's presence'. No reference was made to the fact that the King's own outlay of over £60,000 in stock and subscriptions was now hardly worth £12,000. Admittedly, most had come from earlier capital gains, and some of the King's money had been invested elsewhere; but the King could not be depended upon to take so philosophical a view.

This dismal message, sent by the speediest possible means, took the best part of a week to reach Hanover, and even then the business of moving George and his court was so cum- bersome that his animating presence could not be expected until the end of October, given favourable winds.

A Jacobite *coup d'état* was being freely talked about, and Harley, old and broken though he was, was being assured by his friends that he must be ready to come forward and save the country when the right moment came. 'If it pleases divine providence yet to spare this sinful nation', wrote his nephew, 'I hope you may be the instrument under the divine conduct.'

The Pretender himself did not entirely fail to speak at this crisis to those whom he still regarded as his subjects, but what he said showed him to be as tepid and respectable as he had always been. Copies of his declaration to his English supporters were intercepted by Craggs's postal officials. What might have been a clarion call to a bewildered people against a culpable régime proved merely a dignified request for a bloodless restoration. The most interesting thing in it was the news of the approaching birth of an heir to the Stuart claim; who when his turn came, was to press it more effectively than his father had ever done.[17]

The Pretender's timidity was not entirely due to lack of enterprise. It was true that there were still embers of unquenched Jacobitism in England—or perhaps one should say discontent sometimes exploded in the form of Jacobite sentiments. Soldiers who had had too much to drink called for the Duke of Ormonde's march in taverns, and irritated minor officials sometimes said things would have been better but for King George. There were unemployed politicians of the last reign who thought they were not too old for another round of power. But King James's situation was fundamentally weak. He was now a refugee in Rome because, thanks to Stanhope's diplomatic reinsurance arrangements, he no longer had the countenance of France; and Rome was no place from which to capture English sympathy. Spain was no longer likely to help him. But most important of all, Tories and Jacobites were in no position to criticize harm that came from the South Sea. No matter what Whigs had done to enlarge it (and Aislabie, at any rate, was no Whig) the South Sea was still, in the public eye, the Tory institution of the day of its foundation. Blunt had first made his mark as Harley's financial adviser. Hungerford was a veteran Tory who had appeared as counsel for Jacobite traitors. The Company as a whole had always opposed that bastion of the Revolution Settlement founded by King William, the Bank of England, whence alone rescue now seemed conceivable. The first ideological casualty of the disaster was the conception which had preoccupied Tory politicians for so many years: a counterpoise to the moneyed interest which should yet be within the financial system.

CHAPTER X

Fall (2)

THE ECONOMIC CONFUSION of the last three months of 1720 has perhaps no parallel in the history of England. A tangle of ruined credit sprawled over the country like a vast, overgrown beanstalk, withering. The gentleman in Exchange Alley who said he had bilked his cabman 'on account of having been bilked himself' stands for a universal picture of default. In some cases the default was genuine; in others it was a panic-stricken clinging to cash. Each aggravated the other.[1]

It was not merely that the bubble had burst, with a consequent evaporation of surplus credit and the ruin of a group of speculators. The whole system of credit which had gradually grown up with the expanding economy since the middle of the previous century had suddenly collapsed. England was thrown back on to a currency system which it had outgrown, and could no longer tolerate. 'We are at present', wrote one of the shrewdest analysts of the situation, 'much where we were a hundred years ago.' The shock with which the relapse was felt is a revealing measure of the real progress of the economy.[2]

Paper currency had penetrated deeply even in the provinces. When the Bristol mail was robbed in August between Slough and Colnbrook the loss was put at £60,000—all in paper. No doubt a good deal of this haul represented the professional dealings of the Bristol banks—five of which failed in September and early October—but even this cannot be said of the packet which was stolen at Hounslow about the same time from Isaac Gilpin, maltster, of the little Oxfordshire village of Warborough. It contained shares in Pennsylvania flax plantations and an Essex land improvement company, and the endorsements show that these had been changing hands among other humble rural tradesmen.[3]

One estimate of the credit which, as a contemporary said, had now become 'as mere a piece of waste paper as if a prayer or creed were written on it instead of money' was two-thirds of the whole credit in the country. It must certainly have far exceeded the amount of metallic money in circulation. Outstanding Sword Blade notes alone amounted to hundreds of thousands, if not millions of pounds—denominations of £500, £1,000, or even more were often met with. And besides these was the infinite variety of more or less formal yet contingently negotiable notes emitted by goldsmiths, tradesmen, and private persons, whose capacity to pay became suddenly doubtful: such as Gideon Drake, an Alley operator who had latterly specialized as an estate agent. The holders of his notes 'marked with a sheaf of arrows' were invited to meet at the Sun Tavern on 4 October 'on special affairs'.[4]

While people had grown into the habit of using paper as currency, they had not grown out of the habit of distinguishing it from coin. Nor was there any particular kind of paper which was held generally to be more like money than any other. There was no accepted grammar of negotiable paper. Stock, bonds, notes, bills, receipts—all participated in the general pool of paper currency which had undergone uncontrolled expansion during the boom, and now could only be negotiated with difficulty, if at all. What was generally referred to as the collapse of public credit was not unlike what would happen today if bank notes suddenly, and without being replaced, ceased to be legal tender.

Financial pamphleteering was the one activity which showed no signs of slump, and the innumerable remedies that were proposed demonstrated that the inventive spirit, tortured but resilient, was at least still alive. Much of the advice was unhelpful, like the futile numerology aimed at establishing what South Sea stock was now 'really' worth, and Archibald Hutcheson's suggestion that all bargains made during the boom should be deemed made by lunatics, and so annulled. But two commentators at least fastened on the clue of an undifferentiated paper currency and the facile reception that had been given to Law's maxim that credit and money were the same. One was Sir Humphrey Mackworth, the corrupt old promoter of Welsh mining companies, who had now retired from active business. Paper credit, he insisted, though it was capable of performing the same function as money, was not money, but its representative. What was needed was a government-backed paper currency 'too difficult to be counterfeited', which would by law have the same status as metal money. Povey had much the same thought, and a psychologically more acute device, in his proposal for what would now be called 'token sterling'—a new metal coinage with a tenth of the old bullion content but the same face value, which could be used for redeeming devalued paper and getting the circulation moving again.[5]

But schemes like these were utterly beyond the capacity of the government machine. The moves it could make, even though in the right direction, were limited by its physical resources. On 5 October, the Lords of the Treasury, after a dinner-table conference with some of the South Sea directors, decreed an immediate increase in the interest on Exchequer Bills, to assist their circulation; and after some delay the Mint was set to work urgently striking fresh supplies of coinage, which began to find its way into the economy towards the end of the month. But that was the sum total of direct government intervention. Sheer physical limitation on what could be done administratively was throughout an exaggerating factor, both in the rise and the fall. A prime cause of both had been the facility with which credit could be created, and be abolished.

During the whole cycle the South Sea clerks performed marvels, but the speed of events imposed an impossible task on them. During the boom the pace at which they could issue scrip or record transfers had inevitably been outstripped by the gossamer arrangements made on the credit of what would one day happen formally. Even in October the annuitants who had converted in May had not got their scrip, though many had already sold it. If this total informality of the actual market, compared with the laborious processes of the formal one, had accelerated the boom, it produced chaos in the slump. In the confusion of bargains which were not only unrecorded, but which it would be very disadvantageous for many people to have recorded, it was hard to tell who was truly creditor and who debtor, and for what; or how far intentions had been carried into execution in particular instances. Repudiation was as common as default; recriminations commoner than settlement.

The excess and disorganization of credit were far more important causes of the collapse than the application for the writs of Scire Facias against the Billingsley companies which is often quoted beside them. The tradition of moralizing about the South Sea is perhaps the reason for fastening on this particular incident as the clue to the Company's undoing, because it seems so appropriate that such an act of jealousy should have rebounded on its initiators. But the Billingsley companies did not collapse. The writs were never issued. The York Buildings Company carried on, not wholly without success, for several years afterwards. The slump in the Billingsley shares affected only a segment of the market, and contributed to the final catastrophe only to the extent that it happened at almost the same moment as the South Sea books were reopened and a general settlement was attempted in consequence.

*　　*　　*

The cry that hundreds of families had been ruined had gone up on every side and has echoed down the centuries. 'There never was such distraction', wrote poor William Windham three days after the crash of the Sword Blade. 'You can't imagine the number of families undone . . . many a £100,000 man not worth a groat, and it grieves me to think of some of them.'[6]

This must be accepted with reservations. For many the 'ruin' they now bewailed was simply the converse of the 'wealth' on which they had been congratulating themselves only a few weeks before. Pulteney wrote philosophically that ' 'Tis ridiculous to tell you what a sum I might have been master of; but since I had not discretion enough to secure that, 'tis some comfort to me to have put my affairs in such a way that let what will happen I shall be no loser by it'. But it was not easy for the Duke of Chandos to be philosophical when he found, in a review of his portfolio on the very day Windham wrote his *cri de cœur*, that although he was still £200,000 up, its total value had shrunk over the past month by more than £700,000. Chandos was the biggest money giant of his day, and could afford to hang on in the hope of better times; but even he was finding it difficult to raise an urgently required £70,000, either at home or abroad, and for a poorer man like the South Sea director Edmundson the collapse meant penury. In June he had reckoned himself worth £50,000; at the end of September £10,000, if that.[7]

Such losses in fairy gold, and the innumerable public and private adjustments that were later made, limited the real losses. Nevertheless, the shock was felt by every family of any consequence in England, even if it was far beyond the immediately speculating circle; and on some the effects were crippling and permanent.

The Duke of Portland's investments brought the family King William had made one of the richest in England very near bankruptcy, and prevented it from playing an influential part in affairs for nearly two generations. The Duke had to put in for a colonial governorship, and spent the rest of his life governing Jamaica, whence he dared not return even five years later, so embarrassed were his affairs. The sufferings of the Scottish peerage were in proportion to its enthusiasm for speculation, and may well have contributed to its comparative failure ever afterwards to make an impression on politics south of the Border. The Duke of Montrose, Lords Rothes, Dunmore, Hyndford, Irvine, and Belhaven had all played and lost. Lord Irvine also applied for a colony, and was given Barbados. He died before being able to go there, and it was then given to Belhaven, who had been in the retinue of the Prince of Wales and an especially prodigal gambler in both Paris and London. On the voyage out, the ship carrying Belhaven—ironically enough, it was the *Royal Anne*, of which the director Edmundson had been purser—was wrecked in the spring storms off the Scillies, and he was drowned. Understandably no more ruined Scottish noblemen applied for this post.[8]

The medium business man and minor diplomatist Christian Cole speaks in his correspondence with his bankers as eloquently about the general predicament as any tale of fallen grandeur. On 29 September he wrote to Messrs. Warner and Snow begging for time to pay off his overdraft and imploring them in the meantime not to sell the security they held against it. 'A promise of that kind will make me easy in hopes of paying your full demand with good interest in a little time . . . remember what a confounded bargain I have.' Warner and Snow demanded further security for a month's grace. 'You could not ask anything', was the desperate reply, 'I would not most readily comply with, were it in my power, but in truth I have so foolishly embarrassed my affairs that I cannot without great inconvenience do anything just now.' A week later he was explaining that he was himself unable to collect £10,000 he was owed, although 'it was actually money lent and paid out'. 'I have entangled my affairs to such a degree that it is really out of my power to do what you desire.'[9]

Snow probably foreclosed, for his house survived to earn this tribute from Gay:

> O thou whose penetrative wisdom found
> The South Sea rocks and shelves where thousands drowned,
> When credit sunk, and commerce gasping lay,
> Thou stoodst, nor sent one bill unpaid away.

Bankers could not afford to be merciful, for banks themselves were going down like ninepins—houses, too, with reputations going back to the previous century: Atwill and Hammond, Cox and Cleve, Long and Bland, Nathaniel Bostock, Mitford and Mertens, Daniel and Joseph Norcott, all stopped payment during October. Martin's was badly shaken as a result of the head of the firm's faith in the tips of his old clerk Surman. 'I was as blinded by other People's advice', he wrote, 'as the South Sea directors.' Even the more cautious Hoare's, which had bought nothing between the end of May and an unlucky August flutter of £1,000 in the Fourth Subscription, had to unload a great deal of stock at alarmingly low prices during September and October, cutting their net profit on dealing in South Sea stock over the year to a mere £28,000.[10]

The two chartered insurance companies, the London and the Royal Exchange, found themselves in a position of peculiar difficulty. At the beginning of August their shares had stood at 102 and 166 respectively. At the end of September these figures were 30 and 50. The first instalments for their privileges had been paid over to the Exchequer in July, and the second instalments were due on 22 September. Preparations to raise them were overtaken in the tidal wave caused by the crash of the Sword Blade; there were rowdy general meetings, at one of which Lord Chetwynd, who was presiding, was shouted down, and both companies entered a phase of highly complex financial reconstruction. Their position was made still more precarious by heavy claims on the London for losses at sea in the September gales, and the failure of Sir Justus Beck, one of the leading directors of the Royal Exchange. Nevertheless, at heavy cost to their portfolios and the welfare of the market, they managed to scrape together about a fifth of the amount due, which was paid over to the Exchequer in October. At the same time they stipulated for an amendment of their charters to allow them to write fire as well as marine business. Their survival being so closely connected with the solvency of the Civil List, the necessary instruments were prepared at once and sent urgently to Hanover for the King to sign.[11]

The distress, as has been said, spread far beyond London and the speculating classes. The urban workmen who, especially in London, depended so much on the prosperity of the well-to-do, suffered with their employers and their employers' customers. Work stopped on half-finished ships and partly-built houses. Edmundson's new house in Maunsel Street, Westminster, was abandoned with only the outside walls completed. Sales of ships at Lloyd's were cancelled for lack of bids. Luxury trades, such as high-class tailoring, watches, plate, and vehicles, in which so many Londoners worked, came almost to a standstill. Out of forty coaches on which one London yard was working, twenty-eight were cancelled in September, among them, perhaps, 'the fine crane-necked chariot lined with flowered velvet made new this summer', which was advertised on 27 September as 'to be sold a peni-worth'. A grim index was a decline in coal prices, which had been stable all the summer, even though winter was on the way. Unemployment and food riots were a more serious possibility than Jacobitism so far as the towns were concerned. Edward Harley advised his uncle to stay in the country: 'As things appear to me I cannot see how people in London will have money to buy necessaries, what that will produce among all the handicraft people is easy to guess.'[12]

The countryside had to bear blows of another kind. Land, whose value as the ultimately desirable investment had soared with the South Sea, remained hitched to the star on its downward course. As a result, many landlords who had never speculated themselves and hardly knew the use of notes, found themselves hard pressed on account of credit run up on the inflated value of their estates. A good many had entered into contracts of sale with City men who could not now complete. Blunt had six such contracts on his hands when the blow fell. Surman had even more, owing over £100,000 in four different counties. Francis Eyles had undertaken to buy six properties in Wiltshire; Stephen Child one at Kingston for a price based on forty-six times the rent. Worst placed of all were the vendors to the scoundrel Houlditch, who had paid for hundreds of acres by transferring stock to his victims at the top of the market or by subscribing on their behalf to the later money subscriptions.

Even if the landlord had escaped endangering his estate, he found his Michaelmas rent painfully hard to collect. A Canon of Christ Church reported 'almost a total stop of payments of rents' in Oxford, 'even from those who were never used to fail a day'. Beside this, the 'wonderful luck' of Keill, the Professor of Astronomy, who had actually got back the £3,150 he had ventured with Waller, was not much consolation to the Common Room. Dons, indeed, had been hard hit, collectively and individually. Among several Oxford and Cambridge colleges which had invested in the South Sea, King's, encouraged by earlier successful speculations, had bought at 765 that summer. At Oxford 'Franks, of Merton . . . is thrown into the Castle for debts by his adventures in the South Sea'. The Rector of Exeter's daughter lost the £1,200 her father had left her and had to become a governess. Newton, who had somehow been persuaded to re-enter the market after his cautious withdrawal in spring, lost £20,000, and, although the most imperturbable of men, could never bear to hear the South Sea referred to for the rest of his life. Intelligence was no protection. Lady Mary Wortley Montagu lost not only her own money, but an admirer's, and he blackmailed her unmercifully for years as a result.[13]

Across the North Sea and the Channel the commercial world was demonstrating its oneness in disaster as in prosperity. In Holland the shares of the Dutch West India Company and the numerous insurance schemes sank in October with devastating suddenness. The big Dutch banks were shortening sail by recalling advances made in London, refusing further credit, and selling stock held as collateral. Prince Kourakine, the adventurous Russian envoy at The Hague, who had been one of the heroes of the Kalverstraat and deep in the Welsh Copper Company on Exchange Alley as well, vanished altogether from society. Dayrolles, the British envoy, was a ruined man. Moses Haasverberg's English coffee-house at Amsterdam, where English business men were accustomed to gather and read the London papers over 'English elixir', Epsom salts, and other favourite British beverages in which the proprietor specialized, was sacked and burned by a crowd of infuriated Dutchmen.[14]

In France the situation was, if possible, even bleaker, although some Englishmen still professed to find satisfaction in contemplating it. Since midsummer, with Law resisting all the way, there had been a painful return to orthodox finance, which was completed in October by the formal abolition of the paper currency and the remonetization of gold and silver. With this naturally went a reversal of Law's policy of driving bullion out of the country. All the efforts of the government were directed to repatriating gold and silver held by Frenchmen abroad.

The whole European scene was darkened by the inexorable and anxiously reported advance of the smallpox epidemic northwards across France. By mid-October the cordon was on the Isère. Hideous accounts of the casualties mingled with the stock exchange news, further sapping confidence. 'The fury of the distemper', wrote one correspondent, 'cannot be described. It begins with a light pain in the head and is followed by a cold shivering which ends in convulsions and death.' Thirty thousand were said to have died in Marseilles, and reports suggested that in the south of France civilized life had almost broken down.[15]

Ordinary men were still devout, and layman and preacher alike quickly drew the moral that judgement was being passed on the human vanity and materialism of the past twenty years. It was looked on as particularly significant that the plague had first manifested itself in a merchant ship. The trade that had made men rich was being used by the Almighty to punish their ambition. Such feelings had played their part in destroying confidence in the late summer; now they deepened the depression.

This belief that trade itself was infected harmed more than confidence. The extreme quarantine regulations which all countries now imposed were aimed especially against merchant shipping and supposedly plague-ridden goods. In October twenty-two ships were held up by the British authorities in the Downs, forbidden to unload. The Dutch regulations were more savage still. In the Texel three ships from the Levant were burned complete with their cargoes, and the crews compelled to wade ashore naked to undergo isolation on an islet.[16]

*　　　*　　　*

It was said that someone had been knocked down in Exchange Alley just for laughing at a joke. *Mist's Journal*, which had always been against the government, recommended the brokers to study Seneca. Such bargains as there were, were offered by furtive bears, one of whom was nearly lynched when it was found he held none of the stock he was peddling below the market price. Budgell held an unofficial meeting of South Sea proprietors with the aim of forcing the convocation of another General Court—every man, he declared, should be present at the shaving of his own beard; but he refused to discuss what proposal should be made at a General Court, and the proceedings got out of hand when someone 'who, 'tis said, has lately lost a great deal of money, and was perhaps a little in liquor' declared loudly that the directors were a 'cabal of sharpers'. Billers, Caswall's colleague as Sheriff of London, whose zeal for duty had been strengthened by a 'loan' of £500 from Sub-Governor Fellowes three days previously, took the opportunity of dispersing the assembly by threatening them with the Riot Act.[17]

All eyes were fixed on the Bank of England, where the subscription of rescue provided for under the 'Bank Contract' was being taken in the last days of September and the first week of October. The Treasury, the Prince of Wales, and the Duke of Marlborough ostentatiously paid in large sums. But the cashiers were under strict orders to accept nothing but cash and the very safest paper. Sword Blade notes, in particular, were refused. When the books were closed it was found that names had been put down for only just over two of three millions aimed at, and on this the first call yielded no more than £340,000 cash.

Even while the subscription was still being taken the South

201

Sea's committee of directors was appearing almost every day at the Bank asking for some cash on account and the completion of the undertaking, which they supposed the Bank had given, to buy £3 million shares at 400. They kept up their vigil on the 3rd, 4th, 5th, and 7th, when they reproachfully told the Bank directors that from inquiries they had made the Bank's solicitor seemed to have no instructions about preparing the necessary instruments, although he admitted 'the Secretary of the Bank had mentioned something of it to him'. That was a Friday. On the following Tuesday, when they came again, they were fobbed off on the ground that the Court of the Bank was in session, and saw nobody although they hung about till long past dinner-time. Next day they managed to see the Governor, and reported the result to Secretary Craggs in an indignant letter: 'We pressed in plain terms that they would expedite to which the Governor answered he would take the rest of the gentlemen's directions about it.' The Governor had been equally evasive about an advance on account, 'though we used all the arguments we thought proper on the occasion, they only said they would consider of it and send us word when they had come to a resolution'.[18]

This game of cat and mouse was not entirely due to cruelty on the Bank's part to its humiliated rivals. Behind the scenes the Bank was struggling with one of the ugliest runs in its career. Harley's nephew had foreseen as much as soon as he knew the result of the first Post Office conference and the condition about the transfer of the South Sea Company's account. 'The stipulation about the Sword Blade Company is like to have the same effect as the Bank's formerly breaking Shepheard had, which brought a run upon themselves.' For a fortnight after recording the failure of their rival, the Bank came very near having to close their own doors. All over London they called in loans and bought up bullion, adding further to the devastation of the credit system as they did so. These were the weeks in which the great Sir Justus Beck of the Royal Exchange went down, and a rumour spread that even Sir Matthew Decker was in difficulties. Customers presenting notes at the Bank for redemption—as many did—had interest-bearing notes pressed on them in exchange, if only they would defer their call for cash.[19]

In mid-October, with the arrival of 100,000 guineas in gold from Rotterdam, the Bank was out of danger. But all round them the financial world had been trampled ruthlessly under-foot in the struggle for dear life. By this time South Sea was quoted at 200 nominal; and if one thing was clear it was that a rescue of the South Sea by buying their shares at 400, as had been proposed at the end of September, would be merely quixotic.

During the second week in October, Walpole's banker, Robert Jacomb, whom Walpole had just appointed his deputy as Paymaster of the Forces, discussed the situation with Townshend; and on the 11th he wrote about his conversation to Walpole in Norfolk. This letter is significant both for what it said and did not say. It was devoted to the outline of a plan for restoring the situation by a method which included neither the purchase of shares by the Bank nor a loan to the Company; and not a word was said about the Bank Contract, which was based on these two operations. To Walpole it must have been perfectly clear that his advisers in London foresaw—with what degree of inner knowledge we cannot know—that the Bank would not or could not carry out the obligations of which Walpole had made the note in his own handwriting only a fortnight before, and on which the Company and his colleagues in the government were depending. This knowledge, and the fact that Jacomb was working on an alternative solution, Walpole kept for the time being strictly to himself. These were political trumps, but the time had not yet come to play them. Walpole never displayed his celebrated political patience more effectively than by staying in Norfolk for the next four weeks.[20]

Meanwhile, the South Sea directors were still kept in play by the Bank. On the evening of 25 October they demanded point blank the fixing of a day on which the proceeds of the rescue subscription would be handed over to them. The response was a cool request for a statement of their cash requirements in detail and in writing. On receiving the statement three days later, the Bank doled out £100,000 cash on account and 'presumed the Company did not require an immediate answer', since several public holidays fell in the next few days and the Bank would be closed.[21]

By this time the King was on the move across Germany with Stanhope in his train, and a thoroughly alarmed Sunderland posting ahead of him. 'I know very well', the First Lord of the Treasury wrote on the road to the Earl of Carlisle, 'that when misfortunes happen in most countries, and particularly in England, it's the way to lay it at the door of those who share in the Administration.' But at least there was the Bank Contract. He arrived in London on 1 November and immediately sent for the Bank directors. They did not see fit to tell him what was undoubtedly in their minds, and left him with the impression that the Bank Contract still had at any rate some chance of success. Walpole was not in London to consult.[22]

Ten days later, with affairs still in suspense, the King and Stanhope disembarked at Margate. They had been delayed by a bad crossing, and the royal squadron, at its first sailing, had been driven back by a storm into Helvoetsluys. The City had put up decorations for his arrival, and an illuminated pyramid had been erected outside the Royal Exchange; but the King ignored them, driving straight to St. James's through back streets.[23]

Walpole had arrived in London two days earlier, on 8 November, since it was necessary he should be there to meet the King, as well as to be available for the results of another event which took place on the very day of the royal landing. That day, for the first time in the negotiations beween the Bank and the South Sea, a strong party from the Bank, headed by the Governor, Hanger, appeared at South Sea House without warning. 'The Bank Gentlemen', says the Company's minute of this meeting, 'first asked us if we had considered of adequate security.' Such assurances as could be given on this point were declared by Governor Hanger to be unsatisfactory.

Then, reading from a prepared text, he said that the Company should have the £100,000 made up to the full £340,000 which the first call on the rescue subscription had produced, but that, in view of the state of credit, there would not be a penny more. Having finished, and leaving the South Sea directors no time to recover from their dismay, he handed over a letter formally refusing to take South Sea stock at 400. The Bank Contract was dead.[24]

South Sea stock immediately sank to the new depth of 135. Secretary Craggs gloomily said that the Bank meant to use their whip hand to seize control of the nation's finances. His misgivings were confirmed when Heathcote and his colleagues were summoned before the Treasury Board on 16 November, and met Sunderland's and Aislabie's attempts to bully them into changing their minds with a sullen negative. They absolutely refused to have anything more to do with the Bank Contract; and they did not, even now, reveal the existence of an alternative to it, although they had been negotiating privately with Walpole and Jacomb about it for at least a week.[25]

Sunderland was in the position of a man poised to tread on a stair who finds empty space under his foot. Nothing could be more forbidding than the political situation. The King, who had seen a personal outlay of £66,000 in July shrink in this last plunge to something less than £10,000 nominal, and his whole kingdom in confusion, was in no easy mood. Parliament was to meet in nine days' time and the town was already full of angry and perplexed Members. In spite of the bad impression it was bound to create, there was no alternative but to defer the meeting of Parliament for a fortnight, to give time for reflection.

Now, and not till now, Walpole played his political trumps. He allowed Sunderland and the rest three days more to contemplate their position, and then disclosed to a meeting of Stanhope, Sunderland, Aislabie, and Craggs that he had been making progress towards an alternative solution. This was on 19 November, a Sunday. When the news leaked out on

Monday, it at once had a steadying effect. The ministers had no choice but to commission Walpole to continue his negotiations.[26]

It is difficult to acquit either Walpole or the Bank of systematic and masterly duplicity over the whole affair. No doubt the Bank could plead that as the situation developed they found completion of the contract was beyond their powers; but the point at which both they and Walpole knew this was so was long before the point at which either, for their own purposes, chose to disclose it, and what flowed from it. Beside this, the legal breach of contract itself is insignificant; but that this too had happened was the opinion of counsel whom the South Sea Company afterwards consulted. 'If this contract', wrote the eminent Serjeant Chesshyre, after reading the whole dossier, 'is to be considered by the same rules and measures as contracts of less consequence would be, I do apprehend that this agreement as above set forth is binding on the Bank of England.'[27]

One can understand, then, why Walpole's colleagues, though they greeted him as a saviour, never forgave him. The episode tainted his name for years afterwards, and was flung up in a *Craftsman* article (probably by Aislabie) as late as 1735. Later hints that he had been bribed by the Bank are wide of the mark. Walpole never quite lived down the episode of the Bank Contract because the political world knew it had been the occasion of his decisive and cynical advance to mastery of the situation. In the third week of November he marked his triumph with a long memorandum explaining Jacomb's plan, which he addressed directly to the King and signed himself, though he was not yet a Treasury minister. In nine months he had gone a long way: from advising an undutiful son to rescuing a baffled father.[28]

CHAPTER XI

Winter

THE EQUINOCTIAL GALES did not die down with the year, and December and January continued unseasonably warm, with sudden thundery tempests and heavy downpours. But credit was still frozen solid. It was impossible to send £25 from London to Dublin by normal bill of exchange. As bitter petitions from all over the Kingdom were soon to show, traders and producers everywhere were in real distress. In Dublin beef was fetching a farthing a pound, and the Custom House receipts there in the first week of the new year were less than a twentieth of normal. South Sea paper was suffering with the system it had helped to ruin. In early December South Sea Stock was changing hands painfully for cash at 160-170—several points below the levels from which it had set out so proudly nine months before. For the First Money Subscription, by now nearly paid up in full, 40 per cent. discount was being offered, and the wretched holders of receipts for the Third and Fourth Subscriptions could find no takers at any price.

Nevertheless, as the ministers grew used to Walpole's new plan, they recovered much of their old confidence. By the time Parliament met Craggs was as jaunty, Aislabie as pugnacious as ever. Looked at as a whole, the political situation suddenly seemed not unpromising. The prestige of Stanhope was untouched by any domestic scandal,* and his ambitious

---

* While Stanhope can be acquitted of direct complicity in the affair, there remains a suspicion that he was not above profiting by it. It appears from Surman's accounts that when he settled with Knight in December 1720, Knight reimbursed him for 3,100 South Sea stock transferred to Lord Stanhope by Surman on Knight's behalf. The item is the more suspicious in that the other transferees for whom Knight reimbursed Surman were Spencer Compton and the notorious speculator, Lord Londonderry.

foreign policy was about to pay dividends in a general pacifica-
tion with England as arbiter of Europe. Reduced taxation
would be one of the happy results, and the reopening of the
interrupted Spanish trade another—a chastened Spanish
Ambassador was due shortly to arrive in London. With this,
and possibly a few well-chosen colonial concessions, the
Company's trading credit might yet be revived, and it might
make a serious start in bearing the burdens which, slump or
not, it had undoubtedly taken off the shoulders of the Treasury.
The Whig union of the previous April was standing the strain,
and there was no reason to think the Court phalanx would not
still be reliable. As for the Tories, the Pretender had let his few
sympathizers down with his typical feebleness. An alternative
set of men simply did not seem to exist. If, as might become
necessary, there had to be sacrifices, the once overweening
directors, who could hardly expect to be re-elected anyway,
when the triennial Company elections took place in February,
would make suitable propitiatory victims.

At a meeting presided over by Sunderland on 25 November,
and attended by Walpole, Townshend, and five leading South
Sea directors, the government's policy was made clear. A
veil was to be drawn over the past, and all the emphasis put
on the need for immediate salvage operations, which Jacomb's
plan—to be brought forward by Walpole at the right moment
—would fulfil. Although the necessary City support for the
Jacomb plan had not yet been secured (by 28 November
Walpole had only got authority from a Committee of Bank
directors to mediate with the South Sea Company in the basis
of his proposals, with a view to later discussion at a General
Court of the Bank), Parliament was to meet as arranged on
8 December. A further prorogation would look like weakness,
and Members were already in town. All demands for an
inquiry would be resisted.

The policy would have been statesmanlike if proposed by
men whose hands were even moderately clean; and it is fair to
say that much more was at stake than the personal gains and
reputations of the ministers most deeply implicated. If a

witch-hunt once started there was no knowing where it might end. It might not stop short even at the steps of the throne and the Hanoverian settlement itself, as Craggs and Aislabie, at any rate, had good reason to know.

On the eve of the Session the supporters of the government assembled, as was then usual, to hear the contents of the Speech from the Throne and the intended Address of reply—the Lords at Stanhope's house, and the Commoners, numbering upwards of 100, at Craggs's office in the Cockpit. The Commons learned that they were to be earnestly recommended to consider the best means of restoring public credit, in which they would 'no doubt be assisted . . . by the several great societies of this Kingdom'—words designed as a pedestal on to which the new, so-called Engraftment Scheme, would in due course be hoisted. The absence of any reference to an inquiry into the causes of calamity was immediately noticed, and there were indignant interruptions when Craggs began to read the equally forward-looking terms of the draft Address of reply. From the body of the meeting Thomas Brodrick demanded that the Address should include some reference to an investigation, and although Walpole argued that the slightest hint of such a thing would cause the directors to decamp,* and Craggs tried to take advantage of the confusion to pass on to the next paragraph, Brodrick gained his point by declaring party discipline would be defied next day in the House if it were not included. The chink thus opened was never to be closed.[1]

Provided the inevitable criticism came from recognized opponents, the Ministers were not very much concerned about it. The debate on the first day of the Session was in this respect quite satisfactory. The attack was opened by Shippen, the declared Jacobite, who naturally extended the offensive from the directors to the ministers. Jekyll took the same line, but he, though a Whig, was known to have a personal feud with

---

* The objection was not altogether without point, as events were to prove—and Law was at this very moment on the way from Guermantes to Brussels and final disgrace. His fall was already known. *William Stratford to Lord Oxford, 9.12.20, Portland MSS.*

Aislabie. Molesworth, in a speech which was thought absurd even at a time when a woman was actually burned at the stake, concentrated on the directors, whom he considered should be declared guilty of parricide by Parliamentary fiat, and subjected to the ancient Roman punishment of being sewn up in sacks with a monkey and a snake and drowned. The other opposition speaker, Sir William Wyndham, though admittedly a former Chancellor of the Exchequer, had been a crony of Bolingbroke's, and a very heavy speculator in South Sea stock into the bargain. Altogether the Court majority and the independents seemed unimpressed by the idea that Parliament had any special part to play. When ministerial spokesmen talked soothingly of putting fires out before arguing about the cause of them, and Walpole hinted at, but did not unfold, his master plan, the day was won, Shippen's amendment was handsomely defeated, and the exact drafting of the Address referred to a committee of ministerialists. In the Lords, thanks to Stanhope's prestige and Harcourt's emollience, an Address which contained no reference whatever to the possibility of an inquiry was voted without dissent.[2]

In the safety of his committee, Craggs felt there was a chance of righting the damage done to his Address at the Cockpit meeting of 7 December. The reference to the inquiry which had then been inserted at Brodrick's instance was unduly blunt and prominent, especially as it took precedence over the words on which it was designed to mount Walpole's scheme. Too much might be made of it. Shippen had said the Parliament had begun with a Secret Committee and would end with one; and Jekyll had used ugly words which seemed to belong to the seventeenth rather than the eighteenth century: 'where laws are deficient, the legislative authority may and ought to exert itself. A British Parliament should never want power to punish national crimes.'

Craggs accordingly rephrased the draft Address, putting the undertaking to restore public credit first, and almost submerging the reference to the inquiry in the words: 'we flatter ourselves that our undertaking will be the more easy, since we are determined to proceed with all possible care, prudence, and temper to enquire into the causes of our present misfortunes, and with the maturest deliberation apply the most proper remedies for redressing them'.

If Craggs had congratulated himself on this ingenious piece of draftsmanship, he was soon disillusioned when it came before the House. The chink he had hoped to close became a rift between ministers and their supporters. He dared not even divide when, led by Jekyll, the House turned 'care, prudence, and temper' into 'prudence, temper, and resolution' and tacked to the end a vigorous 'and for punishing the authors of them'.[3]

To restore the situation the Ministers decided to accelerate the development of their own policy. As soon as the now obnoxious Address had been voted they made sure of an opportunity by securing a resolution that on the following Thursday, only six days later, the House would consider the state of public credit. But events were already moving too quickly for this manœuvre. On Tuesday, 12 December, three days before the planned debate, Stanhope, the Secretary of the Treasury, expecting a quiet day at Westminster, was at the Sword Blade Bank collecting cash totalling £250,000 for the two notes which represented his 'profit' on the fictitious stock 'taken in' for him in the previous March. Meanwhile his colleagues at Westminster were struggling with an unexpected motion from Grey Neville, Member for Berwick, that the Company should at once lay before the House a report of all their proceedings in executing the South Sea Act. Craggs tried to bluster, and Walpole declared, truthfully enough, that the suggestion would do nothing but embarrass the restoration of credit. They might as well have addressed the wind. Such steady Whigs as Spencer Cowper, Horace Walpole, and Richard Steele now joined in the outcry for an investigation, and the Tories, rejoicing, held their fire. Steele (who, it must be admitted, had always opposed the South Sea Scheme and had an old private grudge against Craggs on the question of his playhouse licence) spoke of 'cyphering citts' who had brought the country to disaster, and were now 'to be screened by those of greater figure'. This word 'screen' was to echo through the controversy. Cowper, like Jekyll four days before, waved aside the argument that the directors had offended against no law, and it was noticed that of all the Members associated with the Company, Janssen alone had the courage to appear in his place. Again the ministers dared not divide against the motion.

These warning signs were not lost on the directors of the Sword Blade Bank. Two days later Caswall directed the book-keeper, Watkins, to alter several entries of the name 'Stanhope' in the Bank's books to 'Stangape'. But by an oversight the original name was allowed to stand in the indexes to the various ledgers.[4]

Again the ministers dared not divide for fear of displaying their loss of support. When the arranged debate was held, it fell so flat that Walpole decided not to disclose his plan; but as soon as it was over the House, with the returns called for from the Company already before them, showed great enthusiasm in demanding more information, especially about the loans made by the Company on the strength of its own stock and subscriptions. Two days later, on the 17th, a further series of orders was passed calling for the exact details of the money subscriptions and the dealings of the Company in its own stock, particularly the parcel of over £500,000 alleged to have been sold by them in the previous February and March. Not to be outdone, the House of Lords, on the motion of the gifted but unstable Duke of Wharton (who had himself burned his fingers badly) had started an inquiry of their own, and were also sending for papers.[5]

Five days before Christmas, with the Government's plans still undisclosed, Westminster was invaded by a crowd of angry annuitants who had been persuaded to part with their government stock in August and had ever since been agitating for better terms than the Company was willing to offer. They were eventually persuaded to go away, leaving a petition to the Commons—the first of many—behind them. Steele actually spoke to Knight about one of these annuitants who had written to him personally and was told Knight 'rested on his integrity'. Next day, after securing a resolution establishing a standstill on all South Sea bargains, Walpole at last unfolded his scheme. The preliminary resolution was not secured without the manœuvre of coupling it with another condemning 'the infamous practice of stock jobbing', which was designed to rally the country squires. It was introduced by Sloper, Jacomb's predecessor at the Pay Office, who had made great sums as a Mississippian, and was now a keen opponent of financial malpractices.[6]

Perhaps a nautical metaphor conveys Walpole's plan more easily than the horticultural one which was calculated to appeal to landed gentlemen of that time and had the prestige of the previous successful 'engraftment' of 1697. The South Sea Company was aground like a stranded galleon. To refloat her she must both be lightened, and have tugs. The other two great companies, which were still afloat—the East India Company and the Bank—would supply both the motive power and the stowage for surplus cargo. Of the £38 million paper capital of the South Sea Company, £18 million, or nearly half, would be converted on terms laid down into East India and Bank capital, in two equal portions. Thus each holder of South Sea stock would receive in exchange for the appropriate part of his holding, parcels of stock in the other two companies at rates slightly, but only slightly, more favourable than if he had made the exchange through the market as it stood. So far as the Money Subscriptions were concerned (except the First, on which instalments were to continue, but were to be accepted in stock) all further instalments were to be cancelled, and stock issued forthwith at the rate of £1 stock for every £4 that had been subscribed. The subscriber would thus receive stock at 400, which was standing on the market at 170. The stock remaining in the hands of the Company after completing these arrangements and discharging the debt of £7 million due to the government, was, however, to be divided among the shareholders, as a solatium.[7]

The great advantage, Walpole said, was that this would

divide control over the inflated South Sea capital and the
political and economic power it represented between three
boards instead of one; and would improve the position of the
stockholders by giving them, automatically, better-balanced
portfolios. It also relieved the market of the task, now recognized as hopeless, of finding cash for the subscription instalments already undertaken, and put a stop to any more being
created. But it was quickly pointed out that everything depended on the agreement of the Bank and East India boards
to an operation which involved their undertaking to maintain
dividends on something like treble their existing capitals
without acquiring any additional assets or expanding their
business.*

But, above all, hardly anything was done to improve the
immediate position of the annuitants, least of all those who
had been swindled in August and now had the prospect of
stock with a market value of something like eighteen years'
purchase which had been represented as worth thirty-six. For
them Walpole's plan amounted to putting their sadly reduced
nest-eggs into three baskets instead of one—stronger baskets
perhaps, but no more eggs. The debate was uninspiring and
confused. Walpole gave up any attempt to answer the
muddled criticisms that rose from all sides, and as Thomas
Harley wrote the day afterwards: 'If owners of stock and
subscriptions complain, the annuitants cry aloud.' The best the
ministerialist *Applebee's Journal* could muster as from a plain
man was: 'We do not well understand what the meaning
of it is, yet we think it is to settle some Certainty for our
money.'[8]

People had had enough of expertise. 'This year', wrote
Pulteney to John Molesworth disapprovingly, 'has been fatal
to systems.' The market showed a small technical rally, but
Exchange Alley was no longer the centre of attention. The
House of Commons, for the last time in many decades, had

---

* The Bank's capital at this time was £5·5 million and that of the East India Company £3·2 million. The proposals would have raised these to £14·5 million and
£12·2 million.

now come, corporately, to the forefront in national life. The invasion of Westminster on 20 December had been only a beginning. On the 23rd the House received from Worcester the first of the innumerable local petitions about decaying trade and the iniquities of financiers. It was in Parliament and at the South Sea House that events were now in train which were to sweep away more than hopes and fortunes.[9]

★   ★   ★

The month had started quietly enough at South Sea House, in the knowledge of the reassuring line to be taken by the ministers, and orders had been given on 2 December to reopen the transfer books. On that day, too, a committee was appointed to begin negotiations with the other two corporations on the basis of Walpole's proposals. Since the plan was still formally secret,* the terms of reference were left suitably vague, and the membership was the most respectable the Court of Directors could muster. It included neither Blunt nor any of his confederates who had steered the Bill in the previous spring. The directors now pinned their faith in men such as Chapman, Walpole's associate, who was on the board of the London Assurance; the well-connected Harcourt Master (who was, however, tottering financially, since he had invested and lost huge sums of government money for which he would have to account as Receiver-General of Land Tax for the City of London); Janssen, the financial colossus; and John Gore, whose father had been one of the original directors of the Bank of England. Significantly, these were the men who were to escape most lightly when the day of reckoning came.

Once Parliament had met it must have been apparent to everyone at South Sea House that such a day was a distinct possibility. Between the 8th and the 22nd the Court of Directors assembled twelve times. Twice there were two Courts in a day. The transfer books so optimistically opened were closed

---

* Most well-informed people, however, were aware of its main features by the end of November, e.g., Thomas Harley writing to Lord Oxford on 29 November 1720.

again on the 20th, no doubt on advance notice of the government's intention to propose freezing all South Sea bargains on the following day. Time was found to commission the respectable Chapman to greet the new Spanish Ambassador, who had now arrived. But by the middle of the month almost the only business was replying to the apparently insatiable demands from both Houses of Parliament for reports and accounts.

In terms of clerical work alone the strain on the already exhausted staff was tremendous, and it sheds a not wholly unpleasant light on men who must have been very near the end of their tether that the directors were considerate enough to vote handsome gratuities to the deputy accountant, Lockyer, and his clerks, who had done most of the copying. The principal officials, Knight and his deputy, Surman, having made large fortunes, did not qualify for gratuities, but the strain on them was no less great, though of a rather different kind.[10]

Of the many demands made by Parliament during December, Knight considered two as really dangerous. One concerned the loans upon stock and subscription receipts, since the rules laid down had been flagrantly broken. Far more had been advanced to individuals, and on lower security, than the Court had authorized. This difficulty he overcame by recopying the loan ledgers and breaking down the largest sums into smaller amounts against fictitious names. This 'copying' operation he entrusted to his confidential clerk, Clayton.

The other demand was, of course, for particulars of the £574,000 stock—far more than the Company had then possessed—disposed of by the Company during February and March. The work on this Knight reserved to himself and Surman, to whom he 'often expressed great uneasiness' about it. As he frankly told the director Astell, who anxiously asked how he was getting on, he could not obey 'without giving up forty or fifty of the Company's best friends', to whom most of this stock had been given without any payment. This, whether from loyalty, pride, or fear, he had no intention of doing, and, especially about Sunderland's enormous bribe, he declared: 'I would go through thick and thin rather than discover it.'[11]

The parliamentary order had been issued on 17 December, and between that date and Christmas Knight, working with Surman in the privacy of his room at South Sea House, produced the reply from the notes kept by the directors who had served on the Committee for promoting the Bill (Fellowes, Joye, Blunt, Gibbon, and Houlditch) and the celebrated 'green book'. Surman, who later represented himself as no more than an amanuensis copying from Knight's dictation, said that in the process it seemed to him that a great deal of the original was omitted, and fictitious matter inserted instead. His memory of the contents of the original later proved surprisingly good for someone who said he had not actually examined it, and he recollected that the 'green book' contained accounts under the names of Aislabie, Stanhope, and Craggs, none of which appeared in the version produced for Parliament.* The dummy entries gave names of people who had never received stock on the dates in question, so that the slightest inquiry would have exposed the whole fraud. Knight was still hoping for the best, but those directors who knew the truth hesitated about submitting so gross a forgery.

In the midst of all this a General Court had to be held to gain the consent of the shareholders to the engraftment scheme, and this was done at the Merchant Taylors' Hall on 23 December, the day after Walpole had officially disclosed the proposals. The atmosphere was thundery in the extreme. It was noticed that members of the public kept clear of the platform from which the Sub-Governor expounded the plan, handbills having been circulated that several of those present were carrying pistols and meant to use them if, as was rumoured, the directors tried to insist on exacting the full instalments from the money subscribers. Some such modification of the engraftment proposals (which would have cancelled all further instalments and given subscribers stock for money so

---

* It was later more precisely described by another witness as 'a foot long, two thirds as broad, and an inch and a half thick', and so fit to contain State secrets of the most extended kind. There are reasons for doubting whether this witness actually saw the book.

far subscribed, at 400) had indeed occurred to the hard-pressed directors, but in the face of a furious and loudly applauded harangue from Lord Morpeth, who was spokesman of the money subscribers, Sub-Governor Fellowes did not dare do more on this point than plead for time. This was grudgingly granted, together with authority to embark (as in fact the directors had already done) on negotiations with the other two companies. It was altogether a rowdy and disagreeable meeting, and the next day, Christmas Eve, the director Blackwell, the most powerfully built man on the board, had to be rescued in the street by a party of soldiers from a mob bent on murder.[12]

Parliament had now adjourned, but the Commons broke into their holiday on the 29th to receive a mountain of papers submitted by the Company, and ask for more. Among the new demands was one suggested by Shippen for an explanation of the grounds on which the directors had painted the rosy picture of a Christmas dividend of 30 per cent. and 50 per cent. for the next twelve years. No momentum, in fact, was lost during the brief recess. It merely helped the enemies of the Ministry and the directors to recruit and concert their plans for securing an inquiry. Poor James Windham of the Salt Office, who had decided to go to sea as 'fittest for a ruined man', foresaw that the director Ingram, who had ruined him, 'will be out'. Sir James Lowther was clear that the House was 'preparing to examine the ill practices of the South Sea Directors'.[13]

*   *   *

But the ministers too were rallying. On the last day of the old year they announced a scheme for concessions to the Company in Newfoundland (originally promised after the Peace of Utrecht) and in the West Indian island of St. Christopher. Their tactics, they had decided, should be bolder. The first sign of this new attitude was on the day the House reassembled—4 January—when they proposed that the annual Mutiny Bill should be taken as first business, and the financial situation later. It was an acute move because the House, especially its Tory Members, would willingly have discussed the iniquity of a standing army for several days on any normal occasion. Now it was indignantly brushed aside into a Select Committee. The purpose of an apparently harmless order made on the one-day sitting of the 29th—that the names of the directors and their chief officers should be formally laid before the House—then became clear, when Jekyll moved for an immediate Bill to restrain all those on the list from leaving the country and for requiring an inventory of their estates. This was seconded by Horace Walpole.

There was no reaction from the ministers until Shippen widened the scope of the attack by insinuations that there were others in high places no less guilty than the directors. At this Craggs started from his seat and declared he would give satisfaction to anyone, in the House or out of it. In the uproar which followed, the veteran Molesworth quelled the Secretary of State and sealed the alliance between Whig and Tory back benches with a solemn rebuke: 'For my part, though past sixty, I will answer whatever the Right Honourable Gentleman has to say within the House, and I hope there are younger Members enough who are not afraid to look him in the face out of the House.' The next move in the campaign of retribution was carried unchallenged, and the House resolved on a Committee of Inquiry, to be selected by ballot. This alone was considered to seal the fate of one Minister, Aislabie.[14]

During the following week revenge, in the shape of the so-called Directors' Bill, and rescue, in the shape of the engraftment scheme, were pressed forward together. But rescue, challenged at each stage by divisions, moved the slower. 'The new scheme does not seem to go down so glibly', wrote William Stratford, hinting that a good deal of influence was having to be used to get it to move even at the rate it did. On the 11th, with Engraftment only just consigned to a drafting committee, the clerks of the House paraded the benches with glasses to receive the slips on which each Member had written the thirteen names he favoured for the Committee of Inquiry. The Ministers had circulated a list of their own, and it was a measure of their loss of control that only two of their nominees were chosen: Wortley, Lady Mary's dull husband, and Jekyll, on whose political loyalty ministers felt—despite appearances—they could still rely. Bitter though he had been against the directors, he had confined his criticisms strictly to them, and this was almost an advantage now that the ministers had given up their former friends at South Sea House for lost. Neither of the Law Officers was chosen—a notable slur on the Ministry. But even more striking was the fact that, apart from Jekyll and Lechmere, those chosen, though distinctly Whiggish, included not a single politician, while those who had demanded the inquiry were commissioned to make it.* The vote of censure was not only on the Ministry but on the whole political leadership of the nation. 'Every individual', wrote Molesworth soon afterwards, 'is sorely hurt, and carries about with him a perpetual smart that drowns and quite overcomes *the other influence* which in any other case would probably prevail.' For a moment the House had escaped the system of influence and interest to which it was already accustomed, and into which it was soon to relapse.[15]

The Whiggish, yet anti-ministerial and non-political, nature of the Committee was symbolized by its chairman Thomas Brodrick, who was chosen by an absolute majority of the House. He was an Anglo-Irishman well past sixty, who so far as Westminister politics were concerned had neither a political future nor, what was yet more important, a political past. Throughout his career he had been a consistent Revolution Whig, and his only term of public office had been as Comptroller of Army Accounts long ago under Godolphin. The Privy Councillorship conferred on him at the accession of George I had not been a reward for political service given or

---

* They were: Thomas Brodrick (Chairman); Archibald Hutcheson; Joseph Jekyll (Master of the Rolls); Edward Wortley; Serjeant Pengelly; William Clayton; Edward Jeffreys; Viscount Molesworth; Thomas Strangeways; William Sloper; Nicholas Lechmere (Chancellor of the Duchy, but not a minister); Lieutenant-General Charles Ross; Dixie Windsor. All these except the last may be categorized as Whigs. Clayton was an adherent of Walpole.

prospective but a gesture to him as an individual and to Protestant Ireland.

This Protestant Irish interest symbolized by Brodrick and another leading member of the Secret Committee, Molesworth, represented an older and more passionate strain of Whiggery than the sophisticated ruling clique which had gathered round Sunderland and Stanhope. There were, indeed, no more hard-bitten supporters of Revolution Principles than the Irish Whigs, but the vigour of their principles was directly related to the origin of their estates and their precarious colonial ascendancy, which had been carved out of Ireland during the dark days of the Great Rebellion and the Revolutionary War by freebooting fathers and grandfathers. In the years leading up to 1720 they had seen the Westminster politicians cynically encroaching for their own purposes on the Irish administration and patronage upon which the settler ascendancy depended. In 1719 the judicial powers of the Irish House of Lords, over which Brodrick's brother Lord Chancellor Midleton presided, had been first affronted and then abolished in the celebrated struggle with Westminster over the celebrated Annesley Cause.* The Peerage Bill, which had offered so much to the Scottish nobility, and nothing to the Irish, had been a simultaneous source of offence. In the eyes of the colonial Irish gentry the chief blame for all this attached to Sunderland: the absentee Viceroy of 1715-17 and sponsor of the Peerage Bill about which he had quarrelled so violently with Midleton that his nose had bled. This irrelevant enmity had much to do with the ruthlessness of the parliamentary inquiry.

In Brodrick, the House turned to a man of unquestioned integrity and formidable strength of character. He had always opposed the South Sea scheme, both publicly and privately,

---

* This law-suit over an estate in Kildare turned into a major constitutional struggle when one of the parties appealed from the Irish to the British House of Lords, who reversed the Irish decision. In the struggle that followed, the Irish House imprisoned the judges of the Irish Court of Exchequer for enforcing the English decision, and the British House imprisoned the Sheriff of Kildare for failing to do so. The deadlock was only resolved by a Westminster Act abolishing the apellate jurisdiction of the Irish Lords.

and, unlike a great many who were now eager avengers, he had neither lost nor gained. Not only was he a Whig by conviction, but he regarded the South Sea Company as tainted with the Toryism of its origins—'Tories, Jacobites, and Papists (for those they have all along hugged)', had in his view been the chief gainers. He was not a mere martinet, a scourge to the guilty. With considerable skill, he avoided a collision of the Houses in their parallel inquiries. Above all, he was well aware that the credit and even the existence of the Hanoverian régime were now in grave danger. 'Before the end of next Session', he had written to his brother in September, 'I may be called a South Sea man, for I shall not join with those whose losses have so far exasperated them, as to be desirous, out of revenge, to run to extremes, which may endanger the nation.' Where he differed from Walpole was in his conviction that 'skinning over the sore without probing the wound to the bottom' would not do. The régime would be saved not by screening, but by excluding, the guilty. *Vivunt post funera*—they live after their obsequies —was his family motto, and Whiggery's survival of this crisis, when politicians as a class had lost the nation's confidence, owed more to the availability of an upright, independent Whig in Brodrick than to Walpole or any other leader. It can be said that he was narrow-minded in his attitude to financial practices not in themselves harmful, and his punctiliousness certainly blighted the development of financial technique for years to come; but the lesson he taught the City of London was never to be forgotten.[16]

Brodrick's Committee set to work at once. Till now the House had been compelled to proceed by resolution calling for particular documents, which, though it sounded impressive, was a cumbersome way of conducting an investigation and allowed Knight and his henchmen at South Sea House room for manœuvre. It was decided to set up the inquisition in the South Sea House itself, and the Committee held their first session there on Saturday, 14 January, the entire staff being in compulsory attendance. Fellowes, Joye, Blunt, and Grigsby were subjected to examination that day for ten hours. Except for Sundays and the anniversary of Charles I's execution, the sittings there for the next three weeks took place every day and lasted from nine in the morning until eleven at night.

*   *   *

The directors, with an investigating committee now installed on their premises, were not to be spared more formal pilgrimages to Westminster as well. They were to regret bitterly the days when they had so industriously cultivated the peerage. More than a hundred peers—an overwhelming majority of the House—had been induced to take part in the Third Money Subscription. The Dukes of Chandos, Portland, Bolton, and Wharton had been heavy losers. The Earl of Dartmouth had been hard hit. The Lord Chancellor and Lord Harcourt had holdings they dared not part with. A weighty group of peers, led by Lords Cowper, Aylesford, and North and Grey, which had always opposed the scheme, was in full voice. Stanhope and Sunderland, the two chiefs of the Ministry recently so triumphant, saw their only hope of survival in throwing the directors to the wolves.

A debate in the Lords on the day before Brodrick's Committee was chosen showed how completely this was so. Stanhope frankly espoused the policy of the Directors' Bill which Craggs, his fellow-secretary in the Commons, had denounced as preposterous only a few days before. He went even further, declaring that 'the estates of the criminals, whether directors or not directors, ought to be confiscated'. Sunderland, who had far more on his conscience than Stanhope, stood at bay and said he would 'go as far as anyone to punish the offenders'. Bishop Atterbury may have meant to take the edge off these personalities when he piously compared the slump to a visitation of the plague, but they were probably needed to get the resolution that the government's action in appointing the directors managers of the scheme under the Act conformed with precedent. Even so fifteen peers entered their written dissent. On the 12th, two days afterwards, the Lords examined Knight, Surman, and Grigsby and several directors, and solemnly resolved, without a division, that in lending its money on the security of its own stock the directors had been guilty of a breach of trust and ought, out of their private estates, to make good consequent loss to the Company.[17]

It was the talk of the town that they would be hanged, whether there was law for it or not. The Bill compelling them, under pain of death, to make a return of all their possessions, and to remain in the country under heavy monetary penalties, was read for a second time in the Commons on the 10th, and passed its Committee stage next day. The 19th was appointed for its final stages before being sent to the Lords, who in the meantime had invented their own measure disabling the directors from standing or voting in the Company elections of the following month and from sitting on the boards of either of the two other great companies.

The appearance of Blunt for an examination before the Lords on Monday, the 16th, caused some surprise, since there had been rumours over the week-end that he meant to abscond before the Directors' Bill became law. The heavy strain was beginning to tell. On Thursday passers-by in Old Broad Street were treated to the sight of Sir George Caswall and Sir Harcourt Master setting about each other with their canes outside South Sea House. The same day Lord Chetwynd, one of the Company's purchased friends, was shouted down by indignant shareholders during a meeting of the London Assurance at which he was presiding.[18]

Till now Robert Knight had felt that he might yet keep the pursuers at a distance. But at the examination of the 16th there had been searching questions by the Lords about stock 'taken in for particular persons' and not officially recorded. From the evidence of brokers the Lords were beginning to piece together proof that one such person had undoubtedly been the Chancellor, Aislabie. In South Sea House itself the interminable inquisition—now with the full powers of a Secret Committee*

---

* This meant that the Committee was self-contained, and members not appointed to it could not (as was allowed on ordinary committees) join in its proceedings at will.

—was on the same track. Some of the directors were ready to throw up the sponge and appeal for mercy. On Wednesday there was an indignant meeting of the August subscribers. During this desperate week there can be no doubt that Knight appealed to leading ministers, and Sunderland in particular, for protection, and that these appeals were accompanied by blackmail. On Thursday evening a stockbroker named Joseph Shaw, who had been having frequent conferences with Knight, inquired for the Cashier at South Sea House, and was given to understand he was visiting in Westminster. This was probably the day on which Theodore Janssen, appalled by ruin at the age of sixty-two, urged Knight to make a clean breast of all he knew. 'If I should disclose all I know,' was the reply, 'it would open such a scene as the world would be surprised at.'[19]

What he meant, and what he might have told, will never be known with certainty. That Saturday Brodrick's Committee pressed him hard about the disposal of the 'fictitious stock', the forged account for which was still simmering in some private corner of South Sea House, and he was only able to extricate himself by pleading an order to attend the Lords for further cross-examination. That evening was the last for more than twenty years on which anyone in England was to see the man of whom Brodrick's Committee thought it 'proper to observe that it has appeared to them, throughout their examination, that Mr. Knight, Cashier of the South Sea Company, was principally concerned in their most secret transactions'. At eleven o'clock on Saturday night this gifted, ambitious financier, accompanied by his son, left London and embarked silently at Dover for the exile that turned him from a charmer into an embittered curmudgeon. On Monday morning a porter delivered to Surman at South Sea House a letter in which Knight informed the directors that he was now in Calais. The directors' Bill received Royal Assent two days later. 'Mr. Knight's being gone', wrote Lady Lechmere brightly to her father, 'will be a great loss to the Secret Committee, for he was as much in the secret as anybody. . . . I am really very sorry for him, for in all appearances he was a fair, obliging man.'[20]

CHAPTER XII

The End of the Ministry

THE NEWS OF Knight's escape was instantly carried to the House of Commons by Serjeant Pengelly,* one of the members of the Secret Committee, who interrupted a debate on the Lords' Bill for disabling the directors to announce it, and read the letter the cashier had left for his employers. It was dated Sunday evening. 'Self-preservation', it began, 'has compelled me to withdraw myself.' He had done nothing to reproach himself with, in his opinion, except a few acts of indiscretion for which 'I am sensibly touched with what you are likely to suffer'. After recommending the directors to a greater degree of team spirit than they had hitherto shown in adversity, and wishing them 'as well as you could wish yourselves', he provided a sketch of the state in which he had left his responsibilities. It appeared that a large part of the assets consisted of promises to pay instalments by the money subscribers, in lieu of cash, and he strongly advised the Company not to issue stock against these until the cash was forthcoming. So far as he was concerned, he had taken 'but little more than a sufficiency to maintain myself'.

'I have withdrawn myself', he went on with alarming frankness, 'only to avoid the weight of the inquiry, which I found too heavy for me; and I am sensible that it would have been impossible for me to avoid the charge of prevarication and perjury; though I must say that I have deserved better usage than I have had of the Court the last week.' 'I am pressed for time', he concluded, 'so can only assure you that I am, with

---

* Pengelly was Oliver Cromwell's grandson, being an illegitimate son of Richard Cromwell. Here again the fiercer Whiggery of the previous century can be detected in the composition and outlook of the Secret Committee.

all respect, in inclination though not in power, Gentlemen, your obedient humble servant.'[1]

Pengelly's reading of this impudent apology was followed by an explosion of concentrated wrath which swept the Ministry and Company into open crisis. Resolutions were instantly addressed to the King demanding the arrest of Knight, wherever he might be, and the closing of all ports to prevent further escapes. Then the doors were solemnly locked and orders given for the attendance of the four directors who were members of the House—Janssen, Sawbridge, Eyles and Chaplin. While the House was waiting for them, Brodrick was securing a series of resolutions putting the members of his Committee into executive motion. Three of them—Wortley, Hutcheson, and Clayton—were despatched to seize the papers of Surman and Grigsby. They discovered a rich haul of stock, notes, and tallies, amounting to nearly £750,000, but no green book. Two more—Ross and Sloper—were sent to do the same at the Sword Blade Bank, whence they extended their mission to the homes of the proprietors. Finally, Sub-Governor Fellowes, the directors Lambert and Blunt, and the officials Grigsby and Surman were all ordered into the custody of the Serjeant-at-Arms.

Janssen and Sawbridge had now arrived to face what was in fact a drum-head court martial before the infuriated House of Commons. There was no formal evidence against them. It was enough in that atmosphere for General Ross to declare that the Committee had 'discovered a train of the deepest villainy and fraud that Hell ever contrived to ruin a nation'. The House heard Sawbridge and Janssen in their places, and then resolved them 'guilty of a notorious breach of trust',[2] for which they were expelled from the House and committed to custody. It was hard that Janssen, who was comparatively innocent, should have been among the first victims, but his enormous success as a financier had made him a symbol of the new money market. Eyles and Chaplin could not be found that day, but five days later, though Eyles, at any rate, was even less guilty than Janssen and had powerful relations in the

Bank and East India Companies, they met the same fate.

The Ministry were now taking in such sail as they could in the teeth of the tempest, and the sensations of the day were not yet over. That evening, by Order in Council, the government stripped of public office any director that held it, and removed all directors from Commissions of the Peace. Five directors lost revenue posts under this decree,* which also deprived the wretched director Edmundson of the pursership of the man-of-war *Royal Anne*. Only two of them, Hawes and Houlditch, had been guilty of serious malpractices. But Hawes was close to the Chancellor, Aislabie, whose career, too, was now guttering like a finished candle. For some weeks he had taken no part in the debates on his fatal financial policy, and his enemy, Walpole, had in practice already replaced him. Only two days previously the House of Lords had elicited damning evidence of his dealings in South Sea stock, and the Duke of Wharton, always ready to quote scripture for the benefit of those who criticized his godlessness, had observed that 'he hoped some great men would produce some good fruit, else they would break out in blotches that would stick upon them like the leprosy of Naaman the Syrian on Gehazi'. As recently as November Aislabie had been hoping for a peerage that would cover his retreat to Studley Royal and the enjoyment of his considerable fortune. Now his resignation was tersely announced in the same number of the *Gazette* as the reward of £2,000 for apprehending Knight. Nobody regretted him. Vain, blustering and slippery, he is one of the least attractive of eighteenth-century politicians. Even his pious Yorkshire biographer, Walbran, felt that a relation of 'the affairs of state which he skilfully managed, or those political transactions in which he was so long engaged, would be neither just to his memory, or sufficiently intelligible'.[3]

*　　　*　　　*

* Hawes, Cashier of the Customs; Ingram, Treasurer of the Salt Duty; Master, Receiver-General of Taxes for London; Houlditch, Treasurer of the Stamp Duty; Reynolds, Victualling Commissioner. Harcourt Master later also had to resign his commission in the Tower Hamlets Militia, as did the director Raymond, at the request of the Lord Lieutenant, the Earl of Carlisle.

It is at first sight puzzling that Knight's disappearance should have released such a storm, and that in the following months the question of his extradition should have been the subject of passionate attention in Parliament and outside. But any sensation would have been an excuse for violent action of some kind. It was five months since the golden dream had faded, and nothing had yet been done. And there was a more specific reason. As soon as he heard the news, old Robert Harley was convinced that Knight's escape had been contrived by the Ministry because Knight, and Knight alone, was in full possession of their guilty secrets. The rumour was soon everywhere. Knight himself had fostered it, no doubt deliberately, when he complained in his letter about the ill-usage he had recently had from 'the Court'—which could have meant the Court of Directors, but was generally understood to mean the Court of St. James's.

Whether these rumours were true or not, the events of the 23rd were the beginning not only of a witch-hunt, but of a revolution in the relationships between the witch-hunters, the Ministry, and the directors. Hitherto the Ministry and the directors, in public at any rate, had stuck together. Now the Ministry not only abandoned its old friends, but tried to outdo the House of Commons in dealing blows at them. This was partly panic, partly hope that the thirst for blood would be satisfied with the directors and Aislabie as victims. But just as important was the Ministry's increasing dependence on Stanhope. He, having had nothing to do with the inner history of the scheme, was naturally downright in demanding sanctions on the directors whom he considered responsible for the failure.

But Brodrick's Committee were not going to be content with hunting the directors to ruin and the sacrifice of Aislabie. They were already on the track of the Secretary and the Postmaster, of Charles Stanhope and, above all, of Sunderland.

The directors were thus caught between the two fires of Ministry and Committee. The future of the Company now meant nothing to them—they would soon be out of office and could not hope for re-election. Such corporate spirit as even the inner circle at South Sea House had ever possessed had gone. It was each man for himself, to save what he could. Men like Janssen and Jacobsen, whose fault was at worst lending their names to malpractices they must have suspected, could hope to do this by blaming the men more obviously identified with the events of the previous summer. Some hoped they might yet make peace with the Ministry. But for Blunt and his decemvirs the best chance seemed to lie in making peace with the Commons and providing Brodrick with evidence against their old friends, the ministers. Evidence was for all of them their only remaining asset. Even their possessions in Amsterdam had been seized by the prompt action of the British Resident, on the Ministry's instructions.

For the next few months, therefore, nothing was quite what it seemed. The Commons' demands for the extradition of Knight were designed to save him as a witness, not punish him as an accomplice; the Ministry's apparent compliance with these demands was accompanied by secret moves to keep him in exile; those directors who knew most became the allies, and ultimately the protégés, of the Brodrick Committee. The inquiry in the Lords was pressed vigorously by Sunderland, not with the purpose of discovering the whole truth, but to shadow the Commons' Committee and, if possible, forestall their report.

*   *   *

On 24 January, the day after Knight's escape was reported, Deputy Governor Joye began to crack under the Lords' examination and to tell them the story of the bear's skin. On this the directors Houlditch, Hawes, Gibbon, Chester, and Chapman were ordered into the custody of Black Rod, bringing the total of South Sea men now imprisoned by the two Houses to fourteen. On the 26th the directors Astell and Master supplemented Joye's evidence by naming to the Lords, though only from hearsay, several members of the Ministry and the Commons (but, significantly, no peers) as having been implicated, and Stanhope himself moved that the whole

bear's skin transaction was 'a notorious and dangerous cor-
ruption'. The Duke of Wharton and the future Earl of Chesterfield thereupon hired a hearse and drove it through the street
in a mock funeral procession of the South Sea. The gesture,
though not to everyone's taste, was thoroughly apt. Nobody
yet gave a thought to the impossibility of bringing order to
the affairs of South Sea House with half the directors and most
of the chief officials in custody or in flight.[4]

Next day Deputy Governor Joye, who, as the only responsible person in the Company still at liberty, had every justification for being thoroughly rattled, recklessly presented the
House of Commons with Knight's forged account, accompanied by a note that it was 'as received from the Committee
of Treasury, who never laid any account before the Court of
Directors of stock sold until after the receipt of the order of
the House'. This was no doubt an attempt to exonerate the
least guilty directors, though Joye himself had little claim to
be one of them. Whatever his reasons, this action gave Blunt
the opportunity he had been waiting for to come forward as
Brodrick's star witness.

He had been examined by the Secret Committee on the day
Joye presented the forged account, and had told the anxious
Deputy Governor afterwards that he had given nothing away
about the Ministry or the royal ladies. Next day, when his
examination was continued, he told the inquisitors that the
account was false; that names in it were covers for other
recipients, of whom he named Aislabie, Postmaster Craggs,
Sunderland, Charles Stanhope, the Duchess of Kendal, and
Countess von Platen; and, for good measure, that this 'was
generally so understood among the directors'. Tackled afterwards by Joye, he piously said he could not disclose the evidence he had given; that he loved him very well; and that the
best way was to tell the whole truth. 'What!' exclaimed the
bewildered Deputy Governor. 'Royal ladies and all?' Blunt
was at his sanctimonious best. 'Yes', he replied; 'the examination
is very strict and nothing but the whole truth will do.'[5]

On the last day of the month the Deputy Governor had the

cheerless duty of presiding at the election of a new Governor, Sub-Governor, and Deputy Governor of the Company. All day, from nine till six, Joye sat at South Sea House with a glass before him to receive the votes to which he was not allowed to contribute and for which he was not permitted to offer himself. The new Sub-Governor was Sir John Eyles, a kinsman of the Eyles recently ejected from the Commons, but a person of much greater substance, being a director of the Bank and a brother of a director of East India Company, connexions which looked promising for the engraftment scheme, though the new Sub-Governor was, in fact, to be the chief man to frustrate it. In spite of the unpleasant rumours about royal complicity, the King was re-elected as Governor. The next day, at an election held by the new officers, a completely new Court of Directors was chosen, in which several names prominently connected with the Bank were included, and a Bank official, de Gols, was brought in as Cashier to tidy up the chaos left by Knight.

Though the Ministry may already have suspected Blunt's treachery, they now saw a chance of stealing Brodrick's thunder, and were once more in a defiant mood. When, on the day of the Deputy Governor's ordeal at South Sea House, Brodrick sought to prepare an audience for his revelation by moving for circular letters requiring all Members to attend a call of the House a fortnight later, Craggs complacently taunted him for the delay in producing 'the report so much expected'. The Prince of Wales was said to be in high spirits. Ministerial confidence was advertised at an uproarious gathering at the Duke of Newcastle's, where new Tokay, champagne, Visney, and Barba water were drunk, it was said, for thirteen hours on end. Next day—4 February—it was intended to examine Blunt in the House of Lords and find out exactly what he had told Brodrick.[6]

Stanhope was in no condition for such a session. He now knew that his name, if not his reputation, was to be dragged in the mire in the person of his favourite cousin, Charles. He may have suspected Sunderland. It was impossible to ignore the crumbling public confidence in his colleagues or the whispers about the King, his master. He had been on the point of achieving the sort of ascendancy by diplomacy that Marlborough had achieved by war, and now the whole of his political edifice was in peril from financial issues he had never professed to understand.

From the beginning of the examination it was clear that Blunt was keeping faith with his new masters, the Commons. He would not repeat in the Lords what he had said to Brodrick on the 28th, and so warn the ministers how completely their ground was undermined. Hard as he was pressed, he refused all material disclosures concerning ministers and officials in the previous February and March on the ground that he had already given evidence about them elsewhere, and did not wish to be led into inconsistency. Of all the scenes of the South Sea this is probably the most extraordinary. Blunt, with some of his old portentousness still clinging to him; Stanhope, heavy with wine and frustrated ambition; Sunderland, probing to discover how far his guilty secret was already known to his enemies; the mischievous Wharton; the ruined Portland. Even Sir William Sanderson, Black Rod, Blunt's temporary custodian, had ventured £1,000 at his prisoner's invitation in the Third Money Subscription, and most of those present had ventured more. And yet, since he was already the prisoner of the Commons, they could do nothing to him. Again and again he was directed to withdraw, called back, and told he must answer. Each time he prevaricated, and finally refused to take the oath at all. Seething with frustration, the Lords dismissed him and fell to debating what they should do. To this the Duke of Wharton impishly contributed a parallel between the present situation and 'Sejanus, who made a division in the Imperial Family, and rendered the reign of the Emperor Claudius odious to the Romans'. Stanhope's patience was at an end. He rose and denounced Wharton as a degenerate whom his father, like Brutus, would have sacrificed to patriotism if he had lived. Then he staggered and was carried fainting from the House. Three days later he was dead of cerebral haemorrhage.

It was said King George was so moved that he could not eat his supper.[7]

The loss of Stanhope's towering prestige was a deadly blow to the Ministry. Informing Carlisle of Stanhope's death, Vanbrugh lamented there was hardly an untainted politician left, and hoped the report, when it arrived, would not have the effect of finally discrediting all to whom the nation could look for leadership, and leaving a vacuum of power when power was most needed. Sunderland, now for a moment in undivided control, was in almost as unenviable a position as Joye's had been at the South Sea House. Walpole, the only politician except Brodrick with any following in the Commons, was far from being his friend. Impeachment must have seemed even closer than in 1710.[8]

But the other reaper, of more than reputations, was riding ahead of Brodrick. The fortnight's delay with which Craggs had taunted the Secret Committee was, by a remarkable irony, to be almost exactly the term of the cheerful Secretary's own life. The day after Stanhope's death he felt pains in his back and head which soon developed into smallpox. On the 7th he was well enough to execute what must have been almost, if not quite, his last official act in signing a series of circular letters to posts abroad instructing them to press for the extradition of Knight. When Brodrick at last rose, on the 16th, to read his report, Craggs was on his deathbed. Next day he died. He was only thirty-five.[9]

Secretary Craggs, with all his faults, is one of the most amiable figures in this history. Ever since his father had placed him with Stanhope in Spain he had served under that statesman's banner, and now the master was gone, the man, with a final gesture of obsequiousness, followed him to the grave. Some people thought his jovial high spirits were tinged with vulgarity; but most were genuinely fond of him, and thought, with Pope, that 'there never lived a more worthy nature, a more disinterested mind'. 'Il est sensible de l'amitié', Dubois wrote confidentially to the French Ambassador, 'et en est très capable.' In a way this gift for friendship, which verged on gullibility, was his undoing, for the South Sea Scheme provided his optimistic nature with excessive opportunities of obliging people at no cost to himself. His funeral at the Abbey was an impressive affair attended by many peers and politicians, but it was held at night, for fear of riots. Two epitaphs were provided. One by Pope, was inscribed on the tomb:

> *Statesman, yet Friend to Truth! Of Soul sincere,*
> *In Action faithful, and in Honour clear,*
> *Who broke no Promise, serv'd no private End,*
> *Who gained no Title, and who lost no Friend.*

The other was suggested by the herald Le Neve: 'Here lies the last that died before the first of the family.' And it is true that the Postmaster, though stricken by the death of his only son, still persisted in unblushing denial of any complicity in the affair.[10]

*　　　*　　　*

Faced with the certainty of a determined personal attack, Sunderland had to reconstruct his shattered Ministry. There was only one way of doing it. He would have to share power with his old rival, Walpole, whom he had ousted from the Treasury in 1717 and who had never had any cause to be his friend. Even so, he clung to what he could—which for the time being included the Treasury. One of the vacant Secretaryships went to Townshend, as part of the price of Walpole's support; but the other, much to Walpole's disgust, went to Carteret, on whom Sunderland could depend to hold the balance in the Cabinet.

Walpole took no office for himself at the moment. He remained Paymaster—or, as people were now beginning to call him, 'Screen Master'-General. He was edging his way up the most dangerous, because the most exposed, passage in his climb to power, and there is something impressive, even when all allowances are made for the greatness of the prize, in the courage of such ambition. It was of moments like this that a later statesman, Addington, was thinking when he said that a public man should not care a farthing whether he died in his bed or on the scaffold.

In committing himself to doing what he could to save Sunderland from destruction, Walpole saw clearly that the only course was to play for time. The Secret Committee was still at work: the storm had not yet reached its climax, and to make way against it was impossible. It must be ridden out until the calmer time came when that 'other influence', of which Molesworth had spoken, could gradually be brought to bear. In the interval, undoubtedly, there would have to be sacrifices; for the men of the Secret Committee, though they might not be ministerial timber themselves, were dangerous. They had the fire of Shaftesbury, if not his stature. With what inner resolutions Walpole shouldered his responsibilities we cannot know, but one can be reasonably sure of two of them. One was never again to risk much to gain all. The other was never to forgive Blunt or Knight, the men who had turned against the politicians on whom they had battened.

Just as the accommodation was reached between Walpole and Sunderland the news reached London that Knight had been found. The enterprising secretary of the British Legation in Brussels had picked up the fugitive's scent there, and, commandeering a party of Austrian dragoons, had overtaken him on 2 February at the little Flemish town of Tienen. Given another day, he would have been out of Brabant and beyond reach in the dominions of the Bishop of Liège. He was taken back to Antwerp a prisoner and lodged in the citadel, while proceedings for his extradition began.

This, however, proved a matter of unexpected difficulty. The Austrian Government in the Netherlands insisted on their minute respect for the ancient local constitution, or *Joyeuse Entrée*, which laid down the conditions on which Habsburg rule had been admitted in Brabant, and was the 'precious jewel of Brabant liberty'; it included the following article:

So wat persoon binnen onsen lande van Brabant ende van Over Maese gehevangen wort, dat wij dien niet en sullen

doen voeren, noch laeten voeren gehevangen buijten onsen
vorsz lande.

These words, which became the object of passionate study
in London, were ambiguous. The article's original purpose,
undoubtedly, was to prevent Brabanters from being shipped to
other parts of the Habsburg dominions for trial. But it said
rather more than this:

> If any person be made prisoner in our territories of Brabant
> or Upper Meuse, we will not require such a person, nor
> permit him, to be removed out of our aforesaid territories.

The literal interpretation, on which the authorities in Brabant
took their stand, was that Knight could not be sent back to
England either as a fugitive offender (as public clamour
demanded) or as a witness against Sunderland (which was what
the Secret Committee really wanted).[11]

The British Government kept up a great show of activity in
complying with the demands of Parliament and public for
extradition, and the negotiations in Brussels were reported
round by round in London. Leathes, the British envoy,
protested until he was worn out, and his efforts were reinforced
by representations to the Imperial Government at Vienna, but
without success. 'It is with the utmost *indignation*', wrote the
Kent Quarter Sessions in one of the many pronouncements on
the question, 'that we see this *Honourable House* struggling
with unexpected opposition; and labouring under unaccountable difficulties; and we can never sufficiently express our
resentment when we behold the King of Great Britain in vain
demanding the person of a man, inconsiderable for everything
except his crimes, who, as he was no doubt prevailed on to
fly his country to obstruct justice on *greater offenders*, is still
denied on pretences *too weak* to give satisfaction to so wise a
Prince and so discerning a people.' The Commons were
particularly angry when Leathes reported that the Austrians
had supported their position by pointing out the absence of
any specific charges against Knight. He had not even offended

against the Act forbidding South Sea men to leave the country, having chosen to depart two days before it became law. The frustrated Commons appointed a special committee to examine the possibility of economic sanctions against Brabant.[12]

Whether or not Knight could have added much that was genuine to the report which Brodrick was now on the point of launching is uncertain. But what he might say to save his neck and fortune (and this was the price the firebrands were willing to pay for his testimony) would not necessarily be limited by the truth. Only forty years had passed since Titus Oates. There can be little doubt that alongside their official representation to Brussels the government privately and earnestly took steps to see that Knight stayed in the Antwerp citadel until the summer exodus from London brought the adjournment of Parliament and weariness of the whole subject.

Although Walpole was thus committed to a waiting game on the question of Knight, as on almost every other aspect of the crisis, there was one positive action in which he wisely did not permit delay. This was to make a beginning in the process of bringing home to Parliament that whatever they might be minded to do to individuals, they would also have to exercise their authority to save the Company; and he managed to arrange for this before the full force of the storm broke. On 13 February, three days before the Brodrick report was to be delivered, the new Court of Directors handed the Commons their first sobering draught in the shape of a summary of the Company's liabilities for the coming year:[13]

	£ million
Due to the Exchequer:	
(1) In four quarterly instalments, beginning on 25 March, under the South Sea Act	7*
(2) For Exchequer Bills underwritten by the Company and subsequently lent out by them to purchasers of stock	1
Due to the bondholders, as repayment of capital or in part payment of converted government securities	5
Dividends and interest already due	1·5
Total	14·5

* Seven, not seven and a half as originally bid, because less than the full amount of Debt contemplated in the proposal had been converted.

Assets, owing to the controversial nature of the value to be placed on them, were not included in this statement, and it was true that a computation made for the Secret Committee showed the total income of the Company over the next ten years or so at the enormous figure of £205,039,401. But this was based on the assumption that all the money subscriptions would be completed on the original terms and that all the loans made on the security of scrip and stock would be recovered. In cold fact, even the instalments on subscriptions so far due had not been paid in full, and it was the essence of Walpole's engraftment scheme that future ones would be cancelled. As for the loans, it was most questionable whether the borrowers, who included a great many Members of both Houses of Parliament, could ever be forced to repay them to the Company in whose stock they had laid them out so disadvantageously. Owing to its expenditure on bribes and support of the market, the Company's cash position was even worse than it was on paper. In hard reality the only asset, apart from problematical trading prospects, that it could put against obligations of £14·5 million was its income of £2 million a year from the Exchequer. In other words, the Company was hopelessly insolvent.

Since the bulk of the shareholders were the former creditors of the State, a declaration of the Company's bankruptcy would be the equivalent of a national default. No British Parliament after 1688 could contemplate such a thing. Two days after the Company had delivered its statement, Walpole enforced the moral by presenting a message from the King in which a broad hint was given that Parliamentary action would have to be taken to relieve the Company of some of its burdens.

*   *   *

On 16 February, with these reminders of their responsibilities freshly before them, the House of Commons heard first Brodrick, and then the Clerk of the House, read the Secret Committee's report. The process took four hours. The whole story of the sale of the bear's skin was told in damning detail, with a brief acknowledgment to Blunt as the 'one from whom your Committee had the first material information': Sunderland's complicity, attested by Blunt and Houlditch; Charles Stanhope's vast bribe and the subsequent cooking of the Sword Blade Company's books to conceal it; the Duchess of Kendal and Countess von Platen being introduced on the ground floor by Secretary Craggs; Aislabie playing the market in the first half of 1720 to the tune of nearly £150,000; the utter disregard of the Company for its own rules about the loans, as a result of which it had lent more than £11½ million—£4½ million more than had been authorized—and now held the absurd security of about £3½ million of its own stock and scrip. Further reports were promised. It was an appalling and disheartening document, unique in British parliamentary history. Someone moved it should be printed. Walpole, in persuading the House not to authorize this, scored his first little victory.[14]

The report and the royal message suggesting relief for the Company were considered together two days later, and relief and revenge were running once more neck and neck. But this time relief made a solid advance. The House gave directions that the Engraftment Bill, which was still at its drafting stage, should defer for one year the payment of rather more than £5 million of the £8 million due to the Exchequer. So the House began to yield up the public bribe, far exceeding any of those given privately, which had secured acceptance of the South Sea scheme.

Having thus begun, almost without being aware of it, to cast out the beam, they turned to the motes, and on that and succeeding days passed a series of resolutions which collectively made up their verdict on the report. Six of these condemned the malpractices of the directors in lending on insufficient security, disposing of security held against loans, trading by the Company in its own stock, declaring the 30 per cent. dividend without the resources to meet it, and inflating the price of stock against the improperly enlarged money subscriptions. Four of the others were more remarkable.

In form they were findings on the part Ministers and Parliamentarians had played: in substance they created the basis of new crimes for which ministers were to be tried before the Commons sitting as a supreme court of justice.

The trials which followed—for they were no less—were held under the following declaration of the House:

> The taking in, or holding of stock, by the South Sea Company for the benefit of any member of either House of Parliament or person concerned in the Administration (during the time that the Company's Proposals or the Bill relating thereto were depending in Parliament) without giving valuable consideration paid . . . were corrupt, infamous, and dangerous practices, highly reflecting on the Honour and Justice of Parliaments, and destructive of the Interest of His Majesty's Government.

The privilege of the House of Commons—and it was on privilege alone that this resolution was founded—has probably never been stretched so far in modern times. Impeachment, as Walpole pointed out, was the proper procedure, but Brodrick and his allies were in no mood to trust their victims—least of all Sunderland—to the judgement of the peers. The House of Commons had constituted itself, in the fullest sense, the grand inquest of the nation.

The first victim was Charles Stanhope, still Secretary of the Treasury, who was brought before the Commons on 28 February. Five witnesses—Blunt, Houlditch, and the three Sword Blade partners—were examined. Walpole spoke for the defence, and so did young Philip Stanhope, the future Lord Chesterfield of the mid-century, who made an emotional and effective appeal to the memory of the defendant's namesake, the great Earl. Even so, Brodrick was confident. But when it came to the division on whether Stanhope fell within the terms of the resolution it was noticed that Jekyll, Molesworth (who later pleaded a sudden fit of the stone) and Sloper, who were all supposedly ardent members of the Secret Committee, had quietly gone home. There were many other abstentions, and

Brodrick could not afford these three votes on which he had relied. Stanhope was acquitted by 180 to 177.[15]

'It has put the whole town in a flame', he wrote indignantly to his brother in Ireland about this first sign of the 'other influence' reasserting itself. But a week later he was to see flames of a more satisfactory kind. The tussle over Aislabie on 8 March went on until one in the morning. There was an impressive list of charges against him, but one of them was enough—the acceptance, under the bear's skin arrangements, of £20,000 stock, on which the ex-Chancellor had cleared a profit of £35,357. 10s. He still showed fight, and enraged his judges by his defiant admission that he had burnt the account of his dealings with the director Hawes as being a matter of no importance once it had been settled. Walpole did not lift a finger to save him. He was expelled from the House and consigned to the Tower after being found guilty under the resolution; and orders were issued to bring in a Bill for compelling him to disclose his estate. The bonfires were lit all over London when the news was known.

On the 13th Walpole allowed Brodrick to work his will with Sir George Caswall, the 'Lem Knight', and the other partners in the Sword Blade. Their condemnation followed automatically from the acquittal of Charles Stanhope, for if he had not made illicit profits, the intermediaries through whom the sums he had received had reached him fell to be regarded as principals. Caswall was at an initial disadvantage, for he had prepared himself to answer charges of forgery, not of illicit acceptance of stock; and Jekyll himself had some doubts about the legal propriety of the altered line of attack. It did not matter. Without Walpole's help, Caswall's case was hopeless, and a rumour that he had been secretly received by the King on the previous evening made things worse. He followed Aislabie into expulsion and the Tower, where Lord Coningsby, his difficult Herefordshire neighbour, who was also imprisoned there for contempt of the House of Lords, made the low company of the former Chancellor of Exchequer the ground of a formal complaint to the authorities.

The estates of all three partners were ordered to be made responsible for the quarter of a million which had been shared out, in all probability, between Stanhope and the senior Treasury officials.

These triumphs made Brodrick outwardly confident as the last and greatest of the trials approached. But inwardly he must have had misgivings. The trial of a member of the Upper House in the Lower without the possibility of intervention by the peers was unprecedented. Sunderland, though he was the accused, did not appear; but the House and its approaches were packed by almost everyone else of consequence, from the Prince of Wales downwards. Joye, Gibbon, Chester, Houlditch and Surman gave evidence, but Blunt was not exposed to examination again. The struggle raged most fiercely over an obscurely worded note of hand for £50,000 which, it was asserted, Sunderland had given to Knight, and showed that the transfer of shares had been made for genuine consideration. On this point, above all, Knight could have earned his pardon from the Commons, if he had not been safely in the Citadel of Antwerp; and if it is true that a large sum was privately conveyed to the Governor of the Austrian Netherlands for defending the Constitution of Brabant so manfully—as rumour suggested—it was well spent from Sunderland's point of view. Walpole extended himself to the full in defence, and in the absence of the vital witness managed to expose discrepancies in the evidence. The contest was long and desperate, but in the end Sunderland was acquitted by a majority of 51. Even so, 172 votes were cast against him—a grievous number on such a question. Walpole had kept his bargain, but his rival would not be able to hold up his head much longer.[16]

There remained old Craggs, the grey eminence of the affair, the confidant of Marlborough, Godolphin, and Sunderland, who, in Lord Onslow's opinion, was 'the principal agent for the Administration in the *whole* transaction . . . and bore the chief blame for all the iniquity of it'. The Postmaster had journeyed far, and was now in his sixty-fifth year; doubly a millionaire; and the master of a major political interest and many political secrets. In spite of Le Neve's snobbish jest, he was proud to be the first of his family. His three daughters were well married, and the son he had loved had been raised by his efforts alone. Left alone with his money, he had stoutly denied all the charges against him, and was to be the last, and one of the least popular, victims of parliamentary vengeance. The hearing had been fixed for 18 March, but whether Walpole would have thrown a shield over him, and with what success, will never be known. On the evening of 17 March the Postmaster put an end to his life with a dose of laudanum. More than any of the others he typified his self-made generation.[17]

CHAPTER XIII

The End of the Affair

IN THE FIRST week of April Sunderland bowed to circumstances and resigned the Treasury to his rival and protector. Groom of the Stole and a powerful minister he still remained, but the financial departments were at once garrisoned against him. Walpole himself assumed the offices of both First Lord and Chancellor of the Exchequer, thus acquiring day-to-day as well as general financial control. His brother Horatio took over Charles Stanhope's Secretaryship, and another brother, Galfridus, the vacancy at the Post Office. The office of Clerk of the Pells of the Exchequer went to Walpole's eldest son. A clean sweep was made of the junior commissioners; the Chancellor's private secretary was changed; and even the office-keeper from Walpole's last spell at the Treasury was restored. The only survivor of any importance was the venerable Lowndes, whose Treasury career had begun over forty years before, in the year of the Popish Plot. The King was still said to be 'resolved that Walpole should not govern', but, as Carteret told Newcastle, it was 'hard to be prevented'. The time was past when, as Charles Stanhope had once put it to Newcastle, 'I always fancy your Grace's little jobs go more soundly when I am there.' The Duke and others who had business at the Treasury were not slow to draw the moral.[1]

These changes were not enough for the party of retribution, and the brew of scandal was kept boiling. In the three months following their first report the Secret Committee produced six more, crammed with inflammatory detail about the conduct of ministerialists and the obstruction it was encountering in its inquiry. Nor was this all. Brodrick and his colleagues were now at the head of an organized national campaign.

'Our credit throughout the Kingdom', Brodrick had written to his brother in March, 'will sufficiently support us. Let them look to themselves, they stand on a sandy foundation.' The evidence for this was a deluge of petitions, significantly timed to begin just before the trial of Sunderland. Seventy-nine of them, bearing clear signs of orchestration under the slogan, 'Justice for an injured nation', reached the Commons during the spring and early summer from quarter sessions, corporations, and even unincorporated towns like Birmingham and Leeds. Though Scotland and Wales were thinly represented, there was word from as far afield as Pembroke and Caithness; and the heartlands of England left Members of a Parliament that was entering the last year of existence in no doubt of their indignation. Somerset spoke of 'villainous and corrupt management'; Kent of 'execrable fraud'; Warwickshire denounced the directors as a 'set of parricides' and urged vengeance for 'the unparalleled grievances of a plundered people'. Although the campaign was certainly organized, it is equally certain that its organizers worked on deep feelings, and that those feelings were spread throughout the country. Its effect was to alienate from the government the votes of many non-partisan country gentlemen on whom it could normally count.[2]

Simultaneously came a formidable barrage of press propaganda, led by the *London Journal* in a savage series of letters, most of them signed 'Cato'. They were long reprinted as models of invective, and 'Junius' is 'Cato's' lineal descendant. 'They are *Rogues of Prey*, they are *Stock Jobbers*, they are a *Conspiracy of Stock Jobbers*, a name which carries along with it such a detestable deadly image, that it exceeds all humane invention to aggravate it. . . . What we can have of them, let us have, their Necks and their Money.'[3]

Some of the Cato letters were attributed to Molesworth himself; but they were mainly the work of Thomas Gordon, editor of *The Independent Whig*, who appears in *The Dunciad* as Silenus, and John Trenchard, a Grub Street veteran whose style had been formed in Shaftesbury's time. The whole picture

—star witnesses, petitions, snarling propaganda—recalls the crackling Whiggery of 1679, with the stock-jobbers cast as the Jesuits in a new conspiracy against the State, and the real target, not the alleged conspirators, but the government itself.

Walpole, however, could depend on one factor which had been denied to the ministers of Charles II when confronted with Shaftesbury. While there was a generalized sense of grievance, the interests of the various groups of South Sea sufferers were by no means identical. Those who had paid high prices for their stock, whether they had been direct money subscribers, former Debt-holders, or purchasers in the open market, all wished to see the price of the stock recover. But whereas the later subscribers and the annuitants who had converted in August maintained that the Company should sacrifice its profits by modifying the terms on which they had entered, the holders of fully paid stock, and those who had come in on the comparatively favourable terms of Spring, 1720, saw no reason why they should see the potential value of their holdings diminished, which would be the inevitable result of such relief. Though divided on this issue, the stock-holders and money subscribers were at one in clamouring that those who had borrowed money from the Company should be forced to repay it; but these borrowers, who included 138 Members of the House of Commons, were not inclined to pay over cash and receive in exchange stock valued at 400, or more than double the price at which it stood on the market. To complicate matters further, many stock-holders were also borrowers; and many had bought at different prices, or were concerned in more than one subscription. For such people no single remedy urged by a pressure group would do.

On one point only, all groups of investors were united. The State must finally abandon its claim on the Company for the seven millions. But it was on precisely this point that the parliamentary party of vengeance and its following of indignant squires differed from those whose sufferings they made so much noise about. Their cry was that the promise to relieve the nation of debt and the landowner of the land tax must at least be kept. The difficulty was that the Company's ability to do this depended on recovering its loans and extracting its instalments from people who would not or could not pay them.

The new First Lord of the Treasury's position as arbiter between groups who would never reach agreement among themselves was therefore an extremely strong one; and that he knew this was implicit in his reference, in explaining his engraftment scheme, to its having been designed 'not to ease or relieve any one sort of adventurer at the loss or expense of another'. But it was now clear that on further examination the engraftment scheme did not live up to this claim. It maintained the Company's vast obligation to the Exchequer—which with Brodrick in full cry it would have been madness to abandon—while leaving the Company no resources from which to meet it. Above all, it did nothing to remove the gross inequality between the terms of the early and late conversions. The Bank was at best luke-warm about the plan; the East India Company disliked it. The new masters of South Sea House very properly decided they could not recommend it to their shareholders.

While Walpole and Lowndes set themselves to consider what should take the place of the engraftment scheme, it was necessary to proceed against the former directors. The measure for imposing a levy on their estates to make good the Company's losses was known as the South Sea Sufferers Bill, and was presented to the House two days after Walpole took formal control of the Treasury.

The foundation of this remarkable measure was two bulky volumes containing the accounts which each director had been compelled to prepare, showing the state of his affairs in June 1720 and March 1721, with particulars of every transaction in between, so as to indicate the method and extent of his gains. As the Select Committee said in presenting them, they were 'in themselves so voluminous, consist of such a variety of trans-actions and things, such great numbers of persons must of necessity be examined, and so many difficulties will naturally arise, that your Committee humbly conceive that they cannot, in any reasonable time, make such proper observations as will answer the intention and expectation of the House'.[4]

The whole was printed by order of the House, and it is probable that no fuller description of the properties and activity of a representative business group exists in so accessible a form for any period of history. Interests all over Europe, from Andrew Molacoff & Company of Archangel to businesses in Portugal and Leghorn; plantations in the West Indies; a brewery, a timber-yard, a fashionable West End square, estates all over England were all inventoried. So were the jewels of wives and daughters, the china, glass, hangings, pictures, pots and pans in their houses, horses and carriages in their stables; the private hoards of cochineal and pepper; but, significantly, very little hard cash. The Sufferers Bill operated neither on gross assets nor by laying down specific penalties, but as a forfeiture of net assets after allowing—and allowing not ungenerously—for existing liabilities. In addition, it left for future discussion an amount to be allowed to each director for his support.[5]

It was a haphazard as well as unusual method, because those who could produce the most impressive list of liabilities escaped most lightly, and the net 'estate' on which the Bill operated was no guide at all to the financial size of the individual. Hawes, for instance, with his labyrinthine dealings in the Customs revenue and his magnificent collection of antiques, showed indubitable assets of £165,000, the sixth largest of the gross totals, but managed to sweat his balance down to only £40,000. Gore, with assets of £86,000, showed an estate of £39,000. Yet the method produced a kind of rough justice. Those who had salted their money away in land, like Janssen, Blackwell, and Surman, suffered heavily in comparison with men such as Page the brewer, Astell the timber merchant, and Morley the importer of wine and fruit, whose wealth was turning over in business. The gross assets of these last three came to £57,000, £80,000, and £15,000, but their net 'estates' to only £34,000, £27,000, and £2,000.

Operating only on net assets also had the economic merit of

maintaining the credit, both at home and abroad, of the large sector of English business that was linked with the former directors. The gross assets shown in the inventories came to a total of over £3 million at the South Sea men's own valuation. The scope of the Bill extended to £2 million of this; to have imperilled more would have been a blow to English credit from the Baltic to the Mediterranean.

Nothing was said in the Sufferers Bill about politicians; but Brodrick and his allies had no intention of letting their ministerial victims escape without monetary penalties in addition to the loss of their seats and reputations. On 21 April they hoisted Aislabie, 'the director of directors' as he was now called, into the tumbril along with the directors themselves. His name was added to the schedule of those whose estates were to be forfeited, even though Walpole, changing his tactics, did what he could for his old enemy. He appealed in an unresponsive House to Aislabie's family responsibilities and the impropriety of putting 'a person of such eminence' on the same level as mere business men; but he dared not divide, and Brodrick gloated over the prospect of the Lords relishing the amendment 'like chopped hay'.[6]

A week later the avengers fastened on the memory and fortune of the late Postmaster. Old Craggs had left more than a million and a half to be shared among his three daughters and Hariot, his son's illegitimate child. The three elder ladies (Hariot was only seven) were all married to Cornish Members of Parliament—Margaret to Samuel Trefusis, Elizabeth to Edward Eliot, and Ann to John Newsham. Here was a parliamentary interest, a going concern, which Walpole could not afford to neglect. He had spoken up for Aislabie, not out of chivalry for a fallen foe, but in recollection of Aislabie's unbroken control of the two seats for Ripon. Now his first move was to seek leave for the three sons-in-law of Craggs to be heard by counsel, on the ground that they had not yet spoken in the House. This drew the retort from Lechmere that Walpole himself was as good an advocate as anyone could expect, and on 1 May a resolution was proposed that the

Sufferers Bill should apply to the whole increase in the Craggs estate since 1 December 1719. Walpole showed his gathering confidence by dividing against this, and although he was heavily beaten, by 82 votes, he thereby laid an important part of the foundations of the Robinocracy; and the bulk of the Craggs estate survived to support one of the greatest electoral interests of the eighteenth century.*[7]

Walpole's policy of making friends for the future out of Brodrick's victims was taken a step further in his handling of the measure for making the Sword Blade partners liable for Stanhope's £250,000, which had been ordered after the finding of Caswall's guilt. Caswall's interest at Leominster was still intact, and he had useful friends in the City, all of which counted a great deal more with Walpole than the cringing letter he received from the 'Lem Knight' about 'wife, children, and many dependants to be stripped of all the comforts of life and reduced to the utmost necessities'. Sawbridge's connexion at Cricklade was not negligible. So although the Bill against the Sword Blade partners came up again and again Walpole found means to delay it until it lapsed with the end of the Session. At the General Election of 1722 Caswall appeared once more as Member for Leominster, and until his death twenty years later the Robinocracy had no more devoted supporter. Sawbridge left a family which gave London a Wilkesite Lord Mayor and history the celebrated Catherine Macaulay; and Turner, that retiring man, enough to found a hospital when he

* The parliamentary marriages of the four Craggs ladies are sufficiently remarkable to be given in detail. The connexion with the Eliots of Port Eliot formed by the marriage of Elizabeth, was further cemented in 1726 by the marriage of Hariot—then still a child—to Richard Eliot, her aunt's husband's younger brother, and ancestor of the present Earl of St. Germans. Ann Craggs was married three times—first to John Newsham (who assumed her surname), then to John Knight, Member successively for St. Germans and Sudbury, and finally to Robert Nugent, Earl Nugent (who also assumed the surname of Craggs and was for many years M.P. for St. Mawes). Margaret, the third daughter, married first Samuel Trefusis, Member for Penryn, and then Sir John Hynde Cotton, Member for Cambridge. The four ladies thus wived a total of seven M.P.s, six of whom sat for Cornish boroughs. Nor did the story of the Craggs fortune and Parliamentary inheritance end there. When Hariot's first husband died in 1749, she married again, and her son by this marriage, later Marquess of Abercorn, sat in due course for the Eliot boroughs of East Looe and St. Germans. The first Baron Eliot (who also assumed the surname of Craggs) married the director Gibbon's granddaughter.

died in 1734. The Company for Making Hollow Sword Blades in the North of England continued its banking business on a more modest scale until, in the 1740s, it finally disappeared from view.[8]

The party of revenge struggled against these fabian tactics in vain. Early in May, while the House was considering the provisions about Aislabie, Thomas Vernon, his father-in-law, who had himself once been a South Sea director, provided the opposition with some fresh fuel by an ill-advised approach to General Ross, one of the fiercest members of the Secret Committee. Ross at once made a dramatic report to the House, and Vernon was deprived of his seat. Later in the month more feeling was whipped up by a special report from the Committee that Knight's former confidential clerk, Clayton, had been interfering with their witnesses by 'laying his hands violently on this examinant's face, squeezing his jaws very hard, and saying that if this examinant discovered anything he would be the death of him'. Clayton was imprisoned by order of the House, but as the Session dragged on far beyond the time for normal summer adjournment Brodrick saw his hour was over. He withdrew from active leadership of the Committee. In spite of calls of the House and circular letters from the Speaker requiring attendance, Members were steadily drifting away to the country, and the numbers at divisions steadily declined. No squire would willingly stay in London during June, with the corn growing.[9]

The House was already thinning when on 26 May the great question of what each director should be allowed to keep came up at the end of the Committee stage of the Sufferers Bill. The proceedings of this day have been described by the grandson of the director Gibbon, the historian of the Roman Empire, with an accuracy that does him credit, seeing, as he himself admits, that he was 'neither a competent nor a disinterested judge'.

Lowndes's original suggestion that each director should be allowed to keep one-eighth of his net assets was rejected as not leaving scope for distinguishing 'the various shades of opulence and guilt'; and the names were simply considered one by one. All the directors had put in petitions—Blunt's had been greeted with derisive cheers—and some of them had been able to take advantage of the interval to do some lobbying; but in practice the fate of each depended on what Walpole and his gradually consolidating ministerialist phalanx would do for him.

Fellowes and Joye, as the two senior office-holders of the Company, came first. Sloper, with some truth, tried to excuse Fellowes on the ground that he had not been so active 'in the late vile and pernicious practices as some others (owing perhaps rather to the heaviness than the purity of his mind)'; but he was for all that the richest director. His accounts showed that he had taken full advantage of the long prices during the boom, and out of a balance of £243,000 he was allowed £10,000. Fellowes was not a knave. He had stuck loyally to his stock when the slump came, and held no less than £86,000 of it when he was judged. But it is difficult to say he did not deserve this savage penalty, though it broke him. Three years later he died, aged only fifty-three, at the house in Carshalton he had managed to keep.

Joye's guilt was so plain that it was hardly discussed. He had received a suspicious block of shares from Knight at a modest price early in the spring of 1720, and had been indispensable to the whole scheme. Admittedly he had made precious little, most of his profits having been swallowed up in bankruptcies and broken bargains, but he was still worth £40,000, and was allowed only £5,000 out of it. The death of his father, Peter, soon made him a rich man again, but even so it must have been with mixed feelings that he presided, as Guy's principal executor, over the early years of the hospital the sagacious stationer had founded out of South Sea gains. When he died in 1737, he left precisely the amount of his Parliamentary allowance to start a charity school in Blackfriars.

Sympathy for continental protestantism was still a powerful force, and the extreme of leniency was shown to two directors of foreign origin, Janssen and Jacobsen. Janssen, though very rich, was elderly and distinguished, a man of broad culture as well as immense commercial prestige going back to the early days of the Bank of England, on whose board he had four times served. His wife was a sister of Robert Henley, the wit, and his brother-in-law was a Bertie. His accounts showed a decrease in his net assets of £56,000 since June 1720, and he had not unloaded undue quantities of stock during the panic. He had lost his seat in Parliament, and had suffered imprisonment. Above all, he had privately enlisted Walpole's interest. In spite of protests from Jekyll and the fire-eating General Ross, who pressed the Committee to a division, he was allowed the largest sum of any director—£50,000 out of nearly a quarter of a million. Even so, the misjudgement of rejoining the South Sea board in 1719 and the crime of lending it his unique reputation cost him altogether nearly £300,000. Wimbledon had to be sold—it was picked up at a bargain price by the Duchess of Marlborough—but Hanover Square survived, and there he died, twenty-five years later, at the age of ninety.

Jacobsen, the steelmaster, was allowed to keep all but the odd hundreds of his balance of over £11,000. He was Sir Gilbert Heathcote's son-in-law, as well as being fairly guiltless.

Four of the ex-directors—Horsey, Ingram, Tillard, and Edmundson—were not serious business men at all. Two of these had lost comfortable official jobs; all four had lost money and already had good reason to regret the evil hour in 1718 when they had been induced by more important relatives and friends to join the South Sea board. They were allowed at least half their modest estates, and in some cases more.

Genuine tradesmen, with one significant exception, also ran the gauntlet without many bruises. Eyles, the clothier (who was related to a Bank director), kept two-thirds of his £34,000. Page, the brewer, one-third of the same; Delaporte, the thread merchant, after a protest from Molesworth, over half of £17,000; Morley, the importer of wine and currants, practically the whole of his modest balance of £1,869. 10s. 3d. Hugh Raymond, the shipbuilder and late Colonel of the Tower Hamlets Militia, was conceded half his estate, which included an unusual quantity of jewellery, a holding in the Royal

Lustring Company of doubtful value, and a great deal too much South Sea stock for its well-being; so was Hamond, Fellowes's Turkey merchant neighbour at Carshalton. The exception was Astell, the Baltic trader. He had some claims to sympathy, for he had lost not only a good deal of property, but his wife and most of his family as well when his house was burned down in the winter of 1720.* But he had also been one of the most talkative witnesses during the investigation, and for that reason Walpole's friendship was not extended to him. He was at first allowed only £5,000 out of £27,000, though his friends rallied to get the concession doubled when the Bill came before the whole House.

The treatment of unashamed financiers, even those who had good friends and had played no very significant part in the affair, was on the whole harsher. Five City men were fairly blameless in this sense: Gore, Reynolds, Chapman, Chaplin, and Blackwell. Gore and Reynolds were especially well-connected, one as member of a far-flung banking family, and the other as a sinecurist in the West Indies and a property-owner in Lancashire. Gore kept more than half his substantial estate, and Reynolds all but £4,000 of his, as well as his office of Provost Marshal of Barbados, which was especially excepted from forfeiture. But Chapman, though he was a personal friend of Walpole and had concentrated during the critical period more on the insurance schemes (in which he was deeply interested) than on the South Sea, had to be content with £10,000 out of £45,000, and Chaplin, for whom even Molesworth put in a good word, with the same amount out of £39,000. Blackwell, the ex-diplomatist son of the parliamentary general, returned an estate of £83,000, and although the £10,000 originally allowed was raised to £15,000 when the Bill reached a later stage, his gigantic Norfolk estates, carefully accumulated over twenty years, had to be dispersed.

A still darker view was taken of the financiers Read, Master, Lambert, and Turner. Read's considerable wealth seems to

---

* It was, however, heavily insured.

have been founded on pepper, but he had made at least £60,000 by dealing in South Sea stock, and his total balance was over £117,000. All but £10,000 was forfeited. Master, who had graduated from lending money to ship's captains, naval chaplains, and other seafarers, to farming the land revenue of London and Middlesex, had died since compiling his accounts, but the House was so shocked by the evidence in them of how public money had been used for private gain, that they left his widow—the daughter of the Earl of Leicester—and five children by a previous marriage only £5,000. Turner had the misfortune to bear the name of the senior Sword Blade partner, though he appears to have been no more than a fashionable speculator. His assets came to over £40,000, but his debts to almost the same, leaving only £881 for the Committee to consider. They took £81. A dispute took place over the stock-broker Lambert, who pleaded ignorance of what was happening in London through having been so busy enriching himself in Paris. In the end his original allowance of £10,000 (out of £83,000), was, like Blackwell's, increased to £15,000.

With Child and Houlditch the Committee moved yet nearer to the heart of the conspiracy. As Benjamin Tudman's old partner Child had long been an intimate associate of Blunt; Houlditch had served as a director since the foundation of the Company and was a notable crony of Knight's, having handled a great deal of business in Holland for him. Worse still, his transactions in land had been particularly unscrupulous. Child was allowed £10,000, and Houlditch was lucky to be allowed £5,000, £1,000 being the initial suggestion.

There remained, apart from Fellowes, Joye, and, of course, Knight, whose whole property within reach (coming to over £300,000 gross) had already been seized by the Company, seven men who represented the core of the swindle. Gibbon's bill-broking house, with assets running to £112,000, was subjected to the enormous forfeiture of £96,000, which, in his grandson's words 'proclaimed him eminently guilty'. Yet he was able, in the sixteen years which remained to him, to repair his fortunes 'by the skill and credit of which Parliament had been unable to despoil him'. Fortunately for history, he died almost as rich as the South Sea had found him.

Chester the goldsmith, West India merchant, and planter, was worth £170,000 gross—a very rich and a very guilty man. His estates in England and the Indies brought in £1,300 a year in rent alone. He had two country seats and nearly £100,000 in South Sea stock and bonds. Like Gibbon, he had been deeply implicated in the secret allocations to Members of Parliament and others, and, although he had been a rich man long before becoming a South Sea director, he was cut down to £10,000.

Sawbridge had escaped as a Sword Blade partner, but had to suffer as a director, and all but £5,000 of the modest £21,000 at which he put his balance was expropriated. It is some comfort that to this extent at any rate the fraudulent bankruptcy of the Sword Blade was frustrated.

Harley's old financial familiar, Arthur Moore, had the courage to speak up for his former protégés, the officials Grigsby and Surman, but to little purpose. Grisgby, as a professional stock-broker, was fair game, even though the old man was now so infirm that he had been unable to hand in his inventory personally. Somebody quoted a chance remark he had made in his prosperous days that he would feed his horses on gold, and in the end the ex-coffeeman was voted one of the smallest allowances of all, only £2,000. Surman was able to plead his comparatively junior status, and the help he had given in unravelling his superior's misdoings. He also had the grace to admit what was only too clear from his accounts showing a balance of £121,000 (£158,000 gross)—that he had been a considerable gainer by the whole business. But, as with Astell, willingness to talk was no passport to the friendship of the government party on the Committee. Horatio Walpole suggested almost complete forfeiture, and eventually £5,000 allowance was agreed upon. On this, which was only a little less than his admitted fortune in 1719, Surman was able to resume his banking career, first with his old firm of Martin, and finally as senior partner in a firm of his own, Surman,

Dinely, and Cliff. His daughter married a Viscount's son, and he died, respectable and indeed armigerous, in 1759. Of all the South Sea men, with the single exception of Knight, Surman probably had the most bounce.

The climax was, of course, the question of what should be allowed to Blunt, and here the clash between the party of vengeance and the ministerialists came into the open. The leaders of the Secret Committee tried hard to reward their star witness with at least the rags of his £183,000. From the back benches 1s. was suggested. It was a perfect chance for Walpole to outplay the avengers at their own game. He personally led the attack on Blunt, citing earlier instances of knavery to get the scrivener's allowance fixed at a mere £1,000.

Blunt's friends did not desert him, and eventually managed to raise the figure to £5,000 before the Bill passed; but it was the end of his career. He retired to Bath, where not, one may suspect, wholly unprovided, he spent the last fourteen years of his life in comparative obscurity. His only further appearance in history was his citation—the last until very recent times—before the Court of Chivalry for improperly using the arms of the ancient family of Blount of Sodington.* He died before the question could be settled, leaving behind his baronetcy and a progeny which developed into a spreading tree of army officers, administrators, and clergymen, among them one of Queen Victoria's chaplains, the Rev. James St. John Blunt, and Bishop Blunt of Bradford; who was Sir John's direct descendant in the sixth generation.

Blunt was not the most evil nor the most picturesque of the directors. This place, as the Commons clearly felt, must be reserved for Francis Hawes. His house in London was crammed with curios and works of art, and he had two other major establishments, one at Kettering, the other at Reading. His whole fortune had been built out of abuse of official position. The turnover in one of his accounts alone—that with his brother Thomas, which was fed mainly with Navy money—

* Heraldic ambition ran in the family. Tudman had been prosecuted by the heralds for the same offence in 1707. So too Craggs and Surman.

came to over a million in six months. Huge blocks of the Customs revenue in his custody had also been played on the stock exchange for his personal benefit. Above all he had been the evil genius of Chancellor Aislabie, and the agent through whom his most questionable dealings had been conducted. His allowance was later increased slightly, but the Committee put it at £31. 0s. 2¼d. from an estate returned as that much over £40,000.[10]

*　　　*　　　*

Behind Walpole's stiffening defences, Lowndes was making steady progress with the plan for final settlement of the South Sea affair, which crowned his forty-two years' work at the Treasury. Unlike the earlier schemes of reconstruction, which were both based on the principle that private bargains should be left intact, the new plan proposed to rearrange a whole network of private transactions by parliamentary fiat. So glaring was this retrospective interference in the financial affairs of individuals that Parliament felt obliged, in presenting it, to disarm criticism by a footnote to the resolutions in which it was embodied. 'When we first entered into consideration of this extensive and perplexed affair', wrote the Commons, 'we thought it most advisable to leave every man's property to be determined by due course of law; and were of opinion that no relief or abatement could properly be prescribed or given, but from the South Sea Company; but the discontents of people daily increasing, and the uncertain and doubtful events which threatened very great and valuable properties, creating such infinite anxieties and dissatisfactions, as had a most fatal and general influence upon all publick and private credit, the interposition of Parliament became unavoidable; and we found ourselves under the necessity of resuming the consideration of this nice and intricate matter; and to endeavour to remove, as far as possible, the chief and greatest inconveniences.'[11]

This grudging surrender of *laissez-faire* principles may be summarized as follows:

259

1. *Exchequer Liability.* The seven millions originally bid by the Company for its privileges was remitted. As a *quid pro quo* two millions of the Company's stock (and, of course, the related interest payment on it from the Exchequer) was to be abolished. This caused such an outcry that it later had to be forgone.

2. *Loans from the Company.* These were cancelled, and the stock deposited for them as security was transferred to the Company. The borrowers (except those who had deposited no security, who were to pay the whole of their debts) were to pay 10 per cent. of the amount borrowed to the Company, a provision that caused one Member to say, he 'wondered anybody that had borrowed money and refused to pay it could look anybody in the face'. One hundred and thirty-eight other Members, however, were borrowers.

3. *Money Subscriptions.* The last three had already been reduced by resolution of the Company to the rate of £100 stock for every £400 subscribed. They were now reduced to £100 stock for every £300 subscribed—the rate at which the First Subscription had been taken—and the issue was to be based on money so far paid in: there were to be no more instalments.

4. *Annuities and Redeemables.* The Company was required to issue additional stock to all who had converted on the August terms, to give them the same proportion of stock to converted debt as those who had converted in May.

5. *Surplus Stock.* The balance of stock authorized under the original South Sea Act, and remaining after carrying out the above distributions, was to be divided proportionately among the shareholders—a provision which, among other things, gave handsome compensation to original proprietors who had held on to their stock throughout the crisis and suffered nothing worse than shock.

6. All contracts for the purchase of any stock, whether South Sea or other, which had not been completed or settled by 29 September 1721 were to be void if the vendor did not possess the stock in question at the time the bargain was made, and in

any case if not entered in books opened for the purpose by 1 November.

The ultimate settlement varied slightly from the scheme set out in these resolutions, but the following table, severely simplified, shows its effect compared with the original plan for distributing the stock, and the interim change made by the Company in September 1720.

	Original plan £m	Interim adjustment £m	Final adjustment £m
Stock allotted to:			
Original Proprietors .	12·32	12·32	16·68
Money Subscribers .	10·25	3·22	5·40
Annuitants (May) .	3·56	3·56	4·84
(August) .	0·47	0·94	1·91
Redeemables . .	1·98	3·96	7·17
Balance . . .	9·42	14·00	Nil
	38·00	38·00	36·00

Altogether this £36 million capital represented something like £50 million at normal market values: £12·43 million in annuities; £14·39 million in redeemables; and about £10 million cash subscribed, plus the original capital created in 1711 and enlarged in 1719. The effect of the reconstruction was therefore to make the average price at which stock was held 140; but there were very wide divergencies among the various groups of stock-holders. Taking the average of those who had come in during 1720, one can say they had put up about £180 for each £100 of stock, while the former holders of redeemable Debt taken by themselves had put up over £200.* So far as the Exchequer was concerned the cost of servicing the National Debt, in terms of the Company's annuity plus the

* This takes no account of the payment in bonds and cash which were included in the conversion terms. To the extent that these were regarded as capital, and not as windfalls of income, the position of the recipients was better than I have shown. It was improved still further by amendments to Lowndes's Bill and the restoration of the £2 million suppressed stock—see the careful specimen calculations made by Scott.

interest on Debt whose holders had withstood the temptation
to convert, was very little if at all better than it had been at the
beginning of 1720; and indeed, when the final adjustments
had taken place, slightly worse.

★   ★   ★

It was 5 July, more than a month after the normal time for
ending the Session, before the last of the resolutions was voted.
The opposition were worn down, but at least they had the
satisfaction of seeing that Aislabie had not slipped through
their fingers. The Sufferers Bill, in which his name was included, had now reached the Lords, and his friends had high
hopes that he would escape monetary penalties after all. But
Sunderland longed only to get the whole business over with as
little fuss as possible. When the peers had examined a series
of witnesses, and Lord Onslow had remarked that, if they were
to be believed, nobody was to blame for anything, a feeble
effort was made to get the Commons to be more specific about
the written evidence against Aislabie. It led to nothing, and
after hearing two blustering, self-contradictory, and extremely
long speeches from the ex-Chancellor, the House decided
without a dissentient to leave the Bill as it was. They dealt
even less ceremoniously with the clause relating to Craggs's
estate when Sawbridge, under pressure, admitted that the
Sword Blade Company neither received nor expected any
consideration whatever for the note for £37,000 they had
given to the late Postmaster. As a result, the four heiresses had
to share an estate diminished by about £70,000.[12]

Aislabie was left nearly £120,000 with which to support
country life at Studley, and contributed only £45,000—a
reasonable estimate of his bribe and stock exchange gains—to
the pool under the Sufferers Bill. From then onwards he
showed, as his biographer observes, that 'it was not in the arena
of political turmoil alone that Mr. Aislabie's abilities were
manifested'. When Lord Harley visited him at Studley in 1726
he was shown the 'handsome canal recently finished', a quarter
of a mile long, feeding waterfalls and cascades. He cultivated

the neighbourhood as well as his estates, and the horn on which the curfew is still sounded in Ripon market-place was beautified at his expense. His wife scandalized the neighbours by organizing horse races for women wearing breeches and riding astride. More to the purpose, he continued to control both parliamentary seats for Ripon, and members of his family occupied them until he and his son William (who added Fountains Abbey to the property) were in their graves and Studley passed to their cousins, the Robinsons, Earls de Grey and Marquesses of Ripon. On 2 February 1722 Walpole had his last official communication from his predecessor, thanking him for all he had done—'you may see, that by making me free, you have made me your creature and most obliged humble servant'. Accompanying it was the King's private stock account, on which a substantial balance due from Aislabie was unobtrusively settled. He is commemorated beside the lake at Fountains in a temple erected by his son, to Piety.[13]

★   ★   ★

By 25 July, in a dwindling House, Walpole finally got the reconstruction embodied in an address to the Crown, and at once brought the Session to an end. But Parliament was not allowed to disperse. It was immediately reconvened for a special midsummer Session in which, with no more than a rump of Members, Walpole forced through the necessary legislation as the only business.

The speech delivered by the King on 31 July to barely a hundred Members and a handful of peers must be among the shortest on record. He was 'persuaded that at this season of the year your deliberations will be confined to what is absolutely necessary on this extraordinary occasion'. But despite the neatness of the manœuvre, the last stages were brutal. On 4 August the few Members struggling to the House had to run the gauntlet of a mob of public creditors, who thrust leaflets into their hands demanding to be heard against the proposed settlement. Their voices could be heard menacingly just outside the chamber as Ward, an East India Director, and Heathcote presented a petition on their behalf, and in a last effort to revive the atmosphere of scandal Brodrick spoke once more, denouncing the Ministry. But Walpole was now conscious of his mastery, even in face of this formidable combination. Waving at the empty benches, he said the House had given its word to the five-sixths of its Members who were absent that the settlement embodied in the resolutions should be passed into law. He carried a motion to adjourn by 78 to 29, and after a threat of the Riot Act the grumbling crowd dispersed, one of them shouting as he went, 'You first pick our pockets, then send us to gaol for complaining.'

In the next three days the Bill passed through all its stages in the Commons with barely fifty Members present; and after a protest from the irrepressible Coningsby the Lords agreed in a single sitting. On 10 August the King dismissed his Parliament with the good news that commercial relations with Spain had been renewed on the terms of Utrecht and an admonition 'in your several stations to suppress profaneness and immorality'. Messengers from the Secretary of State's office wrecked the presses that had been printing the Secret Committee's reports. The Robinocracy had begun.

Epilogue

IN OCTOBER 1721 Robert Knight made a hole in the wall of his cell at Antwerp and disappeared through it, taking the sergeant of the guard with him. It was said with some colour of probability that the authorities, having been bribed to keep him, had now been bribed to let him go. In the same month John Law, after twenty-seven years' exile, landed at Rochester from the flagship of the British Baltic squadron, on which he had obtained a passage from Copenhagen. As he came on shore he was greeted by the Duke of Argyll, Lord Londonderry and other financially-minded members of the upper class.

Law spent nearly four years in England, securing a pardon for the death of Wilson, but waiting in vain for a sign of forgiveness from France. Apart from Lord Coningsby, who wanted to start an inquiry into the authority for his voyage, the British public regarded him, on the whole, with polite curiosity, and the government thought he might prove a useful instrument. But he was poor now, and beginning to show his age of fifty-three. His letters, in spite of occasional flashes of spirit, began to take on a querulous, cadging tone. But there was none of this in the memoirs of his administration and his comparison of it with the South Sea promotion, which he composed during these years. They have all the old trenchancy and certitude of rightness. 'I improved the Company's resources', he wrote, 'but the South Sea Company did not propose to make its dividends out of its income, and the profit of its trade, but proposed to give back to its proprietors a part of their principal yearly'; and with still more pith: 'The South Sea directors worked against England. I worked for France.'[1]

In the end Walpole wearied of him and sent him on a sleeveless mission to Bavaria. His travels began again, and

265

eventually he settled at Venice, the home of the state lottery, where he had made his first fortune. There he talked finance with visitors in Florian's and explained to all who would listen —Montesquieu among them—how ill used he had been, until he died in 1729. He is buried in San Moise, the rococo church of the Jesuits, under a slab placed there many years afterwards by his grand-nephew, General Count de Lauriston, who found himself in command of the Napoleonic garrison of Venice in 1808.

Knight, the lesser man, fared better. After his disappearance from Antwerp, he turned up in Paris, and the Regent was privately informed through the Duchess of Kendal of King George's personal wish that the demand his Ambassador was making for extradition should be refused.[2] He was in time to witness the end of the Mississippi. In the course of the operations known to history as the 'Visa', twenty-seven commissioners examined and adjusted every recorded transaction in Mississippi stock. Then, in October 1722, 'après le jugement universel du royaume, viendra la conflagration générale'. All the 'registers, journals, extracts, inventories, ledgers, lists and minutes of decision' were made up into eight immense bundles and solemnly burned in an iron cage so constructed that not a leaf should escape destruction. 'On ne veut pas', wrote the lawyer Marais, 'qu'il reste rien de tout cet ouvrage, et on a bien raison de détruire par le feu un travail si injurieux pour la nation.' The commissioners took it in turn to preside during the many days that were needed to reduce the whole accumulation to ashes. It was a ritual purification, the destruction of a dream.[3]

Knight, with the status of an exile rather than a fugitive, turned once more to finance and compiled another fortune, smaller than the one he had left behind, but big enough for a comfortable life. It was a surprisingly tolerant age. Steele sent him a new play to read, with a passage marked about ingratitude. Many English visitors came to his hospitable house in Paris, among them Fanny Vane, the *demimondaine* daughter of the director Hawes, who speaks in the memoir of her career that Smollett put into *Peregrine Pickle* about the 'kindness of M. K——, who had been formerly intimate with my father', when she visited Paris. Eventually Knight formed a close friendship with Bolingbroke, by this time in self-imposed exile at La Planchette, and cemented it with a family marriage between his son Robert and Bolingbroke's half-sister, Henrietta St. John. The marriage was a failure, but young Robert Knight was not. Attaching himself to the Grenvilles, he entered Parliament and crowned a successful political career with the earldom which, if things had gone otherwise, might have been his father's.[4]

Bolingbroke and even Lovat were allowed to return, but so long as Walpole ruled the ban against Knight's homecoming was absolute. Not even an application made by the ex-cashier through Queen Caroline, accompanied, it was said, by a large gift of money, could alter it. The story went that he travelled every year to Calais to look at the cliffs on the opposite shore, and groan, as Lady Irvine oddly put it, 'for the leeks and garlic of England'. He had to wait for twenty-one years, until Walpole in his turn went down before the Secret Committee; and it is conceivable that even after that lapse of time one of the motives for his pardon was the hope of revelations to Walpole's disadvantage.* At any rate the pardon came surprisingly quickly. It was one of the first acts of the new Secretary of State, Lord Gower, in 1742, and a fitting return to the man who had laid the foundations of Gower's fortune by endowing him with a timely piece of the bear's skin long ago.[5]

The ex-cashier lived on for three years more, sour and crotchety now, at the house he had himself built near Epping in 1720, which his son had bought back from the trustees. By the time he died in 1745 most of the original ambience of the Bubble had gone. The Sword Blade partnership had been dissolved by death, Sawbridge alone surviving; Aislabie had been laid to rest in Ripon Cathedral, although an Aislabie still sat for Ripon at Westminster. Only ten of the directors of

---

* In 1741, during Walpole's final crisis, the 'Screen' prints of 1721 against him were reprinted. *Cf.* D. M. George, *English Political Caricature* i 79.

1720 were still alive; and the trustees appointed to liquidate the forfeited estates, though they had taken longer than their French counterparts, had completed their task more than fifteen years before. Their report, accepted by Parliament in February 1729, showed they had realized more than £2 million for the Company's benefit. More than three-quarters of this came from the former directors, and nearly half the rest from Knight.*

Yet the South Sea Company was still alive, and its Governor was still the King. It continued, though fitfully, to focus the dream of British commercial empire in South America, and had succeeded in dragging Walpole into the war which was fatal to the Robinocracy. In 1750, by a treaty supplementing the settlement of Aix-la-Chapelle, the Company at last surrendered the Asiento and its other commercial privileges to the Spanish Crown in return for a lump sum of £100,000; but even so it remained in existence, although its only function was to distribute in dividends the annuity it received from the government as interest on a diminishing portion of the National Debt. The deeply engrained conservatism of the eighteenth century kept it in being for more than a century after it had ceased even to pretend to trade, and it was not until Mr. Gladstone succeeded for the first time to the office of Aislabie that the decision was taken to abolish this curious self-

---

* More precise figures, taken from the Interim Report of the Trustees dated 6 May 1728 in the House of Lords Archives, are (to the nearest thousand):

	£ net paid to Company
Ex-directors	1,510,000
Knight	239,000
Surman	93,000
Craggs	69,000
Grigsby	52,000
Aislabie	45,000
Other assets realized	75,000
Total	2,083,000
Less Trustees' expenses	87,000
	1,996,000

About £300,000 worth of assets remained to be sold at the time this account was prepared.

governing appendage to the National Debt it had once proposed to swallow. In 1854 the South Sea capital, which had by
that time shrunk to the £10 millions at which Harley had
originally fixed it, was converted into mid-Victorian consols,
and the Honourable the South Sea Company finally came to
an end.

*   *   *

The traditional view of the South Sea Bubble as a kind of
historical freak, foisted by men of base birth on an infinitely
gullible public, has its roots in the period of suspicion and
despair that followed immediately on the collapse. The early
stages of this myth are summed up in Swift's stanzas of 1720
about the institution he had welcomed so fulsomely in the
Examiner:

> *As fishes on each other prey,*
> *The great ones swallowing up the small,*
> *So fares it in the Southern Sea,*
> *The whale directors eat up all.*[6]

The perfected myth echoes down into the nineteenth-century
prose—oddly reminiscent of the Gettysburg Address—of John
Francis, the historian of the Bank of England:

> Thus ended the great delusion, alike memorable and
> melancholy. . . . There is nothing to sanctify, there is
> nothing to redeem it.
> The great delusion of the period stands alone in its
> infamy, its disgrace, and its misery; and though we dare not
> venture to hope that the spirit, which shook the country to
> its centre, has passed away . . . yet let it be hoped that, if
> witnessed again in England, a Prince of the Blood may not
> sanction it. . . .[7]

This purely cautionary result is certainly one of the great
consequences of the Bubble in our history. It is a kind of
memento mori, and may well have helped to establish the
tradition—for it is an English tradition, however imperfectly

it is practised—that business and politics are separate, even though overlapping, worlds. But to fix the Bubble's place in history we must look elsewhere—to its setting in the contemporary European scene and to the perspective of the generations before and after it.

There can be no doubt that the wave of confidence on which the Bubble rode was European in character. The full extent of the continental financial crisis, or even the extent of foreign participation in the London market of 1720, will perhaps now never be traced. But there is enough evidence of the scope of the affair in the transactions of a single man—the Huguenot Lambert with his clientele in seventeen European cities, ranging from Hamburg to Naples, and from Venice to Dublin. When Blunt told his colleagues that the eyes of Europe were upon them, for once he spoke no more than the truth.

Turn now to the perspective of generations. An English boy leaving school in the year of the Revolution reached maturity in a world that had radically changed, both in intellectual climate and in the tokens of everyday life. A new political philosophy and a new view of nature had captured the educated mind. Newspapers had become a matter of every day. The language of his boyhood was old-fashioned when he was forty. London had grown—in the last five years of the seventeenth century alone its population had increased by no less than one-fifth. There was the sense of old ways losing ground and of new ones with unlimited possibilities, which we recognize as progress.

This boy's son was to be an elderly man before he would notice any marked change in the standard of English life to which he was brought up. Instead of imagination and overconfidence his world was cautious, cynical, and artificial, clinging to all that was vested and established: a world we can study in slow motion.

During those years London ceased to grow, and its stationary population died at the unequalled rate of forty per 1,000.* Gin is commonly blamed, but gin itself is the symptom of a

---

* Today the London death rate is about 10 per 1,000.

frustrated and demoralized urban population. The commercial world grew timid and unenterprising. The Bubble Act itself remained on the statute book for more than a century, and in 1733 was reinforced by Sir John Barnard's Act forbidding bargains in which the vendor did not actually possess the stock disposed of at the time of the sale. These were symptoms rather than causes of the inhibition of risk capital during these years. The shock had been enough. As Gibbon said of his grandfather, 'his fortune was overwhelmed in the shipwreck of the Year Twenty, and the labours of thirty years were blasted in a single day'. It was true not only of a single man, but of a business generation.[8]

Inventiveness did not cease. In quiet corners of England and Scotland the work that eventually led to the great resurgence of economic activity still went on. But novelty ceased to be fashionable, or to interest business men. In Cornwall the steam engine remained at the stage it had reached under Queen Anne until the business genius of Boulton fertilized the ingenuity of Watt—an interval of seventy years. Fifty years after Captain Welbe had suggested it, Australia was colonized.

As with commerce, so with politics. The strength of the Robinocracy and the successor ministries of the Pelhams lay in their profound conservatism and caution. Gestures and personality in politics, which had counted for so much under Queen Anne, were a handicap under George II. The press, which had played so important a part in Augustan political life, was treated with hostility by Walpole and indifference by the Pelhams; and the status of the journalist declined. There were to be no more Addisons for a long time. The prospects of reform in any major institution, and even such modest administrative improvements, as Walpole's excise scheme, were overwhelmed by the hatred and fear of change. Parliament, having flared into its last demonstration of seventeenth-century ferocity over the directors, settled into its long period of apathetic omnipotence. Above all, Great Britain abandoned, for more than twenty years, the pretensions to European leadership which had been advanced by Marlborough and

Stanhope. Walpole never crossed the Channel or the North Sea as Prime Minister.

The Bubble, therefore, stands between two epochs, and separates them with remarkable distinctness. It grows naturally out of one and stands guardian over the other. In its context, this fatal end to the Commercial Revolution was also its climax: a climax due to intellect and ambition outrunning technological achievement and accessible resources. The possibilities for improving material standards had sprung to mind before the physical means to realize them were available.

The Mississippi and the South Sea represent a Saurian Age in our financial history; they were too big to survive any process of natural selection. If rage for bigness had been avoided, and if the zest and enterprise of the Augustans had been supported by a better technology and more abundant resources, it is not unreasonable to suppose that the Commercial and Industrial Revolutions might have shaded into each other instead of being separated by the forty or fifty years' pause we tend to think of as the eighteenth century. For they were undoubtedly part of the same process. The stability of those years is the stability of arrest, not completeness. The temporary stunting of enterprise was part and parcel of the artificiality of this apparently balanced age in which so little changed.

A pause so long is rare in modern history, and the fact that it was a pause may explain much of the fascination it holds for us. To delete the years of arrest conjures up all kinds of fancies: a conquest and struggle over the Western Hemisphere and the Indies by European powers using machine guns and steam-driven ironclads instead of muskets and wooden men-of-war; Gray musing to the distant rattle of the threshing machine; Garrick acting by gaslight; and Dr. Johnson holding forth in his compartment as the Edinburgh train belches smoke and thunders across the countryside.

Appendix

A South Sea Directory, 1711-1721

THIS DIRECTORY BRIEFLY gives such biographical particulars as I have been able to recover about those who served on the Court of Directors of the South Sea Company down to (but excluding) the election of February 1721; together with those of Robert Knight, Cashier, Robert Surman, Deputy Cashier, and John Grigsby, Accountant. For the few names that are famous or have entries in *The Dictionary of National Biography*, I have given only minimal information. To indicate all the sources used would be burdensome, and I have not attempted it; but I should mention the various volumes of the Harleian Society's publications, notably Le Neve's *Knights* and Musgrave's *Obituary*; Francis's *London Bankers*; and the *Particulars of the Estates of the South Sea Directors*.

Most of the abbreviations used are traditional. *Gov.*, *Sub-Gov.*, *Dep.-Gov.*, and *dir.* where unqualified, mean Governor, Sub-Governor, Deputy-Governor, and director of the South Sea Company. E.I. means East India Company, and Bank, Bank of England. A marginal asterisk indicates the holding of office at the time of the crisis.

ACTON, Francis, *ob.* 1728. *dir.* Aug. 1712-Feb. 1715. Private banker. May have been related to Gibbon *q.v.* Kept shop in St. Michael's Lane and forwarded letters for Swift.

ARGYLL, John Campbell, 2nd Duke of, 1678-1743. *dir.* Feb. 1715-Feb. 1718. Soldier and Statesman. *m.* 1701 Mary Duncombe (name changed from Brown) *d.* of Anthony Duncombe, Receiver-General of Excise. Succeeded as D. of Argyll (Scotland), 1703; helped negotiate Union, 1705; commanded under Marlborough, 1706-9; Commander-in-Chief, Spain, 1711, and Scotland, 1712. Played major role in Hanoverian Succession and commanded against the Jacobites in Scotland

1714-15. Disgraced, 1716. Returned to favour and created D. of Greenwich (G.B.) 1719. With his brother, the Earl of Islay, a friend and kinsman of John Law.

★ ASTELL, William, *ob.* 1740. *dir.* Aug. 1712-Feb. 1721. Timber merchant and dealer in marine stores. Contractor to the Navy in 1720 for hemp, tar, and planks. Correspondents in Elsinore, Carolina, Riga, Lisbon, Königsberg, Archangel and Amsterdam. Estate in Bedfordshire. Gross assets 1721, £80,419.

BATEMAN, James, *ob.* Nov. 1718. *Sub-Gov.* July 1711-Nov. 1718. Financier. *s.* of Joas Bateman, of Hazebrouck, book-keeper (who *ob.* 1704), naturalized under Charles II. *dir.* Bank 1694-9 and concerned in Darien Scheme (impeached, 1696). *dir.* (New) E.I. 1698-9, when concerned in negotiating union with the old E.I. Knighted, 1698. Sheriff, 1701. *Dep.-Gov.* Bank 1703-5; *Gov.* Bank 1705-7. Purchased Shobdon Court, Herefordshire, 1705. Subscribed to Prince Eugene's Loan, 1706. Alderman, 1707. *dir.* Bank 1707-11 and E.I. 1710-11. M.P. Ilchester, 1711-13, East Looe 1715-18. Lord Mayor, 1716-17. Eldest Son (later created Viscount Bateman) *m.* 1720 Betty Spencer, *d.* of Earl of Sunderland. Second son *m.* Ann, *d.* of Sir Robert Chaplin *q.v.* Property in Herefordshire, Surrey, Hertfordshire, and Middlesex.

BEACHCROFT, Robert. 1650-1721. *dir.* July 1711-Aug. 1712. Cloth merchant. Sheriff and knight, 1700. Alderman, 1710. Lord Mayor, 1711-12.

BENSON, Robert. 1676-1731. *dir.* July 1711-Feb. 1715. Politician. M.P. Thetford 1702-5, York, 1705-13. Succeeded Harley as Chancellor of Exchequer, 1711; raised to peerage as Lord Bingley, 1713, and appointed Ambassador to Spain. Recalled 1714.

★ BLACKWELL, Lambert. *ob.* 1727. *dir.* Feb. 1715-Feb. 1721. Diplomatist and financier. Grandson of John Lambert, Parliamentary General and regicide, *s.* of a Governor of Pennsylvania. Consul in Florence 1688-90, and Leghorn 1690-6. Knight 1697. Envoy to Tuscany, Genoa, and Venice, 1697-1705. Acquired first estate in Norfolk 1700, and in succeeding twenty years built up a rent roll in that county of over £4,000 a year. M.P. Wilton 1708-10. Bart. 1718, by which time he had substantially retired from business. A close associate of Janssen, *q.v.* Gross assets 1721, £138,036.

BLUNT, Charles. *ob.* 1720. *dir.* July 1711-Aug. 1712. Nephew (?) of John Blunt, *q.v.* Paymaster of the Two Million Adventure 1711 and manager of the Classis Lottery of 1712. Cut his throat, Sept. 1720.

* BLUNT, John. 1665-1733. *dir.* July 1711-Feb. 1721. Scrivener and financier. A Baptist. *s.* of Thomas Blunt of Rochester (formerly of Strood), shoemaker and freeman, and Isabella Blacke, *d.* of Thomas Blacke of Frindsbury, Kent. Apprenticed to Daniel Richards, scrivener, of Holborn. Free of Merchant Taylors' Company 1689. *m.* Elizabeth Court, of Warwickshire (who *ob.* 1708), 4 *s.*, 3 *d.* Liveryman 1691. Secretary of the Sword Blade Company about 1703. *dir.* E.I. 1710-11. Adviser to the government on lotteries 1710-12. Contributed financial memoranda to Swift's *Last Four Years* 1712. *m.* for second time, 1712 or 1713, Susannah, *d.* of Richard Craddocke, former Governor of Bengal and *dir.* Royal Africa Co. 1684-6 and 1689-95, she being widow of (1) John Banner, salter, of London, and (2) Benjamin Tudman, goldsmith, *q.v.* Acquired extensive real estate in London. Leading exponent of South Sea Scheme 1719-20. Bart. June 1720. Refused to be Master of Merchant Taylors' Co. 1720. Arrested January 1721, and subjected to penalties. Retired to Bath. Prosecuted for misuse of arms in Court of Chivalry, 1732. Gross assets 1721, £184,043.

CASWALL, George. *ob.* 1742. *dir.* July 1711-Feb. 1718. Banker and stockbroker. A Particular Baptist. *s.* of John Caswall, Bailiff of Leominster. Goldsmith banker in partnership with John Brassey in Lombard Street 1700. Director of Sword Blade Co. 1701 onwards. Connected financially with Harley, and used his influence to support him at Leominster, 1710. J.P. Hereford. M.P. Leominster March 1717. Knighted ('The Lem Knight') Feb. 1718. Sheriff 1720-1. Expelled from the Commons and imprisoned March 1721. Again M.P. Leominster Feb. 1722-42.

* CHAPLIN, Robert. *ob.* 1728. *dir.* Feb. 1718-Feb. 1721. Barrister and financier, 3rd *s.* of Sir Francis Chaplin (merchant and Lord Mayor 1677-8). Inherited Shobdon Court, Herefordshire, from uncle 1704, and sold it to Bateman, *q.v.* (whose *s.* his *d.* married), living thereafter in London and Lincolnshire where he owned extensive property (as also in Somerset, Herefordshire and Durham). M.P. Grimsby 1715. Bart. 1715. Expelled from Commons and imprisoned, 1721. Gross assets 1721, £75,678.

* CHAPMAN, William. 1670-1737. *dir.* Aug. 1712-Feb. 1721. Importer of wine and fruit and insurance director. Younger *s.* of Sir John Chapman (Lord Mayor 1688-9). *m.* Elizabeth *d.* of Thomas Webb, Clerk of the Kitchen to William III. Knighted Oct. 1714. *dir.* and (1720) *Sub-Gov.* of London Assurance. Correspondent of Walpole. Eldest *s. m.* (1736) daughter and heiress of James Edmundson, *q.v.*, and was later (1759) M.P. Taunton. Gross assets 1721, £51,015.

* CHESTER, Robert. *ob.* 1729. *dir.* Feb. 1715-Feb. 1721. Goldsmith and West India merchant. *s.* of Edward Chester, of Royston, sometime Sheriff of Herts. *m.* 1702 Katherine Davies. Goldsmith in Lombard St. 1705. Owned extensive estates in Antigua and Barbados. Gross assets 1721, £170,218.

* CHILD, Stephen. *ob.* 1762. *dir.* Feb. 1718-Feb. 1721. Banker. 6th *s.* of Sir Francis Child (banker and Lord Mayor 1698-9). In partnership with Tudman *q.v.* 1697, and succeeded to his business on his death. Lived at Richmond. Gross assets 1721, £64,687.

CLARKE, Samuel. *ob.* 1733. *dir.* July 1711-Feb. 1715. Merchant and financial official. Commissioner of Customs 1686-7, 1694-9, 1705-8. Receiver-General of Land Tax for Herefordshire 1710. Knighted 1712. Involved in allegations of bribery on behalf of Harley, 1715.

CRAWLEY, Ambrose. *ob.* 1713. *dir.* July 1711-Aug. 1712. *Dep.-Gov.* Aug. 1712-Oct. 1713. Ironmaster. On his connexions see *Namier, American Revolution*, p. 11.

DEACLE, John. *ob.* 1723. *dir.* July 1711-Aug. 1712. Woollen draper. A native of Bucks and M.P. Amersham 1715-22.

DECKER, Matthew. 1679-1749. *dir.* July 1711-Aug. 1712. Financier and economist. Born in Amsterdam. Settled in London 1702. *dir.* E.I. before 1711 and 1713-22. Bart. 1716. M.P. Bishop's Castle 1719-22. London correspondent of Dutch banks, e.g., Pels of Amsterdam. Author of *Serious Considerations on the High Duties* (1743) and *Essay on the Decline of Foreign Trade* (1744). Introduced the cultivation of the pineapple. *d. m.* 6th V. Fitzgibbon 1744.

* DELAPORTE, Peter. *dir.* Feb. 1715-Feb. 1721. Thread merchant, descended from Huguenot family (Caen) naturalized 1656. *s.* of James Delaporte, merchant, of London, and lived at Wandsworth. Gross assets 1721, £34,931.

DESBOUVERIE, Christopher. *ob.* 1733. *dir.* July 1711-Feb. 1715. Turkey merchant. 3rd *s.* of Sir Edward Desbouverie (*ob.* 1694). Elder brothers: William (Bart., *dir.* Bank 1700-7, *Dep.-Gov.* Bank 1707-9, *dir.* Bank 1709-11 and ancestor of the Pleydell-Bouveries, Viscounts Folkestone); and Jacob (Bart, M.P. Hythe 1698 and 1713-22). *dir.* Levant Co. 1707. Knighted 1713.

DOLLIFFE, James. *ob.* 1715. *dir.* July 1711-Feb. 1715. Banker. *dir.* Bank 1708-10. Knighted Oct. 1714.

DURLEY, Henry. *dir.* July 1711-Feb. 1718. East India merchant and *s.* of the commander of an Indiaman.

* EDMUNDSON, James. *ob.* 1729. *dir.* Feb. 1718-Feb. 1721. Financial official. Purser of the First Rate man-of-war *Royal Anne.* Dismissed 1721. *d. m. s.* of Chapman, *q.v.* Gross assets 1721, £11,785.

* EYLES, Francis. *ob.* 1735. *dir.* Feb. 1715-Feb. 1721. Cloth merchant. A Wiltshireman. *s.* of Sir John Eyles Lord Mayor 1687-8, and nephew of Sir Francis Eyles (banker, alderman and bart., *dir.* Bank and subsequently *Dep.-Gov.* and *Gov.* Bank 1697-1715). Lived at Earnshill, Wilts. M.P. Devizes (where he owned the market-place) 1715-21 (when expelled the House). Cousins: Sir Joseph Eyles, *dir.* E.I., and M.P. Chippenham 1715-22; and Sir John Eyles, *dir.* and *Gov.* Bank, 1721, *Sub-Gov.* of South Sea Company, and subsequently M.P.

for Devizes (1722) and Postmaster-General 1739-45. Gross assets 1721, £54,379.

* FELLOWES, John. 1671-1724. *dir.* July 1711-Nov. 1718. *Sub-Gov.* Nov. 1718-Feb. 1721. India and general shipper. Related to the Coulson East India family. Brother a Master in Chancery. Unmarried. Associated with Thomas Pitt in diamond transactions 1700. From 1714 lived at Carshalton in a house formerly belonging to Dr. Radcliffe. Bart. 1719. Gross assets 1721, £277,905.

* GEORGE I, King of Great Britain. 1660-1727. *Gov.* Feb. 1718-1727.

GEORGE, Prince of Wales, later GEORGE II, King of Great Britain, 1683-1760. *Gov.* Feb. 1715-Feb. 1718, and 1727-60.

* GIBBON, Edward. 1666-1736. *dir.* Feb.1715-Feb.1721. Linen-draper, clothing contractor, and bill-broker. *s.* of Matthew Gibbon, linen-draper, of Leadenhall St. and Hester Acton. Grandfather of the historian. *dir.* E.I. 1706 and 1710-11. Commissioner of Customs 1711-14, being during this time intimately concerned in financial transactions in support of the government. Also associated with Sword Blade Co. Bill-broking house had extensive international connexions. Gross assets 1721, £112,543.

* GORE, John. 1692-1763. *dir.* Feb. 1715-Feb. 1721. Financier and wine-shipper. Belonged to an extensive London family, being 2nd *s.* of Sir William Gore (Lord Mayor 1702, *dir.* Bank 1694-7, 1698-9, and 1701-6). Brother of William Gore, *q.v.*, and Charles Gore who *m. d.* of Sir William Dolliffe, *q.v.* Also a friend of Francis Stratford, *q.v.*, and of Swift. *m.* Hannah Sambrooke, *d.* of Sir Jeremy Sambrooke. M.P. Grimsby 1747-60. Lived at Bush Hill, Enfield. Gross assets 1721, £86,218.

GORE, William. *ob.* 1739. *dir.* July 1711-Oct. 1712. Eldest *s.* of Sir William Gore, and brother of John Gore, *q.v. m.* 1709 Mary Compton *d.* of Earl of Northampton. M.P. Colchester 1710-15, St. Albans 1722-7, Cricklade 1734-9. Lived at Tring.

* GRIGSBY, John. *ob.* 1722. Accountant of the South Sea Company. Coffee merchant and licensed stockbroker. Appointed

Accountant September 1711, removed Feb. 1721. Lived at Wanstead. Gross assets 1721, £61,978.

★ HAMOND, William. 1664-1741. *dir.* Aug. 1712-Feb. 1721. Wool-dealer and finisher, trading with Levant. Prominent in Levant Co. and knighted in that connexion 1717. Lived at Carshalton, but owned extensive City real estate, including sites in Exchange Alley. Gross assets 1721, £52,862.

HARLEY, Edward. 1664-1735. *dir.* July 1711-Feb. 1715. Lawyer and politician. Brother of Robert Harley, Earl of Oxford, *q.v.*, and Nathaniel Harley, of the Levant Co. Recorder 1692 and M.P. 1698-1722 for Leominster. Auditor of the Imprest 1702-14.

HARLEY, Robert, Earl of Oxford. 1661-1724. *Gov.* July 1711-Feb. 1715. Chief Minister 1710-14, and founder of the South Sea Company.

★ HAWES, Francis. *ob.* 1764. *dir.* Feb. 1715-Feb. 1721. Financial official. Clerk in the Treasurer of the Navy's office 1698. Cashier to Treasurer of the Navy 1716. Receiver-General of Customs 1717. Treasurer of the Muscovy Co. 1720. Lived at Purley Hall, Reading, and Winchester Street, London, which latter house contained, among other things, 62 pictures, a model of a ship in gold, a Last Judgement 'with gold figures', and collections of ivories and early playing cards. The confidant of Aislabie, and father of Lady Vane, the *demi-mondaine*. Gross assets 1721, £165,587.

HAYES, Daniel. 1649-1732. *dir.* Feb. 1715-Feb. 1718. Africa merchant. Member of Court of Assistants of Royal Africa Co. 1706, 1708, 1710-12. Acted for Swift and Prior in the sale of Prior's poems, 1721. Probably father of Charles Hayes, the mathematician and *Sub-Gov.* of Royal Africa Co.

HOARE, Richard. 1648-1719. *dir.* July 1711-Feb. 1718. Banker. Knighted 1702, Sheriff 1709, and Lord Mayor 1712. M.P. for London 1710-15. Banker to the Civil List 1710. Strong opponent of the Bank of England both on its foundation and on renewal of its charter.

★ HORSEY, Richard. *ob.* 1734. *dir.* Feb. 1715-Feb. 1721. May have been an American (cf. Edward Horsey, Governor of Carolina, *ob.* 1738) and is described as 'colonel', though he does not appear in contemporary English lists. Gross assets 1721, £36,420.

* HOULDITCH, Richard. *ob.* 1736. *dir.* Feb. 1718–Feb. 1721. Financial official and woollen draper. Commissioner (1715) and Receiver-General (1718), of the Stamp Office. Had extensive connexions in Holland. Related through his wife to Benjamin Tudman, *q.v.* Lived in Hampstead. Gross assets 1721, £111,025.

* INGRAM, Arthur. *ob.* 1749. *dir.* Feb. 1718–Feb. 1721. Financial official. Related to the Lords Irvine, to whom he probably owed his appointment as Treasurer of the Salt Duties (1718). The family was an ennobled mercantile one descended from Sir Arthur Ingram, Customer of London and Cofferer to King James I. The director Ingram must not be confused with his namesake Arthur Ingram (1689–1736), M.P. for Horsham 1715–21. Gross assets 1721, £28,895.

* JACOBSEN, Jacob. 1680–1735. *dir.* Feb. 1715–Feb. 1721. Steelmaster. Of German origin, inherited steelyard from his uncle, Thomas Jacobsen, London agent of the Hanse. *m.* Anne *d.* of Sir Gilbert Heathcote. Knighted 1718. *Sub-Gov.* London Assurance, 1720. Lived at Walthamstow. Gross assets 1721, £50,928.

* JANSSEN, Theodore. 1658–1748. *dir.* July 1711–Feb. 1718 and Feb. 1719–Feb. 1721. Financier. *s.* of Isaac Janssen, a Huguenot, and settled in England 1680. Naturalized 1685. Broke into paper-making monopoly 1687. *dir.* Bank 1694–9, 1700–1, 1707–11, 1718–19. Knighted 1696. Published *A Discourse of Trade*, 1697. *m.* 1697, Williamza, *d.* of Sir Andrew Henley. *dir.* E.I. (New) 1706. Published *General Maxims of Trade*, 1713. Bart., 'at special request of the Prince of Wales', March 1715. M.P. Yarmouth 1715–21 (expelled the House). Lived at Wimbledon (bought 1717—large library) and Hanover Square. Owned Queen's Square (rent roll £1,358 per year, tenants included a duke, two earls, a bishop and a countess). Banked with Andrew Pels of Amsterdam. State of account shows interests in tin, china, Suidas's Lexicon, and transactions with Earl of Stair and Holy

Roman Emperor, as well as in Genoa, Amsterdam, Antwerp and Paris. Gross assets 1721, £254,109.

* JOYE, Charles. 1659-1737. *dir.* Feb. 1715-Feb. 1719. *Dep.-Gov.* Feb. 1719-Feb. 1721. Baltic merchant. *s.* of Peter Joye, Baltic merchant, of Southwark. Treasurer of St. Thomas's Hospital and senior executor of Thomas Guy. Endowed a charity school in Blackfriars. Gross assets 1721, £45,311.

* KNIGHT, Robert. 1675-1744. Cashier to the South Sea Company. *s.* of Robert Knight, citizen of London (living 1682) and grandson of William Knight of Barrells, Henley in Arden, Warwickshire, an armorial family going back to the fifteenth century and of Elizabeth Randoll. *m.* Martha, *d.* of Jeremiah Powell, of Evenhope, Salop. 1 *s.* 2 *d.* Appointed Cashier, Sept. 1711. Governor of St. Thomas's Hospital, 1717. Acquired much landed property and built Luxborough House, near Chigwell, Essex. Absconded, Jan. 1721; arrested in Flanders, imprisoned, escaped, and settled in France. Resumed financial career, and became a friend of Henry St. John, *q.v.*, arranging a conference between him and the British Ambassador in Paris, 1735. Not allowed to return to England until 1742, when he resumed occupation of Luxborough House. His eldest *s.*, Robert (*b.* 1702), *m.* Henrietta, half-sister of Henry St. John (from whom he was separated) and was M.P. Grimsby 1734-7, Lord Luxborough (Ireland) 1745, M.P. Castle Rising 1747-54, Earl of Catherlough (Ireland) 1763, M.P. Grimsby 1762-8, and M.P. Milborne Port 1770-2: a follower of Grenville, he gained possession of the family estates in Warwickshire where his (illegitimate) descendants continued to the present century.

* LAMBERT, John. 1666-1723. *dir.* July 1711-Feb. 1721. International stockbroker, and commodity dealer. *s.* of a Huguenot. Educated at Camberwell Dissenting Academy with Defoe. *m.* a French wife. Raised money for the government and knighted 1710. London correspondent for Samuel Bernard and John Law. In Paris speculating Aug. 1719 to Feb. 1720, when expelled. Accounts show interests in wine, cloth, lead, oranges, salt, cochineal, shares in the London Bridge Water Works, and dealings in Venice, Cadiz, Paris, Madrid, Malaga,

Hamburg, Orleans, Amsterdam, Montpellier, Genoa, Rouen, Naples, Rotterdam, Antwerp, and Dublin. Held South Sea stock as nominee for many residents in these places. Lived in Mincing Lane. Gross assets, Feb. 1721, £189,451.

MARTIN, Joseph. 1649-1729. *dir.* July 1711-Feb. 1715. Turkey and East India merchant. Consul in Moscow 1702-5. M.P. Hastings 1710-15. Commissioner for French Commercial Treaty 1713.

* MASTER, Harcourt. *ob.* 1721. *dir.* July 1711-Feb. 1721. Money-lender and tax-farmer. *s.* of Giles Master, barrister, and Elizabeth Harcourt. Knighted 1714. Commissioner of the Duty on Hides 1718. Receiver-General of Land Tax for London and Middlesex 1719. *m.* Lady Betty Sidney, sister of E. of Leicester, 1720. Gross assets 1721, £70,760.

MOORE, Arthur. 1666-1730. *dir.* July 1711-Apr. 1713. Politician. Of Irish origin. *m.* the daughter of a wealthy doctor, and concerned in East India trade. M.P. Grimsby 1701-15 (when unseated by Sir R. Chaplin, *q.v.*). *dir.* E.I. (Old) 1706, and Royal Africa Co. 1710. Commissioner of Trade 1710. Expelled from South Sea directorship for clandestine trading 1713. Again M.P. Grimsby in place of Chaplin 1721.

* MORLEY, William. *ob.* 1745. *dir.* Feb. 1718-Feb. 1720. Importer of wine and fruit. Probably a brother of John 'Merchant' Morley, the land-jobber and agent of Edward Harley, 2nd Earl of Oxford. Lodged in St. Mary Axe. Gross assets 1721, £14,007.

ONGLEY, Samuel. 1646-1726. *Dep.-Gov.* July 1711-Aug. 1712· *dir.* Aug. 1712-Feb. 1715. Linen-draper. Lottery Commissioner 1711. Alderman 1712. Knighted 1713, and M.P. Maidstone 1713-15. Said to be worth £10,000 a year. Name passed through his sister (who married into the Henley family) to the Barons Ongley. See also Janssen.

* PAGE, Ambrose. *ob.* 1743. *dir.* Feb. 1715-Feb. 1721. Brewer. Beer contractor to Navy 1711. Owned real estate in home counties. Gross assets 1721, £57,923.

PITT, George, of Strathfieldsaye. *ob.* 1735. *dir.* July 1711-Feb. 1718. Country gentleman and politician. Cousin of Thomas Pitt, Governor of Madras, and godfather of William Pitt, Earl of Chatham. M.P. Hampshire 1701-05, Wareham 1705-10, Hampshire 1710-13, Wareham 1713-22.

* RAYMOND, Hugh. *ob.* 1737. *dir.* Feb. 1715-Feb. 1721. Shipbuilder. Commanded East Indiaman *Duchess* 1705. Captain (1715) and Colonel (1720) in Tower Hamlets Militia. Built South Sea Company's ship *Royal Prince*, of which his brother was Captain, 1718. *dir.* London Assurance 1720. Required to resign his commission 1721, and returned to the sea. Lived on Tower Hill. Gross assets 1721, £92,708.

* READ, Samuel, *ob.* 1733. *dir.* Feb. 1715-Feb. 1721. Pepper merchant, of Hackney. Gross assets 1721, £121,825.

REYNOLDS, Thomas. *ob.* 1762. *dir.* July 1711-Feb. 1721. Financial official and Lancashire landowner. Chairman of the Victualling Commissioners 1715-21 (when removed). Provost-Marshal of Barbados (sinecure) 1717. Gross assets 1721, £40,776.

ST. JOHN, Henry, Viscount Bolingbroke. 1678-1751. *dir.* July 1711-Feb. 1715. Politician. Secretary of State 1710-14. Exiled 1714-23. Retired to France 1735, and became a friend of Knight, *q.v.*

* SAWBRIDGE, Jacob. *ob.* 1748. *dir.* July 1711-Feb. 1721. Banker and stockbroker. Of Warwickshire family, but lived in Kent and Hackney. Associated with Sword Blade Co. 1704. M.P. Cricklade 1715-21. *s. m. d.* of Elias Turner, *Gov.* Sword Blade Co., 1720. Grandson Lord Mayor and partisan of Wilkes. Grand-daughter Catherine Macaulay the historian. Gross assets 1721, £121,689.

SHEPHEARD, Samuel. *ob.* 1719. *dir.* July 1711-Oct. 1713. *Dep.-Gov.* Oct. 1713-Feb. 1719. Financier. Recoinage Commissioner 1697. Prominent in formation of New E.I. Forced to stop payment 1701. Committed to prison for corrupt electoral practices 1701. M.P. London 1705-10. Floated loan for Prince Eugene 1706. Harley's banker. *dir.* E.I. 1710.

STRATFORD, Francis. *dir.* July 1711-Aug. 1712. Baltic trader and friend of Swift, with whom he had been at school and at Trinity, Dublin. *s.* of Richard Stratford, partner of Sir T. Vyner. *dir.* Bank 1698-9. Cultivated Swift and was nominated *dir.* of South Sea Co. by his influence 1711. Raised £40,000 for government. Bankrupt 1712, and had to go abroad 1713.

* SURMAN, Robert. *ob.* 1759. Deputy Cashier of the South Sea Company. Native of Tredington, near Tewkesbury. A clerk in Martin's Bank, and, from 1715, in the Sword Blade Bank. Deputy Cashier at South Sea House, 1718. Granted arms, 1720, and bought land on a large scale. Removed, and subjected to penalties, 1721. Partner in Martin's Bank 1730. Senior partner in Surman, Dinely and Cliff, 1748. Gross assets 1721, £158,262.

TENCH, Fisher, 1674-1736. *dir.* Oct. 1712-Feb. 1718. Country gentleman. *s.* of Nathaniel Tench. (*dir.* Bank 1694-7, and subsequently *Dep.-Gov.* and *Gov.* Bank.) Sheriff of Essex 1711-12. M.P. Southwark 1713-22. Bart. 1715. Lived at Low Leyton.

* TILLARD, William. *b.* 1675. *dir.* Feb. 1718-Feb. 1721. East India merchant. Served in India 1699-1705 (President of Masulipatam and friend of Thomas Pitt). Nephew of Sir James Bateman, *q.v.* Gross assets 1721, £19,579.

TOWNSHEND, Horatio. *ob.* 1761. *dir.* Feb. 1715-Feb. 1718. Merchant and politician. Youngest *s.* of 1st Viscount Townshend and brother of Charles Townshend, Walpole's brother-in-law. M.P. Yarmouth 1715-22, and Heytesbury 1727-34.

TUDMAN, Benjamin. *ob.* 1712. *dir.* July 1711-Aug. 1712. Clothier and goldsmith. *s.* of John Tudman of Throgmorton Street. In business as goldsmith banker at 76 Lombard Street from 1697 and in partnership with Stephen Child, *q.v.*, from 1703. Prosecuted for improperly using armorial bearings at the funeral of his first wife 1707. Second wife later *m.* John Blunt, *q.v.*

* TURNER, John. *dir.* Feb. 1718-Feb. 1721. No connexions traced. He lived in Mark Lane in considerable style and seems to have been a speculator. Gross assets 1721, £19,579.

VERNON, Thomas. *ob.* 1726. *dir.* July 1711–Feb. 1715. Politician and Turkey merchant. Knight and secretary to the Duke of Monmouth, 1685. M.P. Whitchurch 1710–21 (when expelled) and 1722–6. Aislabie's brother-in-law.

WILLIAMS, John. *dir.* July 1711–Feb. 1715. May have been connected with the goldsmith family of Williams, whose business was taken over by Tudman, *q.v.*; but is described as 'of Essex' when knighted in 1713.

WISHART, James. *ob.* 1723. *dir.* July 1711–Feb. 1715. Naval officer and diplomatist. Captain, 1689; Rear-Admiral and knight, 1704; Lord of the Admiralty 1710; M.P. Portsmouth 1711–15. Negotiated shipping quotas in Holland 1711–12. Commander-in-Chief Mediterranean with orders not to engage the enemy 1713. Bombarded Barcelona 1714. Superseded 1714.

References

Where it is necessary to repeat a source frequently in the following references its abbreviation is given in [ ] after the first recital of its full title. This practice has not been extended to familiar abbreviations. Small Roman numerals indicate volumes or parts of volumes. Final Arabic numerals are page or folio numbers.

CHAPTER I

1. Journal of the Rev. Robert Kirk: *London and Middlesex Archaeological Society*, New Series vi 322.

2. De Laune, *Angliae Metropolis*, 1690.

3. Dyer, *The Fleece* 1-3.

4. *The Particulars and Inventories of the Late Sub-Governor, Deputy-Governor, and Directors of the South Sea Company; and of Robert Surman, late Deputy-Cashier, and of John Grigsby, late Accomptant, of the said Company. Together with Abstracts of the same.* 1721. [*Particulars*]. s.n. Joye.

5. Anderson, J., *Annals of Commerce* iii 580.

6. Quoted by Guitard, E., *Colbert et Seignelay Contre la Réligion Reformée*.

7. Defoe, *True Born Englishman*.

8. On this episode see, especially, the memorandum in Public Record Office, London [PRO] SP35 xviii 118 which, though unsigned is attributable to James Johnston of Warristoun, at the time Secretary of State in Scotland.

9. *Hatton's Merchant Magazine*, 1694.

10. Scott, W. R., *The Constitution and Finance of English, Scottish, and Irish Joint Stock Companies to 1720* [*Scott*] i 316-17

11. Add. MS 36,785 quoted by K. G. Davies, *Economic History Review* II iv 3.

12. Nef, J. U., *Rise of the British Coal Industry* i 390.

13. Davies, K. G., *Joint Stock Investment in the Later Seventeenth Century: Economic History Review* II iv.

14. *Scott* i 335-6.

15. Davies, *op. cit.*

16. *Ibid.*

17. Gregory King, in his celebrated calculation of 1696, put the merchant population at 10,000, of whom four-fifths were in domestic and one-fifth in foreign trade. At least a third of the urban population of 1·5 million were Londoners, and it would not be unreasonable to reckon that at least half the mercantile population lived in London—probably more.

18. Hatton, *op. cit.* gives his examples of book-keeping in terms of exporting cloth against the products of the Eastern Mediterranean. See Wood, C. A., *History of the Levant Company.*

19. *The Weekly Journal; or Saturday's Post. With Freshest Advices foreign and Domestick* [*Mist*]. 18.4.1719.

20. *Regina v. Jones* (1703): 2, Lord Raymond 1013.

21. Patent Office Specifications numbers 274 (Waterproofs, 15.9.1691); 315 (Armoured vehicles, 6.3.1693); 317 (Plastic wood, 10.3.1693); 331 (Burglar alarm, 12.1.1694); 276 (Pin table, 17.12.1691); 337 (Pianola, 20.10.1694).

22. See, in particular, Fay, C. R., *Locke v. Lowndes* (*Cambridge Historical Journal* IV ii); and *Newton and the Gold Standard* (*ibid.* VI. ii).

23. *Williams v. Williams*: Parch. 5 W. & M. Anno 1692. Carlton 269; *Clarke v. Martin* 1702 *per Holt C. J.*; 3 and 4 Anne, cap. 9.

24. For Blunt's parentage and early career see the normal reference books on baronets (but not DNB, whose only Blunts are clergymen). I owe the details of Blunt's apprenticeship and membership of the Merchant Taylors' Company to the kindness of the Clerk of the Merchant Taylors' Company.

25. The Craggs pedigree and Somerset Herald's life of the elder Craggs (written when its subject was rich and powerful) are printed in the Eliot genealogies published by the Earl of St. Germans. The story about his son's birth is in Lady Mary Wortley Montagu's *Account of the Court of George I*. Harley, in Stowe MS 1058 testifies to the looks of Mrs. Craggs.

CHAPTER II

1. *Scott* iii, statements K (i), O, and Q.

2. Walcott, R., *The East India Interest in the Election of 1700-01: English Historical Review*, 1956.

3. *Early History of the Funded Debt: C. 9010*; Defoe. *Essay on Projects*; *Calendar of Treasury Books*, 1689; Jenkinson, H., *Archaeologia*, 1912.

4. 8 and 9 Will. III, cap. 20.

5. *Calendar of State Papers Domestic*, 1691 521-2; *Scott* iii 436; *Selden Society* xxviii.

6. Le Neve, *Knights* 436; *London Gazette* 5689.

7. Price, F. G. Hilton, *A Handbook of London Bankers* 22-3; Add. Chart. 24,473 and 24,474 (the latter, with Blunt's signature, is dated April 1704); *London Gazette* 4066; *Scott* iii 435-43.

8. Defoe (?), *The Anatomy of Exchange Alley*, 1719, 37; Price, *op. cit.*

9. Burke's Landed Gentry (1853), 1194; *Harleian Society* lxii 151.

10. Townsend, G. F., *The Town and Borough of Leominster*; Price, J., *Historical and Topographical Account of Leominster*.

11. *Anatomy of Exchange Alley* 36-9; Price, F. G. H., *op. cit.*

12. *A Discourse upon Grants*, 1700; *An Argument Proving that it is More in the Interest of the Nation . . . that the Forfeited Estates in Ireland be Purchased by an Incorporated Company*, 1701; *The Secret History of the Trust*, 1702; *Cal. Treas. Papers* lxxx 4.

13. *London Gazette* 3828; *The Case of the Governor and Company for Making Hollow Sword Blades*, 1709; *Scott* iii 439 ff.

14. *Cal. Treas. Books* 1704 268.

15. *Cal. S.P. Dom. Petition Entry Book* vi. 148.

16. *A Short View of the Apparent Dangers and Mischiefs from the Bank of England, More Particularly Addressed to the Country Gentlemen*, 1707; *Arguments against Prolonging the Bank &c.*, 1707; *Some Reasons Against a Clause for Restraining All Corporations but the Bank of England from Keeping Cash*, 1707.

17. 6 Anne, cap. 22.

18. *Anatomy of Exchange Alley* 38.

CHAPTER III

1. Harley to Moore 19.6.1710: HMC Portland iv 545.

2. Drummond to Harley 8.8.1710, 22.8.1710, 4.9.1710; *ibid.* 559, 572, 583.

3. Macky, J., *Characters.*

4. Uffenbach, Z. von, *Journey to England in 1710* 124; George, M., *London in the Eighteenth Century*, Appendix; Patent Office Specifications 393, 395; Chamberlayne, *Magnae Britanniae Notitia* 1716 38.

5. Nettels, Curtis, *England and the Spanish-American Trade: Journal of Modern History* iii 1; Heathcote to the Board of Trade 28.8.1703. C.O. 137/45 51.

6. For Aislabie's career see Darwen, K. *John Aislabie 1670-1742* in *Yorkshire Archaeological Journal* cxlvii (1950) 262—a careful account with a full bibliography.

7. Uffenbach *op. cit.* 136-8; Hermitage to the States of Holland: Add. MS 17,677, 131; Drummond to Harley 15.6.1711: HMC Portland v 11.

8. Edward Harley's Memoir of the Harley Family: HMC Portland v 641-69; Richards, R. D., *The Lottery in the History of English Government Finance: Economic History* iii.

9. For the Classis, including Blunt's accounts, see the collection in the British Museum under 8223.e.9; Gibbon's account is in PRO T 1/168 20.

10. Lady Dupplin to Abigail Harley 3.5. 1710: HMC Portland iv 683.

11. Paterson to Harley 4.9.1710: HMC Portland iv 583-4.

12. The Patent of the Company's foundation is at B.M. Add. Chart. 16,281.

13. Swift, *Examiner* 7.6.1711; *Letter to a Member &c.* dated 3.5.1711 (the day after the announcement in the House, showing careful orchestration of publicity in advance); *A True Account of the Design &c.* 1711; *A View of the Coasts, Countries, and Islands &c.* 1711. The second of these pamphlets is also remarkable for the reference to Harley as 'Prime Minister'. It is fair to say that Harley denied the making of gains through inside knowledge—see HMC Portland v 464.

14. Defoe to Harley 17.7. and 20.7.1711: Healey, Letters of Defoe 338-349; Defoe, *Essay on the South Sea Trade.*

15. Harleian MSS 7497 and 7498; PRO T/1 168 10.

16. *The South Sea Whim* (*cf.* Swift, *Journal to Stella* 27.10.1711); *Particulars s. n.* Blunt.

17. Fifty-eight guineas for drafting charter—Directors' Minutes 19.12.1711; five hundred guineas for 'paines, charges, and troubles'—*ibid.* 9.7.1712; £3,260. 7s. 6d. for taking subscriptions. *Cal. Treas. Papers* 1.4.1713.

CHAPTER IV

1. Edward Harley to Earl of Oxford 2.2.1720: HMC Portland v 581.

2. Minutes of the Committee of Correspondence 1715: Add. MS 25,550.

3. Directors' Minutes 1711: Add. MS 25,494.

4. *Ibid.* 1711, 1712; Drummond to the Earl of Oxford 13.7.1711: HMC Portland v 49; Swift, *Journal to Stella* 4.1.1712

5. Directors' Minutes 20.9.1711: Add. MS 25,494; Toland, J., *Secret History of the South Sea Scheme* in his Collected Works (1726) i 407. The work is not Toland's, but was found among his papers. It was written by someone in the confidence of a director who was not a member of the inner ring, and is extremely hostile to Blunt.

6. For Knight and his family see Cooper, W., *Wootton Wawen, its History and Records* passim; and *Henley in Arden* 139-60. Also *Harleian Society* lxii 80-1.

7. Swift, *History of the Last Four Years of the Queen*, Davis's edition, 71.

8. Contract dated 10 July 1713—see Denman, Elizabeth, *The South Sea Company* 1711-18: *Journal of Economic and Business History* 1930.

9. Minutes of the Committee of Shipping 10.9.1714 and 13.1.1718: Add. MS 25,562.

10. Cowper, S., *Diary of Mary, Countess Cowper* 4.

11. Darwen *op. cit.*

12. Stanhope to Townshend 25.9.1716 and 9.10.1716, and to H. Walpole 6.10.1716: Coxe, W., *Memoirs of the Life and Administration of Sir Robert Walpole* [*Coxe*] ii 84, 98, 102; Dubois to the Regent 30.10.1716: quoted in Perkins, J. B., *France under the Regency* 384-7.

13. On Surman see Hilton Price *op. cit.*; *Anatomy of Exchange Alley* 36-7.

14. Patent Office Specification 418.

CHAPTER V

1. John Law to Robert Harley 14.6.1711: HMC Portland v 7.

2. Houghton MSS P82.

3. On Law generally the most recent English work is Hyde, H. M., *John Law*, which contains a bibliography. Law's complete works have been edited by Paul Harsin (1934).

4. Graham J. M., *Annals and Correspondence of the Viscount and First and Second Earls of Stair* i 263. This useful selection needs to be supplemented by the extensive despatches of Stair in PRO and BM.

5. *Ibid.* i 265-7.

6. The official despatches are in PRO SP78 clxiv to clxvii; the private despatches in Stowe MS 347.

7. Stanhope to Dubois 18.12.1719: Graham *op. cit.* ii 388-9.

8. Houghton MSS P82 and 83.

9. *Anatomy of Exchange Alley* 39.

10. John Gore to Craggs 3.2.1719 (dated O.S. 1718): Stowe MS 247 9.

11. 5 Geo. I, cap. 19.

12. Petrie, Sir C., *The Jacobite Movement* 294-6.

13. *Anatomy of Exchange Alley loc. cit.*

14. PRO SP35 xix 33, 34, 88; Steele to Knight 7.8.1719, Steele to Law 12.8.1719: *Correspondence of Richard Steele* ed. R. Blanchard.

15. Stair to Craggs 20.8 and 1.9.1719: Graham *op. cit.* ii 125.

16. Stair to Craggs 20.10.1719: PRO SP78 clxv 271; Stair to Stanhope 20.10.1719: PRO SP78 clxv 343.

17. Marais, Mathieu, *Memoirs*, November 1719.

CHAPTER VI

1. Aislabie's speech in *Timberland's Debates* [*Timberland*] iii 174.

2. *Chandler's Debates* vi 211.

3. *Commons Journals* [CJ] 1721 521; *Notes and Queries* 9th Series xii 155.

4. *Coxe.* ii 182.

5. *Timberland* iii 175.

6. *Powell's Weekly Journal* 20.2.1720. For the proceedings of the Directors during this period see *House of Lords Records* [HLR] 1721 Box 167B.

7. *Journal of the Institute of Bankers* 1912 131; *Notes and Queries loc. cit.;* Erasmus Lewis to Earl of Oxford 13.2.1720: HMC Portland v 592.

8. CJ xix 424-451.

9. *Lords' Journals* [LJ] 1721 434

10. Add. MS 17677 KKK 3 462-3.

11. Islay to Mrs. Howard 16.1.1720: Croker, J. W., *Letters of Henrietta Howard, Countess of Suffolk*; de Pye to Lord Strafford 13 and 23.2.1720: Add. MS 31,140 23, 28; Lord Strafford to de Pye 15.2.1720: *ibid.* 25.

12. Stair to Craggs 28.2.1720: PRO SP78 clxvii 129; de Pye to Lord Strafford 15.2.1720: Add. MS 31,140 17.

13. *Letter of Thanks from the Author of the Comparison to the Author of the Argument* reprinted in Boyer, A., *The Political State of Great Britain* [Boyer]; Stair to Craggs 11.3.1720: PRO SP78 clxvii 169; Delafaye to Tilson 21.3.1720: PRO SP35 xx 97.

14. Goldsmith MS 89 10; *Hoare's Bank, A Record*, Appendix.

15. Steele, *The Crisis of Property* (published 1.2.1720) and *The Nation a Family* (dedicated to Sir John Fellowes and published 26.2.1720).

16. Goldsmith MS 89 Transfer documents; Hoare *op. cit.* Appendix; CJ xix 569.

17. Aislabie to Hawes 4.4.1720: Add. MS 27,871 535.

18. *Timberland* iii 125.

19. The royal stock account is at Houghton MS P88 360; the bogus cash-book entries at CJ xix 451.

20. Mrs. Windham to Ashe Windham: HMC Beaufort and Others 200.

CHAPTER VII

1. Craggs to Stair 25.9.1718: Graham *op. cit.* ii 375.

2. Cowper *op. cit.* 128.

3. HLR Box 167A contains the bank accounts of Knight, Grigsby, Blunt and Surman. Surman had two accounts: one, which seems to have been his personal account, with T. and J. Martin; and the other with the Sword Blade, which was probably operated by him under Knight's directions as the main account used by the promoters for the manipulation of the market. There are two copies of this account, one being of the ledger entries in the bank's books and the other a 'mirror' of them used as a pass-book. The interpolated entries relating to the Prince of Wales appear in the former, but not the latter.

4. Plumb, J. H., *Sir Robert Walpole* i 283.

5. Cowper *op. cit.* 144.

6. Extract from Directors' Minutes (7.4.1720): HLR 167A.

7. Stair to Craggs 12.4.1720: PRO SP78 clxvii 273.

8. HLR 167A.

9. *London Gazette* 16.4.1720; *Mist* 30.4.1720.

10. Minutes of the General Court 21.4.1720; Boyer xix 449.

11. Notebook of Thomas Guy (facsimile in Guildhall Library, London).

12. Cowper *op. cit.* 141 ff.; *The Original Weekly Journal. With Fresh Advices, foreign and domestick* [*Applebee*] 16 and 30.4.1720.

13. CJ xix 305-11; *London Gazette* 12.4.1720.

14. Cowper *op. cit.* 158-9.

15. Atterbury to General Dillon 6.5.1720: Stanhope, *History of England* ii Appendix, 14.

16. *The Weekly Journal; or British Gazetteer* [*Read*] 9.4.1720. *Applebee* 7.4.1720; Puckle to Stanhope 11.4.1720: PRO SP35 xxi 10.

17. *Daily Post* [*Post*] 20.2.1720; Notebook in the possession of Mrs. Richard Asher. I am most grateful to Mrs. Asher and her husband, Dr. Richard Asher, for making this notebook available to me. It comprises a complete summary of South Sea finance with certain details which could only have been known to someone intimately concerned. Apart from its intrinsic interest it is a beautiful specimen of the penmanship of the period, and must have been prepared for someone of importance, conceivably Craggs or his heirs.

18. *Applebee* 2 and 30.4.1720; Steele, *The Theatre* xxi.

19. *Post* 26.4.1720.

20. *Particulars, passim.*

21. Stair to Craggs 22.5.1720: PRO SP78 clxvii 454.

22. Sayous, A., *Les Répercussions de l'Affaire de Law et du South Sea Bubble dans les Provinces Unies* in *Bijdragen voor Vaterlandsche Geschiednis en Oudheitkunde* vii 2; PRO SP101 lxix letter of 19.4.1720.

CHAPTER VIII

1. Minutes of the Managers from 12.5.1720 are in Goldsmith MS 89.

2. HLR 167A; Transfer documents in Goldsmith MS 89.

3. Instances of overwork in the Transfer Office are the Directors' Minutes for 21.3.1720, 24.3.1720, and 20.7.1720.

4. Goldsmith MS 89.

5. *Toland op. cit.* i.

6. *Boyer* xix 515-18.

7. *Journal of Institute of Bankers loc. cit.*; Toland *op. cit.* i; Hoare *op. cit.* Appendix.

8. James Windham to Ashe Windham late May and 12 July: HMC Beaufort and others 200.

9. *Poem in Honour of the Birthday of His Majesty King George, 1720*—copy in British Museum; *Post* 26.5.1720; *Applebee* 28.5.1720; *Mist* 21.5.1720.

10. Cowper *op. cit.* 170; *Mist* 21.5 and 18.6.1720; *Post* 26.5 and 8.6.1720; *Applebee* 28.5. and 6.8.1720.

11. Cowper *op. cit.* 159; *Mist* 21.5., 4.6. and 30.7.1720; Plumb *op. cit.* 310-12; *Postboy* 2.6.1720.

12. *Daily Courant* [*Courant*] 16.5, 21.6, 26.6, 5.7, 15.7.1720.

13. *Scott* iii; *Courant* 6.6.1720; *Post* 7 and 18.6.1720.

14. *Courant* 8 and 9.6.1720.

15. *Applebee* 2.7.1720; *Read* 2.7.1720.

16. *Mist* 11.6.1720.

17. CJ xix 572.

18. Guy's Notebook; CJ xix 430.

19. *Applebee* 18.6 and 16.7.1720; *Postboy* 2.6.1720.

20. *Mist* 11.6.1720; *Applebee* 11.6.1720; Houghton MSS P88 360.

21. The complete lists are in HLR 167B.

22. *Journal of the Institute of Bankers loc. cit.*

23. Toland *op. cit.* i. 423.

24. He followed the common practice of using the printed powers of attorney, which could be bought blank in the Alley, to sell at the right moment. See the collection of them in Goldsmith MS 89.

25. Mrs. Molesworth to Mrs. Howard 25.6.1720; Mrs. Howard to Mrs. Campbell June 1720: Croker *op. cit.*

26. *Applebee* 25.6.1720; *Mist* and *Read* 2.7.1720; HLR 167B.

27. Craggs to Stanhope 15.7.1720 in *Coxe* ii 189; *Directors' Minutes* 20.7.1720.

28. Toland *op. cit.* i 429; Sayous *op. cit.*; *Postboy* 7.7., 14.7., and 19.7.1720; *Post* 6.7.1720; *Courant* 7.7. and 16.7.1720; *Applebee* 23 and 30.7.1720; *Evening Post* 9.8.1720; *Read* 23.7.1720.

29. Crawford to Craggs 25.6.1720; same to Stanhope 9.7.1720; Sutton to Craggs 26 and 31.7.1720: PRO SP78 clxviii 69, 147, 216, 232, 251. For the Bernese see *Applebee* 16.7 and 6.8.1720 and Manning's despatches to Craggs dated 17.4, 22.5, 19.6, 10.7.1720 in PRO SP96 xx.

30. The disallowances were reported in all the papers on 12 July.

31. *Mist* 16.7.1720.

32. Craggs to Stanhope 15.7.1720: Add. MS 9149 175; *Post* 23.8.1720.

33. Newcastle to Charles Stanhope 29.7.1720: Add. MS 9149 169.

34. Craggs to George Clarke 30.6, 5.7, and 8.7.1720: Egerton 2618.

35. Craggs to Newcastle, 2.8.1720: Add MS 32,686 166; *Applebee* 6.8.1720.

36. Toland *op. cit.* i. 429.

37. *Read* 18.8.1720; *Applebee* 20.8.1720.

38. *Post* 23.7.1720; *Mist* 16.7.1720.

39. *Applebee* 16.8.1720.

40. *Post* 31.7.1720; Sutton to Craggs 7 and 15.8.1720: PRO SP78 clxviii 280 and 334.

CHAPTER IX

1. Craggs to Stanhope 26.8.1720: Add. MS 9149 184; Craggs to Sutton 25.8.1720: PRO SP 78 clxviii 392; Sutton to Stanhope: *ibid.* 350.

2. Plumb *op. cit.* 315; Pope to Lady Mary Wortley Montagu 22.8.1720: *Correspondence of Pope* ii 52.

3. Surman's bank accounts: HLR 167.

4. Craggs to Newcastle 2.8.1720: Add MS 32,686 186.

5. Toland *op. cit.* 443; Archives Etrangères Pol. Angl. cccxxxii 117-18. Plumb *op. cit.* 317. Jacomb surmised that the restriction on ministerial lists was to 'make a crowd at the books'; but the need to attract cash was at least as potent a reason—*Applebee, Read* and *Mist* for 27.8.1720.

6. *Freethinker* 18.10.1720; *Boyer* xx 375-6.

7. Craggs to Stanhope 2.9.1720: PRO SP78 clxviii 435.

8. Craggs to Stanhope 6.9.1720: Add. MS 9149 187; Jacomb wrote to Walpole the same day, *cf.* Plumb *op. cit.* 318; *Applebee* 10.9.1720.

9. *Boyer* xx 180-2.

10. PRO SP35 xxiii 22 (Blunt sent it to Craggs no doubt with a request for protection); HMC Dartmouth i 326.

11. *Applebee* 3.9. and 24.9.1720.

12. The minutes of this Committee are in Goldsmith MS 89, bound up with the relevant minutes of the Court of Directors.

13. *Boyer* xx 187-8; *Coxe* ii 135; and Committee minutes. It has generally been overlooked that there were two meetings at the Post Office between the Company, the Bank, and the Ministers. At the first, on 19 September, the terms of the 'Bank Contract' were roughed out, but the price at which the Bank was to take South Sea stock was left blank. Walpole's holograph of this version of the 'Contract' is in the records of the Bank of England. At the second meeting on 23 September the price was fixed at 400. Walpole's holograph minute of this is item 13 of Goldsmith MS 89.

14. CJ xix 430; *Applebee* 24.9.1720; Clapham, *History of the Bank of England* 85; *Post* 27.9.1720.

15. *Boyer* xx 188–98.

16. *Boyer* xx 246–64.

17. Lords Justices to the King 21.9.1720: PRO SP35 xxiii 54; Edward Harley to Earl of Oxford 27.9.1720: HMC Portland v 602–3; Pretender's Declaration of 10.10.1720 (N.S.): PRO SP35 xxiii 117.

CHAPTER X

1. *Read* 1.10.1720.

2. *Considerations on the Present State of the Nation*, 1720. The anonymous author was of opinion that 'one with another the manufacturers may be reasonably computed to drive three parts in four of their business with money borrowed at interest'. The pamphlet is well summarized in *Boyer* xx 316.

3. *Courant* 12.8.1720.

4. *Considerations &c. op. cit.*; *Post* 24.9.1720.

5. *Boyer* xx 278 ff., and 426 ff.

6. William Windham to Ashe Windham 27.9.1720: HMC Beaufort and Others 201.

7. W. Pulteney to D. Pulteney 20.11.1720: *Coxe* ii 194.

8. The Duchess of Portland wrote to the Duke of Newcastle in 1726 that 'the difficulties he [Portland] lies under in relation to his private affairs makes the thought of coming back into England terrifying': Add MS 32,687 190. The loss of the *Royal Anne* is described at length in *Boyer* xxii 537.

9. The Coles letters are in Goldsmith MS 89. Warner and Snow survived (as Strahan, Paul and Bates) down to 1856—just short of a bicentenary.

10. *Journal of the Institute of Bankers loc. cit.*; Hoare *op. cit.*

11. *Scott* iii; *Post* 22.10.1720; *Boyer* xx 301, 310, 460.

12. *Particulars* s.n. Edmundson; *Applebee* 1.10.1720; *Mist* 24.9.1720; *Courant* 27.9.1720; HMC Portland v 65.

13. Dr. Stratford to the Earl of Oxford 24.10.1720: HMC Portland vii 280; Halsband, *Life of Lady Mary Wortley Montagu* 103–5.

14. *Postboy* 27.10.1720; *Applebee* 8.10.1720.

15. For the flight of bullion see *Postboy* 4.10.1720; for plague *Applebee* 8.10.1720. Also relevant are the numerous advertisements for iron chests and a timely new edition, corrected, of the law on bankruptcy.

16. *Postboy* 25.10.1720.

17. *Read* 1.10.1720; Budgell's meeting was 17.10.1720 and is reported in *Boyer* xx 317-25. See also T. Harley to Earl of Oxford 18.10.1720 in HMC Portland v 604.

18. Committee Minutes: Goldsmith MS 89.

19. Clapham, *History of the Bank of England* 86; HMC Portland v 603; HMC Dartmouth i 326.

20. Plumb *op. cit.* 325.

21. Committee Minutes: Goldsmith MS 89.

22. Sunderland to Carlisle 19.10.1720: HMC Carlisle 24-5.

23. *Post* 12.11.1720

24. Committee Minutes: Goldsmith MS 89 (which gives 10.11, not 9.11 as in Clapham *op. cit.* 87).

25. Craggs to Stanhope 21.10.1720: SP78 clxix 111; Plumb *op. cit.* 329.

26. *Coxe* ii 194-5.

27. Serjeant Chesshyre's holograph endorsement on the Committee Minutes in Goldsmith MS 89. This opinion affects Clapham's statement (*History of the Bank of England* i 87) that 'there is nothing to support Aislabie's suggestion of illegality, in the Bank's withdrawal.

28. *Coxe* ii 197.

CHAPTER XI

1. Hermitage to the States General: Add. MS 17,677 KKK3 176; Brodrick to Midleton: 10.12.1720 *Coxe* ii 201-3.

2. *Parliamentary History* vii 680. This volume of the P.H. contains a long, useful, but somewhat inaccurate summary of the whole scandal.

3. CJ xix 380.

4. CJ xix 437; *Coxe* ii 203.

5. CJ xix 389-90; *Timberland* iii.

6. Steele to Mr. Barnham Good 22.12.1720: Blanchard *op. cit.* 'Mr. Knight says he would have convinced you you are mistaken had you stayed to hear him.'

7. *Coxe* ii 204.

8. *Applebee* 21.1.1721. T. Harley to Lord Harley 22.12.1720: HMC Portland v 610.

9. D. Pulteney to J. Molesworth 18.12.1720: HMC Various Collections viii 289; CJ xix 393.

10. Directors' Minutes HLR 167.

11. CJ xix 427.

12. *Boyer* xx 591-8; *Read* 24.12.1720.

13. James Windham to Ashe Windham 3.1.1721: HMC Beaufort and Others 201; Sir James Lowther to the Earl of Carlisle 29.12.20: HMC Carlisle 29.

14. *Parliamentary History* vii 393-4.

15. Richard Molesworth to John Molesworth 27.1.1721: HMC Various Collections viii 297.

16. *Coxe* ii 190-92.

17. Hermitage to the States of Holland 4.2.1721: Add. MS 17,677 KKK4 50.

18. *Boyer* xx 598-600.

19. CJ xix 436.

20. CJ *ibid.*; Lady Lechmere to Earl of Carlisle 24.1.1721: HMC Carlisle 28.

CHAPTER XII

1. *Boyer* xxi 91.

2. *Cf.* p. 56 for the deliberate echo of 1711.

3. *Timberland* iii; *Surtees Society* xxi.

4. Lords' Journals [LJ] xxi 405-6; Lady Irvine to Charles Ingram 26.1.1721: HMC Various Collections viii 102.

5. CJ xix 428.

6. *Coxe* ii 207; Lord Harley to Earl of Oxford 18.2.1721: HMC Portland v 616. Wine cost almost as much then as today: Tokay 1gn. and Burgundy 7s. a bottle.

7. *Timberland* iii; LJ xxi 417-18; HLR Parchment Collection 43 contains the original longhand notes of the evidence given by Blunt and others which is printed in part in Darwen *op. cit.*

8. Vanbrugh to Lord Carlisle 7.2.1721: HMC Carlisle 29.

9. Hermitage to the States General 18.2.1721: Add. MS 17,677 KKK4 91, 94.

10. Dubois to Senneterre 13.4.1719 (quoted by Michael, W., *Reign of George I* ii); Horace Walpole to Horace Mann 1.9.1750; See also HMC Onslow 514, Lady Mary Wortley Montagu's *Account of the Court of George I*, and *Boyer* xxii 443.

11. *Boyer* xxi 394.

12. *Ibid.* 407.

13. CJ xix 424.

14. CJ xix 453.

15. *Coxe* ii 207-9.

16. *Ibid.* 213-14.

17. HMC Onslow 504-14.

CHAPTER XIII

1. Carteret to Newcastle 22.8.1721: Add. MS 32,686 193.

2. The seven reports are all printed *in extenso* in CJ xix on 16 and 25 Feb., 21 Apr., 22 and 26 May, 5 and 16 June; *Coxe* ii 212.

3. *Boyer* xxi 3. Boyer reprints the whole series of these letters, later the object of an attempt at prosecution, which succeeded in stopping them. The government acted even more effectively against Mist, who called the King 'a cruel, ill-bred, uneducated old Tyrant' and the Prince 'a drivelling fool'. He was pilloried and 'the paper entitled The Weekly Journal or Saturday's Post, with freshest advices foreign and domestick' stigmatized as a 'false, seditious and traitorous libel'.

4. CJ xix 512-13.

5. *Particulars.* Some of the original inventories are preserved in HLR Parchment Collection 43 and notes of some of the sales in the Guildhall Library, London.

6. *Coxe* ii 215.

7. *Boyer* ii 446-8. The size of the fortunes of the Craggs ladies may be judged from the settlement made by Anne Craggs on her third marriage (to the Irish political climber Nugent). He got £100,000 and she kept £50,000 for herself.

8. Some of the shareholders petitioned Parliament unsuccessfully in 1729 (CJ 28.2.1729) and the Company was involved in litigation in the thirties. Bankruptcy seems to have overtaken the Sword Blade at last in 1742.

9. CJ xix 561 and 568; *Coxe* ii 216.

10. For the proceedings on the Directors see *Boyer* xxi 614-17, 627-30, 641-4.

11. CJ xix 638-9.

12. *Timberland* iii 151-84.

13. Darwen *op. cit.*; *Coxe* ii 219-20.

EPILOGUE

1. Houghton MSS P82.

2. Destouches' report of his conversation with the Duchess of Kendal. Archives des Affaires Etrangères Corr. Pol. Angl. cccxxxv 99-100.

3. Marais *op. cit.* ii 354.

4. Williams *op. cit.* 139 and ff; Sichel, W., *Bolingbroke* ii 341, 355-8, 463 ff. Sichel must be used with caution.

5. HMC Carlisle 77; Pope to Swift 28.11.1729.

6. Swift, *The South Sea Project*, 1721.

7. Francis, J., *History of the Bank of England* i 143.

8. George, M., *London in the Eighteenth Century Appendix*; Gibbon Autobiography.

Index

An entry in heavy type indicates a biographical summary in the Appendix.
Peers are indexed (or, in a few cases, cross-referenced only) under their titles.